Clash of Arms

Clash of Arms
12 English Battles

Julian Humphrys

Jacket: Re-enactor on horseback © Ian Deveney 2004

Copyright © English Heritage 2006

First published in 2006 by English Heritage, Isambard House, Kemble Drive, Swindon, SN2 2GZ

English Heritage is the Government's statutory adviser on all aspects of the historic environment.

Copyright text © Julian Humphrys 2006

10 9 8 7 6 5 4 3 2 1

ISBN-10 1 85074 938 8
ISBN-13 978 1 85074 938 7

Product code 51058

British Library Cataloguing in Publication data

A CIP catalogue for this book is available from the British Library.

Designer: Simon Borrough
Cover design: Beck Ward Murphy
Editor: Naomi Waters
Indexer: Alan Rutter
Project Manager: Beck Ward Murphy

Printed in the UK by Bath Press Ltd

For further information about English Heritage and our sites, please contact:
English Heritage Customer Services
PO Box 569
Swindon SN2 2YP
Telephone: 0870 3331181
Website: www.english-heritage.org.uk

In affectionate memory of Mark Humphrys (1925–2005).

Contents

Introduction

Battles are the punctuation marks of history.   *Winston Churchill*

If this is the case, then anyone writing the story of England will need to use a great deal of punctuation. In his recent guide to English battlefields, Michael Rayner has identified over 500 battles that he believes have shaped our history, and in selecting the battles to be included here I certainly had plenty of choice. Why did I choose the ones I did? Many books of this type tend to include battles that have been selected chiefly on the grounds of their eventual political significance. Thus, for example, Marston Moor, which lost the king the north, and Naseby, which lost him his army, are regularly included in the Civil War sections of such works. However, the 12 battles in this book have been chosen primarily because as well as contributing to a coherent story and providing a 'snapshot' of military history at a given time, each one has, in my opinion, something important to tell us about a particular aspect of warfare. As a result, while this book does include 'standard' battles, such as Hastings, Towton and Sedgemoor, it also covers less well-known encounters, such as Myton, Alton and Tresco, the last of which rarely appears in military history books at all.

The examples in this book will show that many factors can influence the course of a battle – the numbers, training and motivation of the troops involved; the suitability of the weapons with which they are equipped; the intentions, decisions and abilities of their leaders; the effects of terrain; the intervention of the weather … and the impact of luck. Thus, the Saxon defeat at Maldon seems at least partly due to the decision of their leader to force a battle by giving up the strong position occupied by his men. The best-known battle in English history, Hastings, was a clash of two contrasting ways of fighting, with the result long in doubt before the relentless attacks of William's infantry, cavalry and archers eventually wore down Harold's Saxon foot-soldiers. Myton was perhaps the most one-sided battle in the history of Anglo-Scottish warfare. It is a salutary reminder of what is likely to happen when poorly led amateurs are pitted against veterans, as Moray and Douglas's hard-bitten Scottish raiders made short work of a largely untrained army of English townsmen. Shrewsbury was the first battle in which Englishmen used the longbow against one another in any great numbers. Although the future King Henry V received a near fatal lesson in the effectiveness of the weapon that was to bring him his greatest victory at Agincourt, his ability to seize the initiative seems to have been the decisive factor in winning the day for his father.

Towton was the largest battle of the Wars of the Roses. Regional hatreds and family vendettas ensured it was also the bloodiest, fought with an intensity that shocked contemporary observers. Fought in thick mist, Barnet was the very epitome of 'the fog of war', as Warwick the Kingmaker's army dissolved amid accusations of treachery after mistaken identity led two parts of his army to fight one another. Stoke was another clash of contrasting armies. The Yorkist force was primarily composed of lightly armed Irish levies, stiffened by a sizeable contingent of German mercenaries. Its leaders seem to have hoped for defections among the supporters of Henry VII, but in the event they were defeated by the men-at-arms and archers of the king's vanguard. James IV's Scottish soldiers took to the field at Flodden with a brand new weapon – the pike – but inadequate training in its use and unsuitable terrain saw them hacked to pieces by the old-fashioned bills of the Earl of Surrey's English army.

Battles featured in this book.

The dramatic Civil War battle of Roundway Down was primarily a cavalry encounter, with the two sides using very different tactics. The Royalists were victorious and some of the defeated Parliamentarians were driven to their deaths off the steep slopes at the western end of the Down. The battle of Alton was, for its size, one of the finest feats of generalship of the entire Civil War. Sir William Waller pulled together a dispirited and mutinous Parliamentarian army and led it on a night march across country to surprise and outnumber a Royalist outpost and defeat its garrison after some heavy street fighting. The storming of Tresco is a fascinating example of a 17th-century joint operation, spiced up with a healthy helping of inter-service rivalry, as a Parliamentarian amphibious force eventually recaptured the Isles of Scilly, following a tricky beach assault that initially went badly wrong. Finally, there is Sedgemoor. Sometimes written off as a hare-brained scheme with little chance of success, Monmouth's daring plan to surprise the royal army by attacking it at night from an unexpected direction was probably his best prospect of victory given the troops he had at his disposal and, with a little more luck, he might well have succeeded.

All these battles have something unique about them, but none exists in a vacuum. With this in mind the main narrative in each chapter places the battle with which it deals firmly in its historical context, while a number of special sections look at the broader political and military issues of the time. Subjects covered include warfare on the Scottish border, revolts in Wales, the Wars of the Roses and the British civil wars. More specific issues arising out of individual battles are also examined, ranging from medieval heraldry to the military use of churches.

The book also examines how we know what we do about the campaigns and battles in question and takes a critical look at some of the sources available to us. Contemporary accounts will always be important. They can supply the background information to place a battle in its strategic and political context, suggest locations, list participants, explain the plans of commanders or provide a sequence of events. Furthermore, they often supply us with the human details that bring a battle to life: the delight of the Scots when they saw the rabble that was approaching them at Myton; the savagery of the fighting at Flodden as the English billmen cut down the Scots like trees; Sir William Waller being forced to draw his pistols on his own men before Alton; Richard Atkyns' vain attempts to penetrate Sir Arthur Hesilrige's armour at Roundway Down; or the squabbling between Roundhead soldiers and sailors after Tresco. As a result, this book quotes quite heavily from written sources, and each chapter also includes an extract from a contemporary, or near-contemporary, account of the battle being covered, together with information about its author, where known, and a brief discussion of its content.

Needless to say, such accounts must be treated with care. They need to be carefully analysed and compared with other evidence: geographical, archaeological and written. Some writers, such as Polydore Vergil in his account of Stoke, may be unfamiliar with the area they are describing, while others, such as William of Poitiers in his description of the actions of William the Conqueror at Hastings, may be motivated by a wish to flatter their patrons. Medieval chroniclers are notoriously unreliable when it comes to their estimates of numbers in a battle, while Civil War newspapers are invariably influenced by considerations of propaganda. Eyewitness accounts may well be embellished in order to tell a good story, distorted by lapses of memory, or influenced by a desire to present the writers' own actions in as favourable a light as possible. As Lord Seaton admitted when he was asked some years after Waterloo about his role in the great battle: 'We were all so intent in performing our own parts, that we are disposed to imagine that the Brigade or Corps with which we were engaged played a most distinguished part, and attribute more importance to the movements under our own immediate observation than they deserved'.

There are also huge benefits in actually getting out and visiting the sites of these and other battles. Over the past few years, thanks to the work of organisations like the Battlefields Trust and English Heritage, considerable progress has been made in improving both access and interpretation of these battle sites. Battlefields can be extremely evocative – I find it thrilling to stand where history was made at Senlac Hill, or to open the battle-scarred door of Alton Church, and more than a little sobering to stand on the bridge over the Cock Beck at Towton and think about those who may have died there in 1461.

Furthermore, a study of the landscape can be an invaluable tool in helping to understand what may have happened in a particular battle, and why. At Flodden, for example, a walk down the steep slopes of Branxton Hill to the boggy valley below gives a major clue as to why the blocks of Scottish pikemen may have lost their order and momentum as they advanced towards the English lines. A boat trip around the confusing myriad of rocks and islets surrounding Tresco makes it less surprising that some of the Parliamentarians landed on the wrong island altogether in 1651! Clearly the landscape may well have changed since a battle took place. This may have happened naturally – at Maldon a relative rise in the sea level has led to a widening of the River Blackwater – but more often it has been brought about artificially with, for example, the enclosure of fields, the plantation of woodland, the draining of marshes and the construction of houses and roads.

Over the past few years there has been a growing recognition of the immense value of reconstructing the historic landscape in order to help locate and interpret a battlefield, and this work is increasingly being supported by the use of archaeological evidence, often in the form of artefacts, such as arrowheads, buckles or musket balls, recovered by metal detector and carefully recorded. With all this in mind the illustrations in this book include photographs of each battlefield, accompanied by details of some of the things we know or would like to know about the landscape at the time of the battle.

One thing that has been of immense help to me in writing this book has been the opportunity I have had as leader of English Heritage's battlefield-hike programme to discuss most of these battles with hike participants and, in doing so, to find out exactly what people would like to know about them. They are, of course, keen to learn what happened and where, but they also share a passionate interest in the people involved – from the ordinary soldiers who did the fighting to the leaders whose careers and often lives depended on the results of the decisions they made. Bearing this in mind, this book includes a number of photographs of some of the best re-enactors in the country which, together with some carefully chosen contemporary illustrations, illustrate soldiers' appearance and weapons, while the accompanying captions describe aspects of their experience in battle. Each chapter also includes biographies of key commanders. Some are already well known while others all too often appear in accounts of the battles in which they fought as nothing more than names on a map.

A Matter of Honour
Maldon, 10 August 991

The Viking victory over Brihtnoth's Saxons at Maldon is one of the
few pre-medieval battles whose location can be identified with
some degree of certainty. Our main source of information about the
battle is a fine epic poem, probably written shortly after the event.
One of its key themes is that of honour. According to the poem, a
sense of honour led Brihtnoth's retainers to spurn flight and fight
to the death around the body of their fallen leader.

The mud of Southey Channel at low tide looking south east from the causeway from Northey Island.

By the time of the death of Alfred the Great in AD 899, Danish expansion in England had been halted and the country was almost evenly divided between the Saxons who controlled the south and west and the Danes who controlled the north and the east, an area that was to become known as the Danelaw. In 912, Alfred's son, Edward the Elder, began a methodical conquest of the Danelaw, and in doing so he united much of England under West Saxon rule, a process that was completed by his son, Athelstan, who became the first king to rule all of England.

When Aethelred II became king in 978, England was united, prosperous and at peace. However, the year 980 offered a portent of things to come when, in the first of a series of raids of increasing scale and intensity, seven Viking ships raided and sacked Southampton. Although England had flourished during the period of peace, its defences had been neglected. There was no standing field army and the walls of many of the fortified burghs founded by Alfred as defences against the Danes were in need of repair.

In 991, a fleet of 93 Viking ships arrived in the English Channel. It is not clear who led the Vikings – it may have been Olaf Tryggvason, a Norwegian adventurer who was later to seize the crown of Norway, or it may have been Svein Forkbeard, King of Denmark. It may have been both. Whoever the Vikings' leaders were, their objectives were clear: they wanted booty and money. They attacked and plundered Folkestone and Sandwich before paying an unwelcome visit to Ipswich. By August, they were threatening Maldon, having landed on Northey Island and anchored their ships on the Blackwater Estuary.

A 9th-century Viking longship excavated at Gokstad, Norway, in 1880.

The causeway to Northey Island at low tide. In 991 the landscape was very different from that of today. The shoreline was firm and the channel between the mainland and Northey Island was only half its present width. At high tide the lowest part of the crossing would have been under about two metres of water, while at low tide the causeway would have been flanked by beds of thick, impassible mud.

A statue of Ealdorman Brihtnoth on the south wall of All Saints Church, Maldon.

Maldon was a tempting target. It was a prosperous town, housed a royal mint and had some military significance; in 917 Edward the Elder had used it as a base for his campaigns against the Danes of East Anglia. The English response to this new Viking threat was led by Ealdorman Brihtnoth. An Ealdorman was a noble responsible for the defence and government of a particular region of England, in Brihtnoth's case, Essex. Brihtnoth was an elderly man by 991. He had been married for 40 years and one near-contemporary account describes, 'the swan-like whiteness of his head'. Although the core of the force that he led against the Vikings was made up of his hearth-troops – retainers who held estates from him – most of his army came from the Essex militia or fyrd.

On 10 August, Brihtnoth arrived with his forces opposite Northey Island, which was connected to the mainland at low tide by some form of causeway or ford. We have no information about the size of the two armies but, according to the *Anglo-Saxon Chronicle*, the Vikings arrived in 93 vessels. At that time Viking ships were of two main types: one carrying 60 and the other 30 men. If the *Chronicle* was correct in its ship counting – chroniclers did have a habit of exaggerating the Viking threat – this would give the Vikings a minimum force of around 2,800 and a maximum of about 5,600 men. Of course, this assumes that all the ships were fully manned when they set off from Scandinavia, that no ships had been lost or had returned home earlier in the campaign and that no casualties had been suffered in the various raids, so the Viking force could well have been smaller. One can only assume that Brihtnoth's force was at least of a similar size to that of the Vikings. Indeed, it has been argued that the fact that Brihtnoth was prepared to offer battle with what was probably a less well-trained force suggests that he must have outnumbered the Vikings.

Northey Island from the flood bank, looking east. A rise in sea level over the last 1,000 years led first to flooding, then to land reclamation by means of a sea wall.

According to the epic poem, *The Battle of Maldon*, Brihtnoth formed up his army in a wall of interlocking shields. After riding up and down the ranks to encourage his men and check their dispositions, he dismounted and stood with his retainers, presumably at the centre of the line. For the time being at least, battle was impossible. The tide had risen, covering the causeway across the River Blackwater and separating the two armies. As everyone waited for the tide to ebb there followed a period of shouted negotiations, with the Vikings offering to depart in return for the payment of tribute money and Brihtnoth contemptuously refusing.

The mainland from Northey Island.

Eventually, as the tide receded, the Vikings prepared to cross to the mainland but found the causeway blocked by a group of Saxon warriors – *The Battle of Maldon* says just three: Wulfstan, Aelfhere and Maccus. Whether they really stood alone or whether each was in fact the leader of a band of warriors is not known, but the Vikings were unable or unwilling to advance. No doubt an attempt to fight their way onto the mainland would have led to such disorganisation in the Viking ranks that they would have been plum targets for a Saxon counter-attack.

Axe and spearheads found in the Thames near London Bridge in the 1920s. They may well be connected with Svein Forkbeard's attack on London in 1013.

Instead the Vikings asked to be allowed to cross to the mainland unopposed and form up there for battle. Brihtnoth agreed. He has sometimes been criticised for thus throwing away what, on the face of it, seemed an advantageous position, and indeed, the poem does describe Brihtnoth's decision as being motivated by pride or over-confidence. In reality, however, there was little else that Brihtnoth could have done. He was almost certainly in no position to mount an attack of his own across the causeway. Had he refused to let the Vikings cross they would probably have waited until high tide, returned to their ships, sailed away and raided elsewhere. This was Brihtnoth's one chance to destroy the Vikings in battle and he probably felt that he had to take it. He pulled his army back and the Vikings advanced onto the mainland.

Bows were busied, buckler met point, bitter was the battle-rush

The battle began with an exchange of arrows before the Vikings launched their onslaught on the Saxon shield wall. Both sides hurled javelins at their enemies before closing in with spears and swords. At first it seems that the Saxon battle line held firm, but the turning point came when Brihtnoth, who had been in the thick of the fighting, was killed. The poem relates that he was twice hit by spears, and that although he succeeded in killing two of the Danes, a third disabled his sword arm. As Brihtnoth sank to the ground, still encouraging his men, the Vikings moved in for the kill and hacked him to death. One account claims they carried his head away as a trophy. The fall of their leader seems to have broken the resolve of many of the Saxons, who made for the safety of the nearby woods. Indeed, the poem puts much of the blame for the flight on a certain Godric, who is described as leaping onto Brihtnoth's horse and riding off. Believing that it was in fact their leader who was leaving the field, many of the Saxons fled too. According to the poem, at least some of Brihtnoth's hearth-troops fought on to the death. Determined to avenge the death of their leader, they took a heavy toll on the Vikings, who were prevented from attacking Maldon after the battle, and were said to have hardly had enough men to crew their ships when they eventually left.

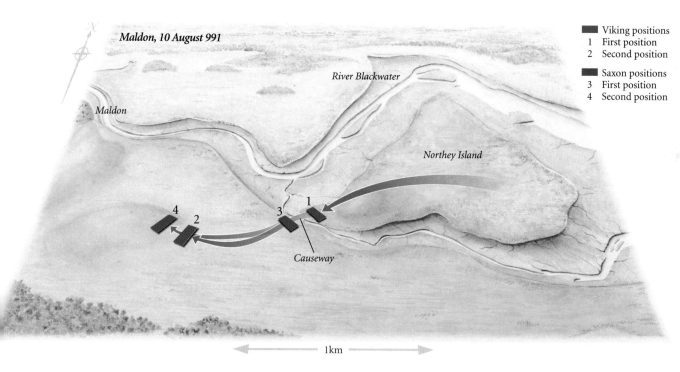

Maldon, 10 August 991

River Blackwater

Maldon

Northey Island

4   2   3   1

Causeway

Viking positions
1 First position
2 Second position

Saxon positions
3 First position
4 Second position

1km

Svein Forkbeard (d.1014) and Olaf Tryggvason (d.1000)

When Svein Forkbeard seized the Danish throne from his father, Harald Bluetooth, in 988, the kingdom of Denmark was more powerful and more secure than it had been for a century. As a result, Svein felt able to leave his kingdom to lead overseas raids, particularly against England, which was rich but extremely vulnerable. Svein's success in extracting tribute money from the English was an important factor in his ability to maintain and extend his power.

We don't know for certain who led the Viking raiding force that clashed with Brihtnoth at Maldon in 991. Although one version of the *Anglo-Saxon Chronicle* mentions Olaf Tryggvason, a Norwegian chieftain, some historians have argued that it was more likely to have been Svein Forkbeard. What is known is that in 994 Olaf joined Svein, who was overlord of Norway as well as King of Denmark, on his invasion of England.

Although the Vikings failed in their bid to seize London, they ravaged the south-east extensively, until they were bought off by the payment of £16,000 tribute. While the Viking army was wintering in Southampton, however, the English king, Aethelred, succeeded in persuading Olaf to break with Svein and seize power in Norway. Clearly Aethelred was hoping that problems in Scandinavia would force Svein to leave England alone. Olaf duly returned to Norway where he secured recognition as king but, in 1000, he was defeated by Svein at the battle of Svold. Legend has it that, in order to avoid falling into the hands of his enemies, Olaf jumped into the sea from his ship, the *Long Serpent*, and was never seen again.

Having re-established control over Norway, Svein returned to England in 1003 where he campaigned until 1005 when famine forced him to leave. His fleet seems to have returned the following year though and exacted further tribute. In 1013, Svein invaded England in earnest. From his base at Gainsborough he soon established control over the old Danelaw, before marching south with his army, causing utter devastation. Oxford and Wallingford surrendered to him and although London initially held out against him, it too surrendered after Svein conquered the south-west.

By Christmas 1013, England had accepted Svein as king and Aethelred had fled to Normandy. Svein, however, did not live long to enjoy his triumph. On 3 February 1014 he died, having reigned as England's king for just five weeks. Aethelred promptly returned from exile, only to die himself in 1016. That October, Svein's son, Cnut, defeated Aethelred's successor, Edmund Ironside, at the battle of Ashington. The two men originally agreed to divide the country between them but, by November, Edmund, who had been badly wounded at Ashington, was dead, and Cnut was accepted as King of all England.

The battle of Maldon had little to do with the eventual Danish conquest of England, which was not completed for another 25 years. The battle is not without historical importance, however. In its aftermath, the first payment of *danegeld* – tribute money to buy off the raiders – was made in Aethelred's reign. The sum of £10,000 was paid to the Vikings after the battle. By 1018 the tribute had risen to £72,000, an astonishing amount given that, according to Domesday Book, the annual revenues from English land in 1086 only totalled £70,000. Perhaps, however, the greatest significance of the battle of Maldon is that it inspired one of the finest battle poems in English literature.

Viking re-enactor wearing a mail byrnie *and a helmet with characteristic 'spectacles', based on one found at Gjermundbu in eastern Norway. Other helmets seem to have been conical in shape, while many warriors may simply have worn caps of toughened hide. Despite their popular image as wild, hairy individuals in horned helmets, there is no evidence that Vikings ever wore helmets with horns. Furthermore, the large number of combs found on Viking sites suggests that they took considerable care over their personal appearance. This warrior carries a two-handed axe. A number of axe heads from the period have been found in England, although the battle of Maldon makes no mention of the weapon. Most warriors were probably equipped with a spear and a circular shield of painted, leather-covered wood. The commonest fighting formation of the period seems to have been a line of overlapping shields known as the* skaldborg, *or shield wall, but for an attack, warriors might adopt the* swinfylka, *or swine array, a wedge-shaped formation designed to punch a hole through the enemy ranks.*

Aethelred II (966–1016)

A coin of Aethelred II from the Royal Coin Cabinet, Stockholm. Minted at Old Sarum in Wiltshire, it presumably found its way to Scandinavia as part of a payment of danegeld.

Aethelred II has gone down in history as possibly England's most unsuccessful and incompetent king. In truth, he was faced with problems that even a ruler of Alfred the Great's calibre would have found difficult to overcome. Aethelred became king in 978 at the age of 12 following the murder of his half-brother Edward the Martyr. Within two years, the Vikings had resumed their raids upon England. These increased in scale and intensity until their aim was clearly no longer the acquisition of tribute and booty but the conquest of all England. At first it seems that Aethelred viewed these raids as merely a local problem and formulated no centralised counter-strategy.

This changed after the battle of Maldon. Thereafter Aethelred used the payment of tribute, *danegeld*, to buy time. This was a well-established tactic – even Alfred the Great had used it – but the danger was, of course, that the Vikings would only use this money to finance further raids. It was therefore essential that Aethelred used the time he had bought as effectively as possible. He tried to strengthen England's defences, which had been allowed to deteriorate in the long years of peace and sought to build a fleet capable of confronting the raiders.

He could never complete the task properly, though, and the Vikings returned, time after time, obliging Aethelred to buy them off with ever-increasing sums of money.

Unable to defeat the Vikings militarily with the resources at his disposal, Aethelred tried diplomacy, recruiting former enemies as allies. He seems to have done this fairly successfully. By backing Olaf Tryggvason in his bid for the crown of Norway, Aethelred obliged Svein Forkbeard, his main opponent, to return to Scandinavia for some time. In 1012, Aethelred succeeded in buying the services (at a huge cost, admittedly) of Thorkell, an independent Danish leader who had arrived with an army in 1009 and overrun much of the south-east of England.

But Aethelred was unable to take full advantage of these diplomatic successes. Both English court and country were split by faction and corruption. Eadric, Ealdorman of Mercia, in particular, is said to have lined his own pockets from the proceeds of *danegeld*.

In 1002 Aethelred married Emma of Normandy in a bid to deny the Danes use of the duchy's ports and coast. This only served to alienate his numerous sons from his first marriage to the Saxon Aelfgifu, though, who saw their inheritance threatened when Emma bore him two further sons. He probably made his worst mistake in November 1002 when he ordered the massacre of Danish settlers in England, thus further splitting an already divided kingdom.

Aethelred's nickname, the Unready, is in fact a corruption of Unraed, a 12th-century play on his name meaning unadvised or ill-advised. It seems particularly appropriate in both senses of the word. By Christmas 1013, with most of his kingdom overrun by Svein Forkbeard's Danish army, Aethelred fled to Normandy with his wife and children, including the future King Edward the Confessor. He returned to England following Svein's death in 1014 but the following year he quarrelled with Edmund Ironside, one of his sons by his first wife and an able warrior. By the time Aethelred died in April 1016 his divided kingdom was virtually at the mercy of the Danes.

England's finest epic battle poem

Details of early English battles are normally very sketchy. For example, the Winchester version of the *Anglo-Saxon Chronicle* simply says of Maldon:

...Ealdorman Brihtnoth came against them [the Vikings] there with his army and fought with them; and they killed the Ealdorman there and had possession of the place of slaughter.

Other versions of the *Chronicle* add little except to note that it was on the advice of Archbishop Sigeric that the decision was made to buy off the raiders with a payment of £10,000. Another contemporary source, the *Life of St Oswald*, simply tells us that:

...an infinite number, indeed of them and of our side perished, and Brihtnoth fell, and the rest fled. The Danes also were wondrously wounded, and could scarcely man their ships.

The battle of Maldon, however, is unique for the presence of a contemporary or near-contemporary source that purports to describe the events of the battle in some detail – an Old English poem known today as the *Battle of Maldon*. The original copy of the poem was destroyed in a fire in 1731 but fortunately a transcript had already been published five years earlier. The origin and date of the poem is uncertain although it appears to have been written shortly after the battle, and it has been suggested that it was compiled for Brihtnoth's widow. Its beginning and end have been lost but 325 lines survive and these tell a coherent story. They merit quoting at length:

> He boastfully spoke, for the seafarers
>
> That you buy off this spear-rush with your tax,
> Than that we should have so hard a battle.
> What need we to vex us, if you will agree?
> We will for this gold a sure compact make
> If thou wilt agree to it – thou that art strongest.
> If that thou be willing thy people to redeem,
> To yield to the seamen at their own choice
> Tribute for a truce, and so take peace of us,
> Then will we with the tax to ship betake us
> To sail on the sea – and hold truce with you.
> Brithnoth made answer – his buckler he grasped,
> Brandished his slender spear – and spoke.
> "Hearest thou, sea-robber, what this people say?
> For tribute they're ready to give you their spears,

A Viking sword, left, spearheads and battle-axe, opposite, found in the London area. The spear, used for both throwing and thrusting, was the commonest weapon in both Saxon and Viking armies. Even Brihtnoth seems to have carried one at Maldon. Swords were expensive to manufacture and were therefore a sign of high status. Double-handed axes, famously depicted in the Bayeux Tapestry, were coming into use by the time of the battle of Maldon.

The edge poison-bitter, and the ancient sword.
War-gear that will bring you no profit in the fight.

　　Bade he then to bear the shields, the warriors to go,
So that they on the river's bank all stood.

Nor could for the water, the army come at the other,
For there came flowing, flood after ebb;
Locked were the ocean-streams, and too long it seemed
Until they together might carry their spears.
There by Panta's stream in array they bestood,
Essex men's rank, and the men from the ships,
Nor might any one of them injure the other
Except where from arrow's flight one had his death.
The flood went out – the pirates stood ready.
Full many of the Vikings, eager for battle.

　　When they saw that, and keenly espied
That bitter bridge-guardians there they met
Then began they to feign – those loathed guests –
And begged that they might some foothold get,
To fare over the ford – the foemen to lead.

　　"Now room is meted you, come swiftly to us,
Warriors to war. Only God knows
Who at the end shall possess this fight's field".
Then went the war wolves – for water they recked not.
The troop of the pirates, west over Panta.
Over the shining water they carried their shields
Seamen to the shore, their bucklers they shouldered.
There against the raiders ready stood
Brithnoth with his band, and with the bucklers bade
Form the shield wall, and make firm the ranks
Fast against the foes. Then was fighting nigh,
Fame in the fight – now was the hour come
When that the feymen [doomed men] must fall.

　　They stood steadfast; Brithnoth stirred them,
Bade each of his men intend to the strife
That would from the Danes win glory.

Went one stern in battle – his weapon upheaved,
His shield for safety – and 'gainst the chief strode –
As resolute against him the earl did go,
Each to the other did evil intend.
Sent then the seafarer a southern dart,
And wounded was the warriors' chieftain.
But he shoved with his shield – so that the shaft burst,
And the spear broke, and it sprang away.
Wroth was the chieftain, he pierced with his spear
That proud Viking who gave him that wound.
Yet prudent was the chieftain; he aimed his shaft to go
Through the man's neck – his hand guided it
So that he reached his sudden enemy's life.
Then he a second swiftly sent
That the breastplate burst – in the heart was he wounded
Through the ring-harness – and at his heart stood
The poisoned point; the earl was the blither:-
Laughed then that high-heart – made thanks to God
For his day's work – that his Saviour granted him.

Loosed then one of the foemen a dart from his hands,
To fly from his finders – that it rushed forth
Through the noble thane of Aethelred.
Close to his side stood a youth not yet grown
Wulfstan's child – even Wulfmeer the younger.
He plucked from his chieftain that bloody spear
Then loosed the hard spear 'gainst that other to go;
In ran the point – so that he on earth lay
Who ere had sorely wounded his chief.
Went an armed Viking against the earl
Who wished the earl's jewels to plunder,
His armour and rings – and well-adorned sword.
Then Brithnoth drew his sword from sheath
Broad and brown edged – and at his breast-plate smote.
Too soon hindered him one of the seamen,
So that the earl's arm he did injure.
Fell then to earth the fallow-hilted sword,
Nor could he hold the hard brand
Or wield his weapon.

    . . . Then the heathen scoundrels hacked him
and both the men who stood beside him,

Ælfnoth and Wulfmær, both lay slain,
when they gave up their lives alongside their lord.
Then those who were minded made off from the fight:
there Odda's sons were foremost in flight…

Translation by Wilfrid Berridge
(For the complete translation, visit www.battleofmaldon.org.uk_

Although its description of the River Blackwater (known as the Panta at the time) and the surrounding area is remarkably accurate and useful in locating the site of the battle, the *Battle of Maldon* has to be used with care by historians as its content may well have been influenced as much by dramatic and stylistic considerations as by a concern for historical accuracy. It seems probable that the details of the battle have been embellished – for example, Brihtnoth's dying words must surely have been placed in his mouth by the author of the poem.

On the other hand, if the poem was indeed composed shortly after the battle, it seems unlikely that it would diverge too far from the facts. After all, many of those who first heard it would probably have been familiar with the personalities and main events of the battle. Whatever doubts there are about the accuracy of its detail, the poem is, at the very least, a valuable source of information about the nature of late 10th-century combat. From it we learn that at least some of the Saxons rode onto the battlefield before dismounting to fight on foot, that both sides formed shield walls, that missile weapons included bows and javelins and, while in close combat, warriors thrust with spears and cut with swords. Interestingly, there is no mention of axes, which are shown being used to devastating effect in the Bayeux Tapestry. Shields seem to have been widely carried and there are three mentions of mail shirts or *byrnies*, but none of helmets.

The poem offers the nearest thing we have to a contemporary, eyewitness report of a battle of this period, although if this is the case one is tempted to speculate about the identity of the reporter. Whoever it was survived to tell the tale and did not live up to the heroic ideal extolled in the poem – that of fighting to the death alongside one's fallen leader.

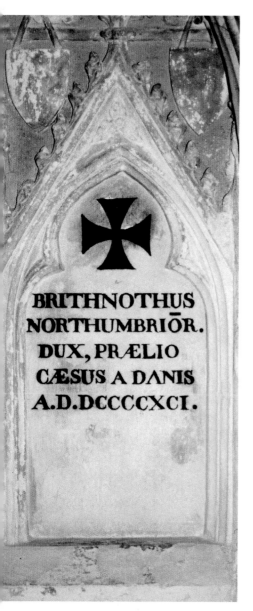

Brihtnoth's tomb in Bishop West's Chapel, Ely Cathedral. Brihtnoth's body was originally buried in Ely Abbey, of which he was a benefactor. It was transferred to the cathedral in the mid-12th century and laid to rest in its present location in 1771. The slightly misleading Latin inscription reads 'Brithnoth, Duke of Northumberland, killed in battle by the Danes AD 991'.

A matter of honour

Spirit must be braver, heart the bolder,
courage the stouter as our strength lessens.
Here lies our leader all cut to pieces,
the great man in the dirt. He has cause to mourn
who thinks to turn now from this battle-play.
I am grown old; I will not leave,
but, alongside my own lord, I
mean to lie, beside so loved a man.

Most debate of the battle among historians has centred on the wisdom of Brihtnoth's decision to allow the Vikings free passage across to the mainland from Northey Island. It is clear that this was not of primary concern to the author of the poem, however, who deals with it in a single line. For him, the key issue was one of honour and, in particular, the response of Brihtnoth's retainers to the death of their leader. Nearly half the surviving poem is spent praising those who fought on and deriding those who fled.

There are many examples in English history of the catastrophic effect that the death of a leader could have on an army. William the Conqueror had to reassure his troops that he was still alive to prevent them from fleeing at Hastings in 1066. Henry Percy risked all at Shrewsbury in 1403 in a bid to kill Henry IV, although in the event it was he who died and his army that collapsed on the news of his death. Richard III died at Bosworth in 1485, vainly attempting to win the day by killing his rival, Henry Tudor. Maldon was no exception, and it seems that Brihtnoth's death led to the flight of much of his army. If the poem is to be believed, however, most of Brihtnoth's personal retainers, his hearth-troops, did fight on to the death. And they did so not in the hope of victory or in order to defend their homeland but to avenge their fallen leader, a sentiment expressed in the poem by one retainer after another:

This I vow that I shall not hence
flee a foot's-pace, but I will go farther,
avenge my master and friend in the fight.
Steadfast heroes round Sturmere need not
taunt me with words, now my patron is dead,
that I travelled home lordless,
turned back from war; but weapon shall take me,
point and blade.

For men like these, it was a matter of honour.

Battle of Attrition
Hastings, 14 October 1066

Probably the best-known battle in English history, Hastings had huge political and social consequences for the future of England and her people. Because of the way it has been depicted in the Bayeux Tapestry, the battle has sometimes been seen as a triumph of 'modern' Norman cavalry over 'old-fashioned' Saxon infantry. In fact, the two armies seem to have been extremely well matched, with the result that Hastings turned into a day-long battle of attrition.

The domestic buildings of Battle Abbey on the crest of Senlac Hill. The location of the Abbey is the prime piece of evidence for establishing where the battle was fought, for William ordered that the abbey should be built around the spot where Harold fell. When William discovered that the monks were trying to build it in a more convenient location he immediately ordered them back to this hilltop site. The land was probably uncultivated heathland in 1066. Ground levelling and later terracing has altered the gradient of the hill, which was originally much steeper. The marshy ground at the foot of the hill has been subsequently drained by the construction of a series of ponds.

William of Normandy regarded Harold Godwinson's accession to the English throne in 1066 as both a political challenge and a personal insult. In his eyes, the fact that Edward the Confessor may have named Harold as his successor on his deathbed did not invalidate Edward's earlier promise that he would leave the throne to him, or Harold's own oath, probably made to William in 1064, that he would help him become king upon Edward's death.

Norman ships crossing the Channel, as depicted in the Bayeux Tapestry. William's own ship, the Mora, *is identifiable by the carved figure of a boy with a horn on the stern.*

After consulting with his close advisors, who considered that an invasion of England was viable, William set about enlisting support for such a scheme. He set his case before Pope Alexander II, who gave the plan his formal blessing and sent William a papal banner that was carried at Hastings. It seems that, initially, many Norman barons were decidedly lukewarm about the invasion. William's force of personality, however, his track record as a successful military leader, the blessing of the Pope and, crucially, the offers of large tracts of land in England won many of them over, and William set about assembling a fleet to transport his army across the Channel. By August, William's fleet was assembling at Dives-sur-Mer. It seems to have numbered about 700 ships, the majority provided by participants in the invasion. William's half-brothers Robert of Mortain and Odo of Bayeux are said to have supplied 120 and 100 respectively.

Harold Godwinson (c.1020–66)

Harold was the second son of Godwin, Earl of Wessex, who rose to prominence in the service of King Cnut. His Danish mother, Gytha, was Cnut's sister-in-law and the Scandinavian names of Harold and three of his brothers reflect their mixed parentage. In 1042, Godwin supported Edward the Confessor's succession to the throne and, in 1045, King Edward married Harold's sister, Edith. In 1043, Harold was made Earl of East Anglia, and a few years later his lands and responsibilities were further increased due to the scandalous activities of his elder brother, Swein, Earl of the South-West Midlands. Swein's many outrages, which included the abduction of an abbess and the murder of a cousin, led to his exile, and much of his earldom was given to Harold. In 1051, quarrels with Edward the Confessor's Norman supporters led to the temporary exile of the Godwinson family but they forced their way back into court the following year, and when

Godwin died that Easter, Harold became Earl of Wessex. The Godwinsons were easily the wealthiest family in the kingdom and their income even outstripped that of the king himself. Harold was thus able to attract a large following throughout the country.

Harold also built up a considerable reputation as a soldier. In particular, he put a stop to the activities of Gruffyd of Wales, who had been raiding England for nearly 10 years. In the winter of 1062, Harold led a lightning attack on Gruffyd's territory, completely surprising the Welsh and nearly capturing their leader. The following year, Harold and his brother Tostig, Earl of Northumbria, attacked Wales in a two-pronged assault: Tostig by land from the north and Harold by sea from Bristol. Gruffyd's disillusioned supporters killed their leader and sent Harold his head.

Significantly, Harold is also said to have travelled to Normandy,

probably in 1064. While no English sources mention this journey, Norman sources claim that Harold was sent by Edward to confirm that he, Edward, had made William his heir. The Norman story, which is vividly depicted on the Bayeux Tapestry, was that Harold fell into the clutches of Guy of Ponthieu after being shipwrecked but was freed by William. Then, after joining William on his Breton campaign, Harold is said to have sworn that he would assist William in his claim to the English throne.

In 1065 the *thegns* of Northumbria rebelled against the rule of Tostig, Harold's brother. Possibly because he wished to broaden his support beyond mere ties to the Godwin family, Harold supported the *thegns* in their bid to replace Tostig as Earl of Northumbria with Morcar of Mercia. Tostig was driven into exile, where he plotted revenge. On 5 January 1066, a dying Edward named Harold his heir, in contradiction to his previous promise to William of Normandy. Harold was immediately accepted as king by the *Witanagemot* – Saxon England's council of magnates. The following day, he was hurriedly crowned in Westminster Abbey. Harold's brief reign was spent attempting to defend his kingdom against a succession of enemies. It is a testimony to his determination, energy and powers of leadership that he very nearly succeeded.

The site of the altar of Battle Abbey church, which is said to have been constructed on William's orders on the spot where Harold fell. The hilltop may have been levelled quite extensively for its construction.

Meanwhile, Harold knew that he faced a number of challenges to his kingship. In addition to William, Duke of Normandy, Harald Hardrada of Norway had a claim to the crown, and there was also the problem of Harold's own exiled brother, Tostig. Indeed, Tostig was the first of Harold's enemies to make a move, raiding the south coast with a fleet of 60 ships before heading up the east coast of England. However, he was driven off by the forces of Edwin of Mercia and Morcar of Northumbria, and sailed to Scotland with the remnants of his fleet.

It seems that it was when Harold received news of Tostig's activities that he mobilised both the *fyrd* – England's part-time defence force raised on the basis of land ownership – and his fleet. Relying on Edwin and Morcar to defend the orth, Harold waited for the Norman invasion, lying with his fleet off the Isle of Wight while the *fyrd* guarded the coast.

But William did not come. Some chroniclers suggest that William's fleet was held up at Dives-sur-Mer by unfavourable winds, but it is possible that William was deliberately waiting until the English army ran out of supplies. It says much for both William's administrative abilities and his powers of leadership that he was able to keep his own army, perhaps as many as 10,000 men, together at Dives for so long. Finally, on 8 September the English army did run out of supplies and Harold was forced to disband it, sending his ships back to London. With Harold's fleet gone, William had a free run of the Channel and, on 12 September, he moved his fleet 150 miles north to St Valery-sur-Somme, where the crossing to England was much shorter.

Shortly after disbanding his forces Harold received bad news. Harald Hardrada had crossed the North Sea with a fleet of 300 ships and, joined by Tostig, defeated Edwin and Morcar at Fulford and entered York. This was a particularly dangerous situation for Harold, as many of the inhabitants of the north were of Viking origin and there was no reason why they should not prefer a Scandinavian king to one from Wessex. Harold acted quickly. After spending two weeks gathering together a fresh army he hurried north, covering nearly 200 miles in just five days. On 25 September, he caught the Norsemen by surprise at Stamford Bridge, just eight miles from York. He destroyed their army, killing both Hardrada and his own brother, Tostig. But he had little chance to enjoy his victory, for on 1 October came the news that William had landed in Sussex.

On 27 September, William had crossed the Channel and landed with his army at Pevensey. They camped for the night in the old Roman fort of Anderida, before moving east to Hastings, where his men erected a fort using timber they had brought with them for the purpose. William

A Norman soldier, as portrayed by a modern-day re-enactor. Although the Bayeux Tapestry gives the impression that Hastings was primarily a battle between Saxon infantry and Norman cavalry, it seems likely that the majority of William's men were in fact infantry. This soldier wears a conical iron helmet with nasal guard and a mail hauberk made up of interlocking iron rings. He carries a painted wooden kite-shaped shield and holds a sword designed for cutting and slashing. Most soldiers on both sides probably had some form of spear as their primary weapon. Not all of William's infantry would have been as well equipped as this individual, while the Bayeux Tapestry suggests that at least some of Harold's troops may well have been dressed in an identical fashion.

Pevensey Castle. The outer walls were built by the Romans at the end of the 3rd century AD and provided William with a secure base on his landing. In 1066 the castle stood on a narrow peninsula, as much of the low-lying land in this picture was under the waters of Pevensey Bay.

wanted to bring Harold to battle as soon as possible for the longer he waited the more time the English king would have to raise more troops against him. William, therefore, ravaged the country around Hastings, part of Harold's old earldom, in a bid to provoke Harold into fighting. The plan worked. Harold headed south with as many men as could follow him, reaching London in five days. He waited there for perhaps six days for more troops to join him, before setting off on 11 October to confront William. It is clear that, had he waited longer, more troops would have been able to join him. He may have been hoping, however, either to surprise William or to bottle him up on the Hastings peninsula, while his own army grew stronger and his fleet, which had sailed again, prevented the Normans from receiving supplies or escaping back to Normandy. The Norman historian, William of Poitiers sums up the situation:

The king was the more furious because he had heard that the Normans had laid waste the neighbourhood of their camp and he planned to take them unawares by a surprise or night attack. Further, in order to prevent their escape, he sent out a fleet of seven hundred armed vessels to block their passage home.

On the evening of 13 October Harold's army, which presumably had picked up reinforcements as it marched south from London, emerged from the Andredsweald forest onto Caldbec Hill where it spent the night. If Harold had been hoping to make a surprise attack early the next morning he was to be disappointed, for William's scouts had spotted his arrival. The Normans stood to arms all night, and in the morning, William advanced from Hastings to Telham Hill, less than two miles from the English camp, and prepared for battle. It seems that it was thus Harold who was taken by surprise by William's move, for one version of the *Anglo-Saxon Chronicle* states '…and William came against him unawares, before his people were set in order.'

Now that there was no chance of defeating the Normans by a surprise attack, Harold drew up his forces as swiftly as he could in a defensive position, almost certainly on Senlac Hill. This position was a strong one, with the rear protected by ravines and forest, the flanks by sharply falling ground and the front by steep slopes above a marshy clay valley. If the Normans were to defeat him it would have to be by a frontal attack.

The English army, perhaps 8,000 strong, was deployed in a thick line on the crest of the hill. It was possibly eight men deep but as our estimate of his army's strength is only a guess, this deployment, too, can only be a guess. Presumably Harold took up a position in or behind the centre of the line, surrounded by his household troops beneath the dragon banner of Wessex and his own personal standard of a fighting man. Harold's brothers, Gyrth and Leofwine, together with other Saxon nobles were also present in the battle, each with their own household troops and retainers. Presumably they would have been stationed at various intervals along the line to lead the *fyrd*. Their household troops, or housecarls, would have gone with them, so it is not impossible that the better-armoured *fyrd*smen were positioned in the front ranks, supported by groups of housecarls at regular intervals.

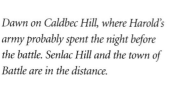

Dawn on Caldbec Hill, where Harold's army probably spent the night before the battle. Senlac Hill and the town of Battle are in the distance.

Norman cavalry attack the Saxon shield wall. Although the majority of the Saxons in the Tapestry are shown with Norman-style kite-shaped shields it seems likely that substantial numbers would have carried round shields. The English are said to have used the war cries 'Godemite!' (God Almighty!), 'Olicrosse!'(Holy Cross!) as well as chanting 'Ut, ut!' (Out, out!).

The English were drawn up in a shield wall, an established tactic where the front rank held their shields closely together. On the Bayeux Tapestry they are even shown as overlapping. How this worked in practice is not clear for, although it is an excellent formation in which to fight with spears, there would have had to be gaps in the line – a housecarl with a two-handed axe needed room in which to swing it.

Marching down from Telham Hill, William's army seems to have deployed into three bodies. It is generally accepted that the Bretons, under Alan Rufus were on the left, the Normans were in the centre, and troops from France, Flanders and Picardy were on the right under Eustace of Boulogne and William fitzOsbern, although even the evidence for this deployment is open to interpretation. The Bayeux Tapestry gives the impression that the Norman army, which also numbered about 8,000 men, was largely composed of cavalry supported by archers. However, the Tapestry's creators chose to depict it in this manner in order to appeal to the aristocratic audience for which it was made – in one scene they even show mounted knights besieging a castle!

In fact, a substantial proportion of William's forces would have consisted of armoured infantry. Each section of his army was deployed with archers and crossbowmen to the front, infantry in the second line and cavalry to the rear. Clearly the plan was to soften up the English lines with volleys of arrows before the infantry moved into the attack with the cavalry waiting to exploit any gaps.

Norman archers, from the Bayeux Tapestry. William also employed crossbowmen at Hastings. His bowmen were almost certainly unarmoured, and the figure in mail, the only archer to be shown like this in the Tapestry, may well be a captain.

The battle began at approximately 9am, as William's archers and crossbowmen moved forward to bombard the English line with a hail of missiles before his infantry and cavalry attacked the English line. William of Poitiers takes up the story:

The duke and his men, in no way dismayed by the difficulty of the ground, came slowly up the hill… the Norman foot drawing nearer provoked the English by raining death and wounds upon them with their missiles. But the English resisted valiantly, each man according to his strength, and they hurled back spears and javelins and weapons of all kinds together with axes and stones fastened to pieces of wood. You would have thought to see our men overwhelmed by this death-dealing weight of projectiles. The knights came after the chief, being in the rearmost rank, and all disdaining to fight at long range were eager to use their swords. The shouts both of the Normans and of the barbarians were drowned in the clash of arms and by the cries of the dying, and for a long time the battle raged with the utmost fury. The English, however, had the advantage of the ground and profited by remaining within their position in close order. They gained further superiority from their numbers, from the impregnable front, which they preserved, and most of all from the manner in which their weapons found easy passage through the shields and armour of their enemies. Thus they bravely withstood and successfully repulsed those who were engaging them at close quarters, and inflicted losses upon the men who were shooting missiles at them from a distance.

Hastings, 14 October 1066

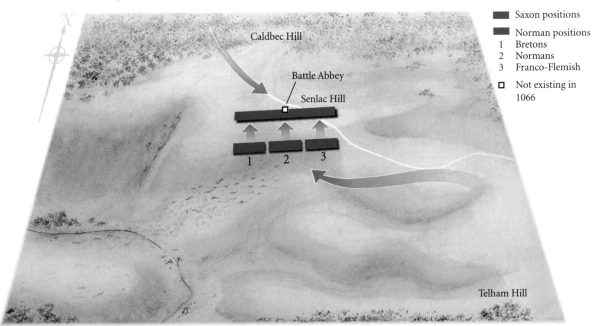

William raises his helmet to show his men that he is still alive. He carries a rough club or 'baculum' as a symbol of authority.

Amongst the weapons that 'found easy passage through the shields and armour of their enemies' must have been the fearsome two-handed axe, which is portrayed so graphically in the Bayeux Tapestry. As casualties mounted and the English shield wall still held firm, the Bretons on William's left suddenly gave way and poured back down the slope. With their flank exposed, the Normans in the centre began to fall back too, and soon William's entire army was in danger of collapse. To make matters worse, the rumour spread that William himself had been killed. As the Bretons retreated they were pursued by a section of Harold's army. This may have been a case of indiscipline amongst the English *fyrd*smen or it may have been an organised counter-attack but, in either case, it was clearly a critical moment in the battle. William acted swiftly:

Seeing a large part of the hostile host pursuing his own troops, the prince thrust himself in front of those in flight, shouting at them and threatening them with his spear. Staying their retreat, he took off his helmet, and standing before them bareheaded he cried: 'Look at me well. I am still alive and by the grace of God I shall yet prove victor.'

The Bayeux Tapestry does indeed show William pushing back his helmet, while Eustace of Boulogne, carrying the papal banner, points at him. Rallied by William, his soldiers turned on their pursuers, who were now scattered on open ground, and slaughtered them, although the Tapestry implies that some of the English troops managed to make a stand on a hillock on the Norman left before being cut down. Despite these losses, which may have included King Harold's two brothers who fell in the battle, the English line still held.

According to William of Poitiers, the Normans now used the tactic of a 'feigned retreat' to draw more of Harold's men down from the relative safety of Senlac Hill. While this does seem to have been an extremely difficult and risky manoeuvre – there was always the chance that those Norman soldiers not taking part in it might think that it was the real thing and panic – the Normans had used this tactic in previous battles (and were to again at Cassel in 1071). It was probably executed on a fairly minor scale during the battle, with small groups of knights using the tactic to win a localised success.

As evening drew near and the English line still stood unbroken, William is said to have ordered his archers to shoot their arrows into the air so that they fell amongst the men behind the shield wall. Contemporary accounts do not mention this – it is first referred to by Henry of Huntingdon in the 12th century – but the Tapestry does depict large numbers of archers coming forward at this point, and many of the shields of the Saxon troops are shown bristling with arrows. Although they are not shown in the Tapestry, crossbowmen seem to have taken a toll of even the most heavily armoured men. Guy of Amiens, the author of the *Carmen de Hastingae Proelio*, a Latin poem about the battle, wrote:

…the bands of archers attacked and from a distance transfixed bodies with their shafts and the crossbowmen destroyed the shields as if by a hailstorm, shattered them by countless blows.

In the end, the relentless combination of arrow fire and attacks by infantry and cavalry seem to have thinned the English ranks sufficiently for the Norman knights to break through the shield wall. It was at this stage of the battle that Harold, possibly wounded in the eye by an arrow, was hacked to the ground by a group of knights and killed. The Saxon line, already crumbling, finally disintegrated. While some of Harold's household troops may have fought on, in true Maldon fashion (*see* Chapter 1), around the body of their fallen leader, the majority of his remaining men fled. Some may have turned and made a last stand in what William of Poitiers called a steep valley intersected with ditches,

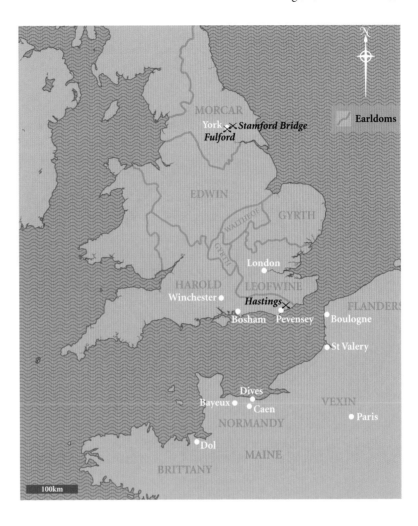

England and Northern France at the time of the Norman Conquest.

sometimes referred to as the Malfosse (the 'evil ditch') but, for the English, the battle was lost.

Although William had triumphed at Hastings, he was not to enter London for another two months. Moreover, it took a further five years campaigning before he established control over all of England. Yet Hastings had been a decisive victory. The English had lost not only their leaders but also their best chance to stop the invasion in its tracks.

Why did William win? Needless to say William of Poitiers would have us believe that it was because of William's inspired leadership: 'He dominated the battle, checking his own men in flight, strengthening their spirit, and sharing their dangers'. Clearly this must have played a part in the Norman victory – William's intervention in rallying his broken troops was clearly critical – and we cannot ignore the possible effects of the feigned withdrawal. Harold's death may have caused the English to flee but it seems that by then they were already broken.

Ultimately, William probably won because he had more tactical options. All Harold's infantry could do was to stand and take whatever the Normans threw at them. Without cavalry, the English were unable to take full advantage of the rout of the French left, whereas the Normans were able to use their knights to devastating effect once the English shield wall broke. Furthermore, the presence of substantial numbers of archers in William's army meant that in the gaps between hand-to-hand combat he was able to keep up the pressure on the English line by switching to missile fire. Nevertheless, the fact that the battle had lasted so long suggests that the two armies were relatively evenly matched, both in terms of numbers and fighting ability. William had won but, as was said of a certain battle 750 years later when Englishmen once again stood on a ridge to face the French, it had been a close run thing.

The Bayeux Tapestry and the death of Harold

This remarkable 'tapestry' is in fact a 68m long embroidery, showing the Norman version of the events leading up to and culminating in the battle of Hastings: Harold's voyage to France; his oath to support William; his seizure of the English throne; William's preparations for invasion; the battle itself. Part of the Tapestry is clearly missing, with the result that it now finishes rather abruptly with the defeated English fleeing off the end but it may well have originally concluded with William on his new throne. This would not only have made narrative sense; it would have balanced the first scene in the tapestry, which shows an enthroned Edward the Confessor. The Tapestry was probably embroidered in Kent for William's half-brother, Odo of Bayeux, who figures prominently in the Tapestry, and was completed around 1070.

Without doubt, the scene that has attracted by far the most interest is that showing the death of Harold, and over the years there has been considerable debate about which figure represents the king. It is now generally accepted that the falling figure with an axe represents Harold. He is shown being cut through the thigh and this is described in a number of accounts of the king's death. However, it has been argued that the figure with an arrow in his eye also represents Harold, and what we in fact have is a scene showing first his wounding by an arrow and then his death. This ties in with the story that Harold was hit by an arrow, which was certainly circulating as early as 1080, when Amatus of Montecassino wrote about it. The fact that the two figures are so very different in appearance must in itself cast some doubt on this theory and, as MK Lawson has pointed out in his book, *The Battle of Hastings, 1066*, we also need to remember that the Tapestry we see today is the work not only of 11th-century embroiderers, but also 19th-century restorers.

The English shield wall crumbles and Harold (with axe) is cut down, as shown in the Bayeux Tapestry.

The earliest record we have of the Tapestry's pre-restoration appearance is a series of drawings made by a French draughtsman, Antoine Benoit, in 1729. Benoit's work clearly shows the figure with a shield holding not an arrow but something much longer without flights. It appears, therefore, that at some stage a restorer, knowing the story of the death of Harold, has turned this mystery object into an arrow and also diverted its path so that it appears to be hitting the figure in the eye. This suggests that the individual with a shield was never meant to be the king. Furthermore, nothing should be read into the fact that the word 'Harold' is above his head, for in other parts of the Tapestry names are some distance away from their subjects. It has also been pointed out that a line of stitch holes can be clearly seen protruding from the 'real' Harold's eye and there may originally have been an arrow there. This too seems to relate to the work of later restorers, however, for in 1819 an Englishman, Charles Stothard, made a set of drawings of the Tapestry for the Society of Antiquaries and carefully noted all the stitch holes. At that time the figure had none. It therefore seems likely that, wherever the story that Harold was hit in the eye originated, it was not, as has sometimes been suggested, from a misreading of the Bayeux Tapestry.

William of Normandy (1027–87)

William was born in Falaise in 1027, the son of Duke Robert of Normandy and Herleva, the daughter of a local tanner. Although his parents had never married, as the Duke's only son he was recognised as his successor, with the approval of King Henry I of France and the Norman baronage. Even so, when his father died in 1035, leaving him Duke of Normandy at the age of eight, his prospects of survival cannot have seemed good. Yet survive he did, and, in 1047, he defeated his cousin Guy of Brionne, who was trying to take over the duchy at Val-es-Dunes near Caen, the only major battle he was to fight until Hastings. In 1050 William married his cousin, Matilda of Flanders, a union that was to produce nine children. The following year Henry I of France and Geoffrey Martel of Anjou formed an alliance against the young duke, and William was forced to repel invasions in 1053/4 and 1057. However, in 1060, both his enemies died and William was at last able to seize the initiative, as King Henry's successor was a child and Anjou was rent by a succession crisis. In 1063, William conquered Maine, which had previously been under Anjou's control.

Three years later, a mixture of skill and good fortune enabled William to secure the throne of England, which he believed had been promised to him by the childless Edward the Confessor. He was crowned at Westminster on Christmas Day 1066 but had to fight for nearly five years before he could overcome the last English resistance to his rule. His 'Harrying of the North' – the systematic devastation of the northern counties in response to a series of rebellions – led to widespread starvation. The confiscation of estates from rebellious English opponents and their subsequent redistribution to his supporters led to the creation of an all-new French speaking ruling class, something William had not envisaged in 1066.

The last 12 years of his reign were beset by problems in Normandy and quarrels with his eldest son Robert, and William was obliged to spend the bulk of his time in Normandy. In 1087, while campaigning along the Seine, the horse he was riding stumbled and he was thrown onto his saddle, suffering serious internal injuries, from which he died six weeks later. William left his ancestral lands in Normandy to Robert and England to his second son, William Rufus. He was buried in St Stephen's Abbey in Caen where his corpulent body was found to be too big to fit into the stone sarcophagus that had been made for it. When an attempt was made to force the body into the sarcophagus, it burst.

The 14th-century gatehouse of Battle Abbey. Like most of his contemporaries, William I was a complex mix of brutality and piety. He caused wholesale death and destruction during his campaigns to subjugate England, then founded an abbey to atone for his sins.

History or propaganda

As for William, their leader, he surpassed them in both courage and wisdom, and should rightly be placed above some of the Greek and Roman leaders so highly praised in the records, and treated as the equal of others. His leadership in the battle was noble, preventing men from fleeing, inspiring courage in others, sharing danger, more often ordering his men to follow him than to advance. From this it is clear that his courage opened the way for his soldiers and encouraged their boldness. A not inconsiderable part of the enemy army lost heart merely at the sight of this astonishing and frightening horseman, before they had sustained any injury. Three horses were killed under him. Three times he intrepidly leaped to the ground and hastened to avenge the death of his warhorse. This shows his quickness, his strength of mind and body. The fury of his sword pierced shields, helmets and hauberks; he struck down several soldiers with his shield alone...

William of Poitiers is one of the main authorities for the course of the battle of Hastings, for although he was not present, he was William the Conqueror's chaplain and had previously fought alongside many of the men who had been at Hastings. He therefore had a good understanding of military matters and would have been able to discuss the battle with the main protagonists. But, as this extract shows, his primary purpose was not to provide future generations with a factual account of the battle – it was to extol William's virtues.

Did a considerable part of the English army really lose heart at the sight of William? All the contemporary and near-contemporary accounts of Hastings are prejudiced to some degree by considerations of national pride, the desire to make a moral point or please a patron, or even just the desire to tell a good story. William of Malmesbury, for example, has been described as the greatest English historian after Bede. He researched widely in the libraries of the cathedrals and abbeys of England, and also brought a critical approach to the source material he unearthed. However, he regarded the Norman Conquest as the judgement of God on a sinful people, which is clearly reflected in his claim that:

The courageous leaders mutually prepared for battle, each according to his national custom. The English, as we have heard, passed the night without sleep, in drinking and singing... On the other side, the Normans passed the whole night in confessing their sins, and received the sacrament in the morning.

Given that the English had covered over 50 miles in two days, it seems unlikely that they would have passed the night without sleep!

War on the Scottish Border

The years following the Norman conquest in 1066 saw intermittent fighting between England and Scotland, much of it over possession of the earldom of Northumberland. In 1138 David I of Scotland invaded England, ostensibly in support of his niece Matilda in her war against Stephen, and, although he was defeated at the Battle of the Standard near Northallerton in 1138, he was able to secure both Northumberland and Cumbria. The Scots held onto them until 1157, when David's grandson, Malcolm IV, was forced by Henry II to return them to England. There was further fighting in 1173–4 when King William the Lion of Scotland took advantage of a rebellion against Henry to invade Northumberland, only to be surprised and captured by the English at Alnwick.

For much of the 13th century there was peace between the two countries but the 'Great Cause' – the dispute over the crown of Scotland following the death in 1290 of Margaret, the sole heir of Alexander III – was to have a profound affect on Anglo-Scottish relations and ushered in a period of more than 40 years near-continuous warfare. Edward I, who had hoped to control Scotland by marrying Margaret off to his son, saw a fresh opportunity to extend his power northwards when he was asked to judge between the 13 candidates for the throne.

Having secured recognition of his overlordship from most of the principal claimants, Edward duly chose John Balliol as the new King of Scotland.

It soon became clear that Edward regarded Balliol as little more than a vassal. When Balliol attempted to exercise his independence by signing a treaty with France, Edward invaded Scotland in 1296, storming Berwick and capturing Balliol. However, the Scottish cause was then taken up by William Wallace and Andrew Moray who inflicted a humiliating defeat on an overconfident and careless English force under Jean de Warenne at Stirling in September 1297. Edward responded by raising an even larger army and, in July 1298, a lethal combination of archers and cavalry destroyed Wallace's army of spearmen at Falkirk. Gradually, in a series of campaigns over the next six years, Edward crushed nearly all Scottish resistance. In 1305 Wallace, who had fought on in relative obscurity was betrayed, captured and sent to London where he was hanged, drawn and quartered.

Only six months after Wallace's execution, Edward was faced with a new challenge when the vacant Scottish throne was seized by Robert Bruce, who had murdered his chief rival John 'the Red' Comyn at Greyfriars Church, Dumfries, in February 1306 and had himself crowned king at Scone in March. Edward I immediately ordered yet another invasion of Scotland, and in June his advance guard defeated Bruce at Methven. Bruce went into hiding with a price on his head, while Edward mercilessly hunted down his family and supporters. Edward's policy of treating the Scots as rebellious subjects was generally counter-productive and it enabled Bruce, who had been decidedly lukewarm about the idea of Scottish independence when Balliol was king, to portray himself as a national hero.

The turning point came in 1307 when Bruce defeated the Earl of Pembroke at Loudon in May. Two months later, Edward, preparing to invade Scotland once again, died at Burgh by Sands. Although his successor, Edward II, was personally brave and an experienced soldier, he was no leader and, lacking his father's single-minded determination, he allowed Bruce to seize the initiative. Despite enjoying far greater resources than their opponents, the English were never able to fortify Scotland as they had done Wales in the 1280s. Bruce fought a guerrilla war, avoiding battle and destroying the isolated English strongholds one by one. In the summer of 1310, Edward invaded Scotland but the Scots, employing scorched earth tactics, fell back before him until, starved of supplies, the English were obliged to withdraw. By now Bruce

Border warfare 1100_1550.

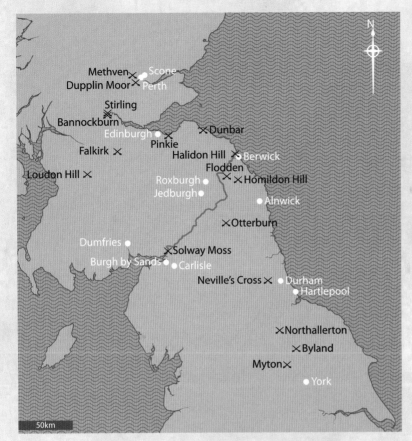

laid siege to Berwick in 1319, only to be thwarted when the daring raid into Yorkshire by Moray and Douglas, two of Bruce's lieutenants, and victory at Myton caused many of his nobles to return home to defend their estates. Further humiliation followed in 1322 when an English army, returning from yet another unsuccessful invasion of Scotland, was surprised and routed at Byland near Helmsley. Scottish raids continued until, in 1328, Roger Mortimer and Isabella, who had deposed Edward II the previous year, finally recognised Bruce's kingship in exchange for a payment of £20,000.

Bruce did not live long to enjoy his triumph for he died, eaten away by leprosy, in 1329. His death allowed Edward III, who had seized power from his mother, Isabella, and Roger Mortimer to ally with some of Bruce's old Scottish enemies. And, in 1332, Edward Balliol, the pro-English claimant to the Scottish throne defeated forces loyal to Bruce's son David II at Dupplin Moor. The following spring Edward III recaptured Berwick after his archers had made short work of a Scottish relief force at Halidon Hill. Balliol was crowned king and ceded much of south-east Scotland to the English, thus ensuring another century of intermittent warfare and frequent cross-border raiding.

The Scots were helped in their attempts to recover their lost

felt confident enough to take the war across the border, raiding so destructively that the northern counties of England were forced to resort to bribery in order to persuade him to leave them alone.

More and more English strongholds fell in Scotland until, by 1314, the only major castle still holding out was Stirling. In 1313 Bruce's brother Edward had come to an agreement with the castle's governor that Stirling would surrender, if it was not relieved within a year. Bruce was furious. He knew that Edward could not allow Stirling to fall in this way. An English

invasion was now a certainty and a pitched battle against a huge English army inevitable. However when it did come, at Bannockburn in June, Bruce's tactical superiority and the fighting spirit of his infantry won the day over the much larger but poorly led English army.

Bruce's victory secured his grip on the Scottish throne and gave him almost a free hand over the next few years. Raiding almost at will, the Scots devastated Tynedale, burned Hartlepool, sacked Durham and, in 1318, recaptured the crucial border town of Berwick. Stirred into action Edward gathered another army and territory by the English preoccupation with their war with France. By 1341 David II had returned from exile, Perth and Edinburgh had been recaptured by his supporters, and Balliol had retreated to England. The gradual expulsion of the English from Scotland continued through the 14th century despite David's defeat and capture at Neville's Cross near Durham in 1346 after he had invaded England in support of his ally France. During the 15th century the Scots took advantage of events in England to make further gains. In 1408 Jedburgh was recaptured in the aftermath of the Percy rebellion. James II retook Roxburgh in 1460 – a mixed blessing, as he was killed when a cannon being fired in celebration blew up next to him. Finally, in 1461, Berwick was recovered when Margaret of Anjou handed it over to the Scots in exchange for their support against the Yorkists. When Richard of Gloucester recaptured the town in 1482 it was, with the exception of the Isle of Man, all that remained of nearly two centuries of attempted English conquest.

Wars, raids and counter-raids continued for over half a century. James IV's invasion of England in support of his French allies ended disastrously with his death at Flodden in 1513. In the early 1540s, religious differences and Scotland's alliance with France led to tension between the two countries, and when James V snubbed an offer by Henry VIII to meet at York, relations descended into war. In November 1542, in retaliation for a raid led by the Duke of Norfolk, James V sent a large army south, only for it to be routed by a small English force at Solway Moss. After James's death, which many attributed to the shock of this humiliating defeat, Henry VIII attempted to force through a marriage between the infant Mary Queen of Scots and Edward, his son and heir – the so-called 'rough wooing'. When the Scots repudiated an earlier marriage agreement, an angry Henry raided Scotland, causing extensive devastation. The Duke of Somerset, Protector of the Realm after Henry's death, continued this policy. In 1547 he defeated the Scots at Pinkie outside Edinburgh but was unable to profit politically from his victory, and Mary was sent to France.

In the second half of the 16th century, while there was officially peace between the two nations, many of the hard-bitten borderer families continued to behave as they had done for centuries – pursuing blood feuds and raiding across the border with monotonous regularity – a situation that was only really addressed after James VI of Scotland's accession to the English throne in 1603. Indeed, in the last years of Elizabeth I's reign, lawlessness on the border had reached such a point that it was seriously proposed in England that £30,000 be spent on the refortification of Hadrian's Wall!

Edward I (1239–1307)

Unlike his peace-loving father, Henry III, Edward I was a natural warrior. He fought in his first tournament in 1256 and died half a century later, leading his army on yet another invasion of Scotland. During the political unrest of the late 1250s and early 1260s he changed sides several times before eventually supporting his father against the baronial opposition led by Simon de Montfort. At the battle of Lewes in 1264 his cavalry routed the left of Montfort's army but made the mistake of pursuing their beaten enemies off the field of battle. When they eventually returned they found that the rest of the royal army had been defeated. Edward gave himself up as hostage to ensure his father's safety but the following year he escaped by outriding his escort outside Hereford. Taking command of the royal forces, he then showed some skill in trapping and destroying Montfort's outnumbered army at Evesham.

In 1270 Edward went on crusade and was famously stabbed in the arm by an assassin outside Acre. Unfortunately the story that his wife Eleanor saved his life by sucking the poison from his veins appears to be without foundation. He heard of his father's death while returning home in 1272 but stayed on the continent until 1274 to deal with the affairs of the Duchy of Aquitaine, English territory at the time. He also found time to take part with his entourage in an extremely violent tournament at Chalons-sur-Marne, dishing out a fearsome hammering to the Count of Chalons who had unwisely attempted to pull the powerfully built English king from his horse.

As a ruler Edward instigated a number of improvements to the royal justice system but spent much of his reign, and indeed much of his money, engaged in a succession of wars, mainly brought on by his desire to be ruler of the whole of Britain. He turned his attention first to the principality of Wales, using his superior resources to overwhelm the resistance of Llewelyn ap Gruffudd in 1276–7 and defeating an uprising five years later. Edward reorganised Welsh law, created English-style shires, founded new towns and built a series of powerful castles to maintain English military dominance.

In 1287 he raised taxes to fund a second crusade to the Holy Land but the fall of Acre in 1291 meant that there was nowhere to go, and Edward prepared to spend the money elsewhere.

He did not have far to look. The death in 1290 of Margaret, the child Queen of Scotland, scuppered his plan to control that country by marrying her to his son but the succession crisis that followed gave him a second chance to influence affairs north of the border. Adjudicating between a number of rival claimants to the Scottish throne, Edward chose John Balliol but the high-handed way in which he then treated him led the Scots to assert their independence. Although he was already at war with the King of France over Aquitaine, Edward responded by raising another army and invaded Scotland in 1296. Although his forces were generally successful on the battlefield, Scotland was too large to be ringed with castles as Wales had been, and Edward was still at war when he died, deeply in debt, in 1307.

Massacre of the Innocents Myton, 20 September 1319

Perhaps no other medieval battle demonstrates so graphically the importance of leadership, experience and training. At Myton a hastily assembled rabble of English townsmen, husbandmen and clerics, led by an archbishop, was trapped and cut to pieces by an army of hard-bitten Scottish raiders.

The possible site of the medieval bridge over the Swale at Myton, about 230m downstream of the existing bridge, which was built in 1868 and rebuilt in 2002. It is possible, however, that the medieval bridge was actually a similar distance upstream of Myton.

Scottish raiders

Soldiers looting depicted in a 14th-century French manuscript. Destructive cross-border raids were a common feature of the Anglo-Scots wars of the 13th and 14th centuries.

In the decade after the battle of Bannockburn in 1314, at which the English had been decisively defeated and driven out of Scotland, the Scots raided England almost at will, avoiding battle but carrying off loot, cattle and prisoners. Many northern English towns were forced to buy them off by paying ransoms. Jean Le Bel, a Hainault chronicler who accompanied Edward III on a campaign against such raiders in 1327, gave a vivid description of these hardy warriors:

When they want to pass into England, they are all mounted, except for the camp followers, who are on foot; the knights and squires are mounted on good, large rouncies, and the other Scots on little hackneys. They bring no carts because of the mountainous terrain, nor do they carry any supplies of bread or wine. They are so little addicted to luxury that, in time of war, they can subsist well enough for a long time on half-cooked meat, without bread, and good river water, uncut with wine. They do without pots and kettles, since they cook their meat inside the hides of the animals which they have skinned, and they well know that they will find a great abundance of cattle in the country they are raiding. So they carry no other supplies, except that each one carries a large flat stone in his saddle bags and ties behind him a sack of oatmeal. When they have eaten so much of this badly-cooked meat that their stomachs feel weak, they throw this stone in the fire, and mix a bit of their oatmeal with water. When the stone is hot, they make a sort of biscuit on it, which they eat to restore their stomachs. So it is no marvel that they make longer marches than other people... they enter into England, and burn and devastate the country, and find so many cattle that they do not know what to do with them all.

It was such hardy guerrilla warriors that the English faced at the battle of Myton. In 1318, the Scots captured Berwick-upon-Tweed, the border town controlling the east road into England. As well as being a strategic setback for the English, it was also a serious blow to their prestige, for the town had been expensively refortified by Edward I in the last years of his reign. In order to continue the war against Scotland, King Edward II moved his court to York in October 1318, gathered together a large army at Newcastle and, in August 1319, laid siege to Berwick.

Rather than risk battle against this powerful English army, Robert Bruce decided to employ diversionary tactics to relieve the town and dispatched a force to ravage the north of England. Led by Thomas Randolph, Earl of Moray, and Sir James Douglas, two Bannockburn veterans, the Scots crossed into England near Carlisle and headed south.

Plundering and burning as they went, they crossed the Pennines and moved into Yorkshire, eventually reaching Boroughbridge and camping to the west of the river Swale near Myton, only 13 miles from York. At this point, the English learnt from a captured Scottish spy both the location of the Scottish army and the fact that Moray and Douglas, in a typically bold move, were planning to abduct Edward's Queen, Isabella, who was staying close to York. In the absence of the king and his leading earls, it was the Archbishop of York, William Melton who took charge of the situation, quickly sending Isabella off to Nottingham for safety. Then, assisted by John Hotham, Bishop of Ely, and Nicholas Fleming, Mayor of York, Melton set about raising a force with which to confront the Scots.

An atmospheric effigy of King Edward II from his tomb in the north ambulatory of Gloucester Cathedral.

Berwick-upon-Tweed. Berwick's position on the Anglo-Scottish border gave it immense strategic importance. The town was stormed by the forces of Edward I in 1296 and changed hands on at least a dozen occasions before being taken by Richard of Gloucester in 1482. The town's medieval defences were strengthened in the reign of Henry VIII, although most of the surviving ramparts are Elizabethan.

It was not the first time that an Archbishop of York had recruited an army to fight the Scots and it was not to be the last. In 1138 Archbishop Thurstan had raised an English army, which defeated the Scots at Northallerton. Three centuries later, in 1346, Archbishop William de la Zouche defeated and captured David II of Scotland at Neville's Cross. On both occasions, however, experienced soldiers from the nobility actually led the armies in the field – Walter Espec and Roger Mowbray at Northallerton and Henry Percy and Ralph Neville at Neville's Cross. Furthermore, Thurstan's levies had been strengthened by contingents of knights and archers at Northallerton while in 1346 the English, who had been anticipating a Scottish invasion, had already raised a well-balanced force of men-at-arms and archers. William Melton had no such advantages in 1319. The key northern earls were away with Edward at the siege of Berwick and, crucially, they had taken their men-at-arms with them.

William Melton (d.1340)

Little is known about Melton's youth – he was born near Hull and seems to have spent some time at Oxford University. In 1297, he entered royal service in the household of the future Edward II, where his financial acumen earned him rapid advancement. By 1307, he was Keeper of the Privy Seal and Treasurer of the Wardrobe – key administrative positions – and rewards came in the form of a host of religious appointments, culminating in January 1316 with his election as Archbishop of York. Melton travelled to Avignon for his consecration but this was delayed due to the death of the pope and, despite frequent appeals by the king, did not take place for 18 months.

The appointment was a reward to Melton for his service but it also made the most of his considerable abilities, for his responsibilities as Archbishop were administrative and diplomatic as well as religious. He was commissioned to negotiate with the Scots on a number of occasions and, in 1339, he was one of those charged by Edward III to raise troops to resist a French invasion.

Melton vigorously upheld his ecclesiastical rights, clashing with the Archbishop of Canterbury, and once even excommunicated the Bishop of Durham for resisting his powers of visitation. Yet he was no mere politician. He carried out his duties as archbishop honestly and thoroughly, often at considerable personal risk, for after Bannockburn the Scots raided almost at will throughout the north of England for nearly 15 years.

After the death of Edward II, his principal patron, Melton seems to have taken a lower profile. He did not attend the coronation of Edward III, although he did marry the king to Philippa of Hainault in York Minster in 1328. Cleared in 1329 of complicity in Edmund of Woodstock's plot against the king's mother Isabella and her lover Mortimer, he briefly held royal office again in the early 1330s before dying in 1340.

It is clear that Melton was a talented administrator of great piety and considerable personal bravery but these qualities counted for little at Myton in September 1319, when his hastily assembled force was confronted by an experienced Scottish army led by two veteran commanders.

A statue of Archbishop William Melton on the West Front of York Minster.

As a result, when Melton left York for Myton on the morning of 20 September it was with a motley force of 'laymen, clerks, and men of religion.' It is impossible to be certain about the size of the two armies as contemporary sources are notoriously inaccurate over this matter. In his poem, *The Bruce*, written in 1375, John Barbour put the size of the rapidly assembled English army at 20,000, far outnumbering that of the Scots. It is difficult to see where Melton could have found so many men, though, particularly as York's entire population in the first half of the 14th century has been estimated at no more than 11,000 people. It is likely that Melton had far fewer men than the 10–15,000 suggested by modern historians and the outnumbered Scots even fewer still.

The archbishop's plan was to catch the Scots by surprise. He seems to have been concerned that, if the Scots learned of his approach, they would simply withdraw, taking their booty with them. Furthermore, he must have realised that, even though he had the advantage of numbers, if it did come to battle then the element of surprise would give his inexperienced force its best chance of victory against the battle-hardened Scots. In reality, however, there was little chance that the Scots would be caught napping. Douglas in particular was a veteran of the guerrilla warfare of the years leading up to Bannockburn when his very survival had depended on watchfulness and speed of reaction. It seems almost certain that he and Moray would have dispatched some of the *hobilars* (mounted infantry) mentioned in accounts of the battle to watch nearby roads and bridges and warn of any approaching enemy force.

A contemporary chronicler, the Monk of Malmesbury, describes the English advance and the Scottish reaction to it: The English

…went stealthily and without noise, to take the enemy by surprise, because if they were warned they might perhaps take flight. Nevertheless they were well enough warned, yet they did not flee. For when they perceived our men advancing in disorder, they said: "These are not soldiers but huntsmen; they will not achieve much".

Had the Scots been up against a well-organised, well-equipped English army, it seems likely that they would have slipped away. When Moray and Douglas were informed of the nature of the force that was heading towards them, however, they resolved to stand and fight. They formed up their spearmen into a single schiltron – a tightly packed formation initially developed to repel cavalry – and created a smokescreen to hide their deployment by setting fire to some haystacks.

In order to reach their enemies the English had to cross the River Swale by the bridge at Myton. Whether they then 'marched all scattered through the fields and in no kind of array' in search of the Scots or whether they were themselves attacked before they had time to form up properly after crossing the bridge is not certain. Nor is it known exactly where the Scots were deployed. It is possible that they were drawn up too far to the west to prevent the English from crossing the Swale. But it is equally possible that they were relatively near to the bridge and, hidden by their smokescreen, were deliberately waiting for the English to cross the river before suddenly attacking them. William Wallace had done something similar at Stirling in 1297 when he allowed the English infantry to cross the bridge there before sweeping down and cutting them off from their cavalry.

Myton, 20 September 1319

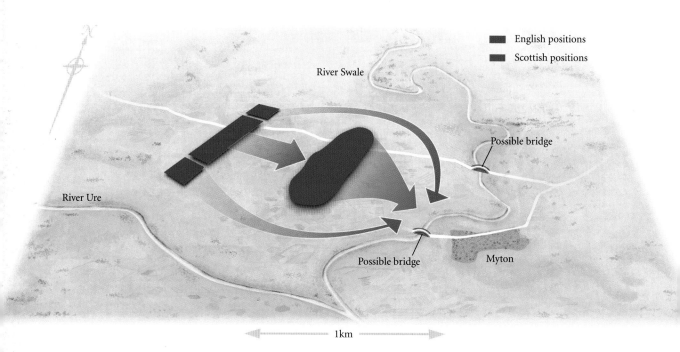

■ English positions
■ Scottish positions

River Swale

Possible bridge

River Ure

Possible bridge

Myton

1km

Archery training depicted on the 14th-century Luttrell Psalter. *Lack of training, together with a shortage of men-at-arms, were key factors in the English defeat at Myton.*

What is clear, however, is that having lost the element of surprise, Melton's force stood little chance against the veteran Scots who were now about to go on the offensive themselves. As the Malmesbury chronicler put it:

They were indeed men picked from the whole of Scotland for their fighting ability, fit for every task. Many of our men, on the other hand, were untrained in the art of war, and were readier to flee than to fight.

The probable position of the Scottish army, about one mile north-west of the modern-day village of Myton, on slightly raised ground above the flood-plain of the Swale. The landscape was essentially open and unenclosed at the time of the battle with the two rivers providing the only obstacles.

Sir James Douglas (c.1286–1330)

One of the most courageous, daring and ruthless commanders of his age, James Douglas joined Robert Bruce when he made his bid for the Scottish throne in 1306 and played a leading part in the often brutal warfare that followed as the would-be king struggled to oust his English enemies and eliminate his Scottish rivals. In 1308, operating out of Ettrick Forest, he surprised the garrison of Douglas Castle while they were in church, slaughtering most of them and seizing the undefended castle. Realising that he could not hope to hold it against the vastly superior forces ranged against him, Douglas executed his prisoners in the castle cellars, mixed their blood and limbs with emptied sacks of provisions and polluted the castle well with salt and dead horses.

In February 1314 Douglas captured Roxburgh Castle in a daring night attack, his men concealing themselves under their cloaks and using a rope ladder to scale the castle walls. Later that year he was knighted on the field of Bannockburn, where he may have commanded a division of the Scottish army and pursued Edward II in his flight from the field. He then served with the Earl of Moray in the attacks on northern England that followed. In the summer of 1315 he captured and looted Hartlepool and plundered the Benedictine Priory of St Bees before being wounded at the siege

of Carlisle. In 1316 he was nearly captured when a surprise attack on Berwick went wrong and he had to escape in a small boat, but he assisted in its capture two years later. In 1317 he again defeated the English who had hoped to take advantage of Bruce's absence in Ireland by invading Roxburghshire.

After his part in the victory at Myton, Douglas' military successes continued. In 1322, he served under Bruce and Moray at Byland, when a surprise uphill attack drove the English back in flight and almost led to the capture of Edward II. In July 1327, Douglas and Moray again raided England, pillaging County Durham and, in a daring night attack on the English camp in Weardale, came near to capturing the young King Edward III himself. The Scots ran rings round the cumbersome English army during the campaign, reducing Edward to tears of frustration, before returning unscathed to Scotland.

The tomb of Sir James Douglas in St Bride's Church, Douglas village.

Before his death in 1329, Bruce asked Douglas to carry his heart to Palestine in redemption of his unfulfilled vow to go on a crusade. Sir James set out in 1330, bearing with him a silver casket containing Bruce's embalmed heart. He got as far as Spain where he fell fighting the Moors on 25 August. He was later buried in St Bride's Church, Douglas village. Since that day, the Douglases have borne a human heart in their coat of arms.

'Black Douglas', as he was known to the English, was described by the Scottish poet John Barbour: 'when he was cheerful he was attractive, meek and sweet in company but if you saw him in battle, he had another face altogether'.

And flee they did. As the tightly packed ranks of Scottish spearmen advanced towards them the English broke. They streamed back, panic stricken, towards Myton, only to find their escape route barred by Scottish infantry who had mounted up and ridden round the flanks of the retreating English. Many tried to escape by swimming the Swale and some drowned in the attempt. Many more were either killed or captured in the meadows of Myton Pastures before the onset of night enabled others to escape. One account claims that 4,000 English died in the rout with a further 1,000 drowning in the Swale but a Scottish source that puts the English loss at about 1,000 may be nearer the mark. Amongst the dead were a substantial number of clergymen, earning the battle the ironic nickname of 'the Chapter of Myton'. William Melton and John Hotham managed to ride to safety but the Mayor of York was not so lucky. He was cut to pieces on the battlefield. Scottish losses were minimal.

The Scots had not intended to fight a set-piece battle in England but Myton turned out to be an unexpected bonus. They returned home with large numbers of prisoners who could be expensively ransomed at a later date. More importantly, the devastation caused by the raid forced Edward to abandon the siege of Berwick so that the northern earls in his army could return home to defend their lands. Bruce's diversion had been a brilliant success.

The White Battle

The Scots went over the water of Solway ... and privily they steal away by night, and come into England, and robbed and destroyed all that they might, and spared no manner [of] thing until they come to York. And when the Englishmen at last heard of this thing, all that might travel – as well monks and priests and friars and canons and seculars – come and meet with the Scots at Myton upon Swale... Alas! What sorrow for the English husbandmen that knew nothing of war, they were quelled and drenched in the River of Swale. And their holinesses, Sir William of Melton, Archbishop of York, and the Abbot of Selby with their steeds, fled, and come into York. And that was their own folly that they had that mischance, for they passed the water of Swale; and the Scots set on fire three stacks of hay; and the smoke thereof was so huge that [the] Englishmen might not see the Scots. And when the Englishmen were gone over the water, so come the Scots with their wings in manner of a shield, and come toward the Englishmen in a rush; and the Englishmen fled, for they lacked any men of Arms; for the King had them all almost lost at the siege of Berwick; and the Scots hobilers went between the bridge and the Englishmen. And when the great host had them met, the Englishmen almost all were there slain. And he that might wend over the water was saved; but many were drenched, Alas, for sorrow! for there was slain many men of religion, and seculars, and also priests and clerks; and with much sorrow the Archbishop escaped; and therefore the Scots called it 'the White Battle'.

The fact that the English army at Myton was led by an archbishop and contained so many clerics in its ranks ensured that the battle was described in some detail in the chronicles of a number of religious houses. This account, however, is taken from *The Brut or the Chronicles of England*, an anonymous work that became the most popular of all late medieval chronicles. It derives its name from Brutus, the fictional Trojan prince whom the 12th-century writer Geoffrey of Monmouth had claimed was the first ruler of Britain. *The Brut* originally concluded in 1307 but was later extended to 1333, and it was translated from the French at the end of the 14th century. Such was its popularity that in English and Welsh the word *brut* was often used to describe any chronicle.

A cleric with a crossbow, from the 14th-century Luttrell Psalter. *He has placed one foot in a stirrup at the end of the bow, attached its string to a hook on his belt and will span the weapon by straightening his back. A crossbow shot a bolt with greater penetrative power than an arrow from a longbow and could be extremely accurate in the hands of a well-trained soldier. Its relatively slow rate of fire could place its user at a disadvantage on the battlefield, however. In siege warfare, it could be a highly effective weapon.*

Revolt in Wales

Owain Glyn Dwr's emergence as the leader of the last major Welsh rising against English rule was by no means inevitable. He was married into one of the leading Marcher families, the powerful Norman barons who held extensive estates on the Welsh borders or Marches. He had spent time in London and in the 1380s he had loyally served Richard II against the Scots. In the end, it seems it was the escalation of a dispute with an English neighbour, Grey of Ruthin, that drove Owain to rebellion. He found plenty of support. English legislation had reduced the Welsh to second-class citizens in their own country – Welshmen were barred from the most important trading centres and, following the deposition of Richard II who had shown some favour to Welsh landowners, power and wealth were placed even more firmly in the hands of the English.

Although Owain was a mere knight he was far from poor and, crucially, he could claim descent from two Welsh princes. For Welshmen he offered a genuine alternative to the House of Lancaster. In September 1400 his supporters proclaimed him Prince of Wales, and attacks were made on English towns in the north of the country. Henry IV raised an army to suppress the rising but was frustrated by appalling weather, difficult terrain and Owain's extremely effective guerrilla tactics. When the English government responded by enacting even more anti-Welsh legislation the rebellion spread. In 1402 Owain won a crushing victory at Pilleth over Edmund Mortimer, the leading Marcher lord who also had a claim to the English crown, then recruited him to his cause. Despite the defeat of his potential ally, Harry Hotspur, at Shrewsbury, most of Wales was under Owain's control by mid-1403. In 1404 the key castles of Aberystwyth and Harlech fell to Owain who sealed an alliance with the French. He held a parliament at Machynlleth where he was probably crowned Prince of Wales.

In 1405, with French help on its way, Owain drew up an agreement with Edmund Mortimer and the Earl of Northumberland to divide up England and Wales once Henry IV had been defeated. Mortimer was to become king, and Owain was to rule Wales and the border country. However, that year the Welsh suffered defeats at Grosmont Castle and Pwllmelyn near Usk, where Owain's brother, Tudor, was killed, and 300 Welsh prisoners are said to have been beheaded.

Nevertheless, helped by a large French army that had landed in Milford Haven in August, Owain continued to make progress, burning Haverfordwest and capturing Cardigan and Carmarthen before marching into England. He set up camp 10 miles from Worcester on Woodbury Hill, where he was faced by Henry IV's army, camped on the opposite ridge. After a week-long stand-off, Owain's army began to run short of supplies and was forced to retreat into Wales. By 1407 his rebellion was running out of steam. Prince Henry was proving an effective military leader and a large portion of the French army had returned home. In 1408 the English retook Aberystwyth Castle and Owain's ally the Earl of Northumberland was defeated and killed at Bramham Moor. The following year Harlech fell to Henry and the rebellion gradually petered out. Owain, however, was never captured and the date and place of his death remains unknown.

Seizing the Initiative

St Mary Magdalene Church is thought to have been built close to the centre of the action, on the site of a mass grave. Built a few years after the battle of Shrewsbury so that daily prayers could be said for the souls of the fallen, it was later converted into a College of Chaplains with a moat, garden and accommodation for a master and five chaplains. The remains of the ponds that provided fish for the college kitchen can still be seen.

Shrewsbury, 21 July 1403

Sometimes the outcome of a battle can be turned on its head by the actions of an individual. Shrewsbury was the first battle in which English longbowmen faced each other in any great numbers and the army of Henry IV soon ran into trouble at the hands of Hotspur's experienced archers. But, in an early example of his skills as a soldier, the future Henry V seized the initiative and won the day for his father.

When Henry IV seized the throne from Richard II in 1399, he had done so with the help of the Percys, the most powerful family in the north of England. Yet, only four years later, the same family were in open revolt against the man they had helped to make king. Their rebellion was ostensibly about money. The Percys believed that they had not been properly paid for their military service on behalf of the crown and things came to a head when the king instructed them to hand over the Earl of Douglas, one of the Scottish prisoners they had taken at the battle of Homildon Hill in August 1402. Henry was entitled to do this, for it was the sovereign's right to ransom prisoners, but the Percys refused, saying that they would ransom Douglas themselves and use the money they got for him to cover their costs. But the rebellion may also have had its roots in the family's frustrated ambitions and also their suspicion that Henry IV was trying to dilute their power by favouring other nobles such as George Dunbar. In any event, the Percys hatched a plot with Owain Glyn Dwr to overthrow Henry and replace him as king with the young Edmund of March.

In early July 1403, Sir Henry Percy – or Harry Hotspur as he is better known – and his uncle, Thomas Percy, Earl of Worcester, headed south with 160 followers and marched into Cheshire. They announced that Richard II was still alive, condemned Henry IV's usurpation and set about raising an army. Cheshire was a good place in which to recruit, for it had been fiercely loyal to Richard, had supplied his archer bodyguard and had been the only region to oppose Henry IV's seizure of the throne. The Percys succeeded in raising a substantial force, including a good number of Cheshire's famous archers and, joined by some troops from north Wales, made for Shrewsbury where they planned to link up with Glyn Dwr.

Harry Hotspur (1364–1403)

An effigy of Sir Henry 'Hotspur' Percy at Wells Cathedral, Somerset.

Sir Henry Percy was born in Alnwick in 1364. The eldest son of Henry Percy, the Earl of Northumberland, he was knighted by Edward III in 1377 and rapidly demonstrated an aptitude for warfare, helping his father to recapture the vital border town of Berwick in 1378.

After serving in Ireland and crusading in Prussia, he returned to the north and, in 1385, was appointed Warden of the East March. This was a particularly important and valuable post, as ever since Edward I had tried to bring Scotland under his control the Borders, or Marches, had known little peace. Even when the two countries were not at war, many of the families on both sides of the border acted as though they were, and cross-border raids and skirmishes were commonplace.

The monarchs of both England and Scotland tried to control this sensitive area by appointing wardens to defend the border, deal with disputes and prevent their compatriots from breaking any truces that had been agreed. The wardens could raise troops at royal expense, even in peacetime, so the office of warden brought with it power as well as prestige. By the end of the 14th century, the Percys regarded the two wardenships of the Western and Eastern Marches, as almost theirs by right.

After a short spell in Calais, where almost inevitably he led a series of raids into Picardy, Hotspur returned to the Borders. In 1388, Hotspur, who gained his nickname from the speed with which he rode into battle, caught up with a Scottish raiding force under Sir James Douglas at Otterburn. In a confused battle, much of it fought at night, Douglas was killed but Hotspur was captured by the Scots. He was quickly ransomed, however, and, on his return to England, appointed Warden of the Western March. Peace with Scotland and France reduced his opportunity to win glory on the battlefield but he made up for it in a series of tournaments, at which he excelled.

In 1399 Richard II tried to reduce the power of the Percys in the north by giving offices to their rivals, the Nevilles. As a result the family backed Henry Bolingbroke in his bid for the crown. While Northumberland, Hotspur's father, helped to negotiate Richard's abdication, Hotspur accompanied Henry Bolingbroke south, beating off an attack in Cheshire by forces still loyal to Richard II. Henry IV lavishly rewarded the Percys for their support, at least in terms of the offices he gave them, and they secured extensive military authority on the Borders and in north Wales. In 1401, Hotspur recaptured Conwy Castle from Owain Glyn Dwr and he defeated a Scottish raiding force under the Earl of Douglas at Homildon Hill the following year. However, the king's slowness in compensating the Percys for the money they had spent in these activities was ultimately to lead to Hotspur's rebellion and death at Shrewsbury.

The Percys played for high stakes and paid the price. Hotspur's father, the first Earl of Northumberland, was killed at Bramham Moor; his son, the second earl, was slain at St Albans; and his grandson, the third earl, died at Towton (see Chapter 5). His great-grandson, the fourth earl, survived the battle of Bosworth by decidedly un-Hotspurlike conduct – he avoided committing his forces at all. But even he died violently, killed by a mob in a tax riot in 1489.

Henry IV's army spent the night before the battle near the Augustinian Haughmond Abbey. Situated on high ground only two miles away, the abbey overlooks the battlefield.

Henry, who had been heading north to assist the Percys against the Scots, was in the Midlands when he heard about the rebellion. He also headed west for Shrewsbury, seeking to bring Hotspur to battle before he could join forces with Glyn Dwr. On 20 July, Hotspur arrived outside the town only to find it already occupied by royal troops, possibly under the Prince of Wales. Hotspur pulled back to the aptly-named village of Berwick where he spent the night. With him was his prisoner from Homildon Hill, the Earl of Douglas, who had thrown in his lot with his former enemy. The following day the king's army, which may have camped outside Shrewsbury in the vicinity of Haughmond Abbey, advanced against Hotspur, who had left Berwick and drawn up his army on a low ridge just to the north of the current Battlefield Church. According to the *Annals of Henry IV*, the rebels:

...chose, as it seemed, the more advantageous ground, as the King's army, should it wish to engage, would have to advance across a broad field thickly sown with peas, which they had further twined and looped together so as to hamper an attacking force.

It is not known how the rebels were deployed but the *Annals of Henry IV* state that Henry's army was drawn up in three divisions, with the vanguard commanded by the Earl of Stafford, the main body under the king himself and the rearguard commanded by Prince Henry. They were probably deployed in the traditional manner with the main body flanked by the vanguard on the right and the rearguard on the left. According to the *Annals*, Henry's army consisted of '14,000 excellent men' but figures in medieval chronicles are notoriously unreliable. Records do show that he did have at least 2,500 archers, for he had paid their wages, along with those of nearly 500 men-at-arms on 17 July. In a last-minute bid to avoid bloodshed the Abbot of Shrewsbury attempted to mediate between the two sides. Much of the afternoon was spent in negotiation but no agreement was reached and, late in the afternoon, the two armies prepared for battle.

Looking north towards the rebel positions.

The fighting seems to have begun with a ferocious archery duel. As the royal army advanced up the slope towards the rebel position, Hotspur's Cheshire and Welsh archers unleashed a storm of arrows against them, and Henry's bowmen replied in kind. The Burgundian chronicler Jean de Waurin wrote:

…it seemed to the beholders like thick cloud, for the sun which at that time was bright and clear then lost its brightness so thick were the arrows…

English longbowmen had never fought each other in large numbers before and soon the soldiers of both sides were being given a taste of what their French and Scottish enemies had endured for decades:

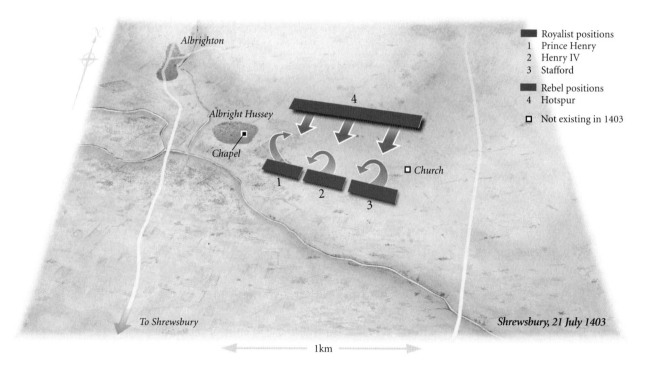

Albrighton

Albright Hussey

Chapel

Church

To Shrewsbury

Shrewsbury, 21 July 1403

1km

Royalist positions
1 Prince Henry
2 Henry IV
3 Stafford

Rebel positions
4 Hotspur

☐ Not existing in 1403

Re-enactment of an early 15th-century longbowman in action. Englishmen were expected to keep a bow and practise with it regularly, as to draw the weapon required great skill and technique. A war bow was constructed from a single piece of wood – Spanish yew was considered the best – with a length between about 1.6m and 1.8m. Bowstrings were normally made of hemp, while arrow shafts were usually made of poplar or ash. Being made from a heavier wood, an ash shaft had a shorter range but greater penetrative power. A variety of arrowheads could be fitted. A fit, experienced archer could shoot an arrow out to a range of up to 300 yards, and have six in the air at one time.

…the archers of Henry Percy began the fight and the place for the missiles was not on the ground… for men fell on the king's side as fast as leaves fall in autumn after the hoar-frost. Nor did the king's archers fail to do their work, but sent a shower of sharp points against their adversaries…

Among the casualties was Prince Henry, who was hit below the left eye by an arrow. He refused to leave the field, however, and continued to lead his men. It seems that King Henry's army came off worse in this murderous exchange, though, and some of his men began to give ground. This may have encouraged Hotspur to lead his men forward and a period of savage hand-to-hand fighting ensued. According to de Waurin:

…they put their hands to swords and axes with which they began to slay each other, and the leaders of the advance guards striking their horses with their spurs and with lances couched struck each other…

As the battle hung in the balance, the men of Prince Henry's division were about to make a decisive intervention. The *Annals* tell us that they were the first to join battle with Hotspur's forces. They were probably experienced soldiers, having been campaigning in Wales, and they drove off the forces opposed to them before wheeling to attack Hotspur's division in the rear.

Thus it happened that his division reached the main body of the enemy before the rest, breaking their line, and overthrowing all opponents. Passing right through he faced about, and thus closed them in between his own division and that of the King. The rebel army fell into a state of great perplexity, not knowing whether they were fighting against the King's party or their own.

The *English Chronicle* reports:

When Sir Henry Percy saw his men fast slain he pressed into the battle with 30 men, and made a lane in the middle of the host till he came to the King's banner, and there he slew the Earl of Stafford and Sir Thomas Blount and others: and at last he was beset about and slain.

Warkworth Castle, Northumberland, home of the Percy earls of Northumberland. To the right is the imposing keep. Begun by Hotspur's father at the end of the 14th century, it has been described as one of the masterpieces of late-medieval architecture and is a majestic statement in stone of the power and wealth of the Percys.

It has been suggested that Hotspur launched this charge earlier, when he saw Henry's vanguard retreating, but if the battle was going his way it seems unlikely that he would have attempted such a move. The *English Chronicle* implies Hotspur's charge was an attempt to rescue a deteriorating situation (as Richard III was to do at Bosworth when he tried to cut down Henry Tudor). One chronicler, Adam of Usk, suggests that Hotspur failed to reach Henry because a number of decoys had been dressed as the king. Some accounts suggest Hotspur was killed by an arrow, which struck him in the face.

Encouraged by the king, his soldiers took up the shout of 'Henry Percy is dead!' No doubt the rebels looked round anxiously, hoping that Hotspur, like William at Hastings, would make himself known and reassure them that he was still alive. But there was no sign of him and, as the news of his death spread across the battlefield, the rebels lost heart and took to their heels, pursued by the triumphant Royalists. Hotspur's rebellion had collapsed and Henry had survived the biggest challenge to his throne.

Casualties in the battle are believed to have been high – perhaps as many as 3,000 on each side. Hotspur's uncle, Thomas Percy, who had been captured during the battle, was beheaded in Shrewsbury and his head displayed on London Bridge. The Earl of Douglas, who had lost an eye at Homildon

Hill, lost a testicle at Shrewsbury but survived to fight another day. Hotspur's body was taken away and buried at Whitchurch but when the king heard that rumours were circulating that Hotspur was still alive, he had his corpse exhumed and displayed it in Shrewsbury, propped up between two millstones. For Prince Henry, who recovered from his wound below the eye, it had been a valuable, if painful, lesson in the destructive power of the longbow – a lesson he would use to deadly effect 12 years later at Agincourt.

A sketch of the instrument used to extract the arrowhead from Prince Henry's face after Shrewsbury in surgeon John Bradmore's written account of how he treated the wound.

Henry IV (1366–1413)

King Henry IV by an unknown 16th-century artist.

Henry was born in 1366 at Bolingbroke in Lincolnshire and, as the son of John of Gaunt, he stood to inherit the Duchy of Lancaster, the richest estate in England. In 1380, he married Mary Bohun, heiress to the earldom of Hereford, as a result of which he was later styled the Earl of Hereford. In 1387, he joined the Lords Appellant (in effect, the baronial opposition to Richard II) and defeated the king's favourite, Robert de Vere, at the battle of Radcot Bridge. There was even some talk of deposing Richard, but as nobody could agree on a successor he was allowed to keep his crown.

In the early 1390s, Henry took a break from English politics and added to his reputation as he crusaded with the Teutonic Knights in Prussia and went on a pilgrimage to Jerusalem. However, on his return, he quarrelled with the Duke of Norfolk, both accusing the other of treason, and King Richard took the opportunity to banish the pair of them in 1398. While Henry was in exile his father, John of Gaunt, died and, despite having promised not to, King Richard seized his estates. The following year Henry returned to England with a few hundred followers and although his initial intention had been simply to recover his inheritance, such was the support he received that he decided to depose Richard and seize the crown himself. He was to spend much of the rest of his life struggling to hold on to it.

One of Henry's problems was that by criticising Richard's extravagance he laid himself open to the same charge. His parliaments complained bitterly about the expense of his household, the annuities he gave to his supporters and the costs of the wars he waged. A shortage of funds hamstrung his attempts to put down Owain Glyn Dwr's rising in Wales and may have led to his inability to remunerate the Percys sufficiently for their services. Although he defeated Henry Percy the younger at Shrewsbury in 1403, it took him a further five years to pacify Wales. The Percys were only finally subdued when Henry Percy senior was defeated and killed at Bramham Moor in 1408. By this time, however, the king was a sick man, suffering from a number of illnesses. These included a skin disease that some claimed was a divine punishment for executing the Archbishop of York in 1405 (Henry had discovered the archbishop had been plotting against him). In 1411, Henry fought off an attempt to make him abdicate in favour of his eldest son but died two years later. He is buried in Canterbury Cathedral.

A statue of King Henry IV on St Mary Magdalene Church at the battlefield site.

King Richard II, surrounded by his Cheshire archer bodyguard.
From a late 15th-century manuscript of Froissart's Chronicles.

Bowmen of Cheshire

It is perhaps not surprising that Hotspur's Cheshire archers got the better of their opponents at Shrewsbury for the bowmen of that county had long been noted for their skill. As early as 1334 a body of 200 Cheshire archers under the command of a John Ward had been chosen for the bodyguard of Edward III. Such was the status of the archer in Cheshire that his social standing has been described as equal to that of a man-at-arms in the rest of the country. His status was also reflected in his pay, for a Cheshire archer received 6d a day whereas an archer in neighbouring north Wales only received 3d.

Richard II, who was also Earl of Cheshire, continued the practice of recruiting archer bodyguards from the area. Paid from the king's own finances, they were very much his own private force. They even had their own badge, for while most of Richard's retainers sported the white hart, his archers wore a device of gold and silver crowns. As Richard's reign became more and more insecure, he employed a personal bodyguard of 312 archers, divided into seven 'watches', each watch guarding the king's bedchamber all night once a week. Richard also used his archer bodyguard for political purposes. They ringed Westminster Hall in 1397 during the trial in parliament of three of the Lords Appellant and later escorted the Earl of Arundel to the scaffold. By the end of Richard's reign, his archers were feared and loathed outside Cheshire and, after Henry IV seized the crown in 1399, many had to obtain special pardons from the king.

'...mercy had no place...'

And on the other side the Lords Percy, warned of the coming of their enemies, ordered forward their vanguard led by the Earl of Douglas, and then when they came in sight of each other the archers dismounted uttering a loud and horrible cry which was dreadful to hear, and then began to march at a good pace in good order against each other, and the archers to draw so fast and thick that it seemed to the beholders like thick cloud, for the sun which at that time was bright and clear then lost its brightness so thick were the arrows, and this was helped by the dust which flew about together with the breath of the men who began to get heated, so that the air was quite darkened. After the arrows were exhausted they put their hands to swords and axes with which they began to slay each other, and the leaders of the advance guards striking their horses with their spurs and with lances couched struck each other. And the men and horses were slain in such ways as it was pitiable to see. None spared his fellow, mercy had no place, each one tried only to escape and put himself at the head of this party, for their was no friend or relation, but each one thought of himself, so they fought with such equality of bitterness that it was a long time before one could conjecture to whom would remain the day and victory.

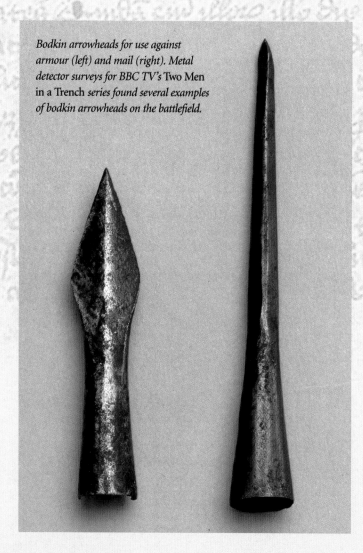

Bodkin arrowheads for use against armour (left) and mail (right). Metal detector surveys for BBC TV's Two Men in a Trench *series found several examples of bodkin arrowheads on the battlefield.*

Jean de Waurin was a Burgundian chronicler who, in the early 1470s, compiled *A Collection of the Chronicles and Ancient Histories of Great Britain* – a history of England from the earliest times to 1471. Waurin wrote his account of Shrewsbury over half a century after the event and is not always reliable over names and places. For example, in his description of the commanders of Henry IV's army, he fails to mention Prince Henry at all. De Waurin is far more interesting, however, when it comes to his descriptions of what it was like to be in the midst of a late-medieval battle. He had been with the French army at Agincourt, so he would have had first-hand knowledge of the effects of an arrow storm. Perhaps more importantly for his description of Shrewsbury, he had also witnessed an archery duel for he had been present at the battle of Verneuil in 1424, where the French army contained a large contingent of Scottish archers. De Waurin later wrote that:

the archers began to shoot at each other so vigorously that it was horrible to watch.

He could have been describing Shrewsbury.

Henry V (1387–1422)

The son of Henry of Bolingbroke and Mary Bohun, Henry was born in the gatehouse tower of Monmouth Castle, probably in 1387. Following his father's seizure of the throne in 1399 Henry was created Prince of Wales. His teenage years were nothing like the misspent youth so memorably portrayed by Shakespeare. Indeed, his principality turned out to be something of a poisoned chalice, as his father, Henry IV, was almost immediately faced with a major rebellion led by Owain Glyn Dwr. The young Henry was to spend nearly a decade first as nominal and then as actual commander of English military operations in Wales. During this time he learned valuable lessons in military finance, command, logistics and siege warfare – lessons he was to use with devastating effect when it came to war with France – and proved himself a talented and inspiring leader of men.

After inheriting the throne in 1413, Henry decided to take advantage of divisions in the French court by pursuing English interests in France, eventually claiming the French throne itself. In 1415 he invaded the country and laid siege to Harfleur at the mouth of the Seine. The town surrendered after a longer siege than had been anticipated and Henry's subsequent decision to march across Normandy to Calais almost ended in disaster when his depleted army

was intercepted at Agincourt by a powerful French force. Henry's archers won him the day, however, turning a campaign which might otherwise have been seen as an expensive anti-climax into a national triumph. This increased not only English appetites for further conquests but also parliament's willingness to pay for them.

In 1417 Henry led a full-scale invasion of Normandy and while he will always be remembered for his victory at Agincourt, it was this meticulously prepared campaign that perhaps best demonstrates his abilities as a soldier. Henry, who had also built up his navy, made great use of ships to protect, transport and supply his men, not only across the Channel but also up the major rivers of Normandy. His experiences in Wales had made him an expert in siege warfare, adept in the use of artillery. One by one the towns of Normandy were battered into submission until, in January 1419, the capital, Rouen, surrendered after a six-month siege.

French resistance had been undermined by civil war between the Armagnac faction and the Burgundians, who controlled the ineffectual Charles VI of France. When the Duke of Burgundy was assassinated by his rivals in September, the new duke made an alliance with Henry. By the Treaty of Troyes it was agreed that Henry

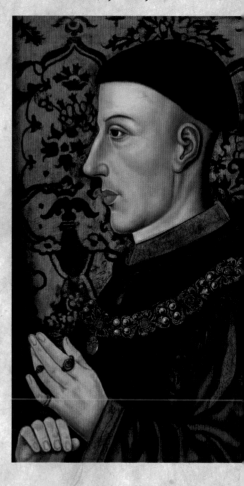

King Henry V by an unknown 16th-century artist. There is no sign of the scar that Henry presumably would have had on his left cheek following his wounding at Shrewsbury.

would marry Catherine, Charles VI's daughter, and would be recognised as Charles's heir and also made Regent of France. The Armagnacs, however, were not yet defeated, and it was while campaigning against them in 1422 that Henry contracted dysentery and died. His father-in-law, Charles VI of France, followed a few weeks later, leaving Henry's infant son as King of both England and France.

The Wars of the Roses

Although popularly seen as a long dynastic struggle between the Houses of Lancaster and York, the Wars of the Roses were essentially three separate wars, each with different causes. The first was caused by Henry VI's inadequacies as a ruler and the ambitions of Richard of York, who demanded the leading role in government. The tense situation was exacerbated by a number of bitter family rivalries, such as those between the Nevilles and the Percys. In May 1455 York and the Nevilles attacked the royal court at St Albans and killed a number of leading Lancastrian nobles. In July 1460 York captured Henry VI at the battle of Northampton and raised the stakes by claiming the throne. A compromise was reached by which Henry remained king with York as his heir but Henry's wife, Margaret of Anjou, refused to countenance the disinheritance of her son and raised an army to fight for the Lancastrian cause. York was defeated and killed at Wakefield in December but the crushing victory by his son, Edward IV, at Towton in March 1461 effectively settled the issue. Nevertheless, Lancastrian resistance lingered on in the north for a further three years.

The second war of 1469–71 was primarily caused by the discontent of the mighty Richard Neville, Earl of Warwick, formerly Edward IV's chief supporter. Warwick saw his influence being eroded following the king's marriage to Elizabeth Woodville and he rebelled in 1469. In July he captured Edward after the battle of Edgecote and briefly held him prisoner, only to be forced by popular pressure to release him. In 1470, following the failure of a second rebellion, he made an extraordinary alliance of convenience with his old enemy, Margaret of Anjou, forcing Edward into exile and temporarily restoring Henry VI to the throne. In 1471, however, Edward returned to England and brought his enemies

to battle separately, defeating Warwick at Barnet and Margaret at Tewkesbury. Having disposed of both Henry VI and his son, Edward then ruled unchallenged until his early death in 1483.

The final phase of fighting was triggered in 1483 by Richard III's usurpation of the throne and his probable murder of his nephews, the deposed Edward V and Richard of York. These actions fatally split the Yorkist establishment and enabled Henry Tudor, a relatively unknown exile, to emerge as the champion of both the York and Lancaster houses, a position he strengthened by promising to marry Edward IV's daughter, Elizabeth. Later that year Richard

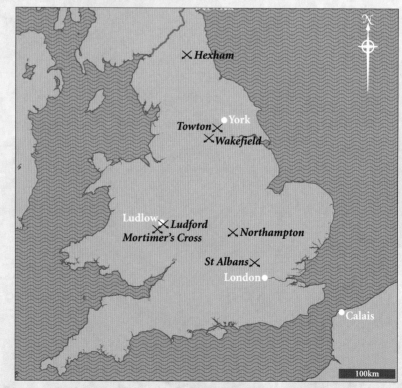

Wars of the Roses 1455–1461

defeated a rebellion by many of Edward IV's former servants, led by his own former ally the Duke of Buckingham. Richard had already alienated much of the political nation by favouring men from his own power block in the north. Grants of rebel land and property to his supporters added to the unpopularity of his regime, at least in the south of the country. As a result, when Henry Tudor launched his bid for the throne in August 1485, although few nobles were prepared to risk life and property by overtly joining the rebellion, Richard also found it difficult to mobilise support. Nevertheless, at Bosworth on 22 August, Richard confronted Henry with ostensibly a much larger army, only to find that key commanders failed to fight for him, preferring instead to let matters take their course before committing themselves. Richard was killed, and Henry seized the throne, successfully defending it at Stoke two years later.

The image of the Wars of the Roses as one long period of bitter bloodshed is mainly due to Tudor historians who exaggerated the evils of the period in order to contrast them with the peace and prosperity of their own age. In fact, while campaigns could be nasty and brutish, they were usually very short. Philippe de Comynes may have been overstating the case when he commented that '…if any conflict breaks out in England one or other of the rivals is master within ten days or less' but the fact remains that in more than 30 years of so-called warfare there were fewer than 15 months of actual campaigning. Furthermore, fighting was more about the elimination of rivals than the conquest of territory; sieges of towns were rare, and England was generally spared the scorched-earth tactics employed by its soldiers in the Hundred Years War. As a result, de Comynes could conclude:

'… out of all the countries which I have personally known, England is the one where public affairs are best conducted and regulated with least violence to the people. There neither the countryside nor the people are destroyed, nor are buildings burnt or demolished. Disaster and misfortune fall only on those who make war, the soldiers and the nobles.'

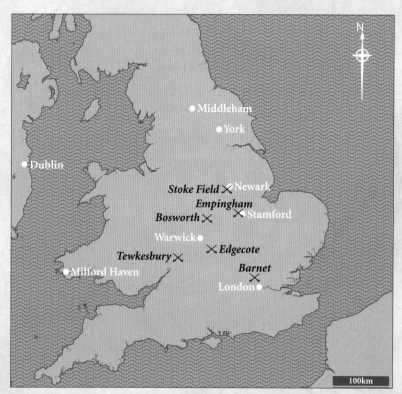

Wars of the Roses 1469–1487

Fight to the Death
Towton, 29 March 1461

Some battles shocked even contemporaries by the intensity with which they were fought. Towton was such a battle. Regional hatreds and family vendettas ensured it was fought with a ferocity that, together with the enormous size of the armies involved, helped make it the bloodiest battle of the Wars of the Roses.

View from the rear of the Lancastrian position, looking south towards the ridge where Edward's army drew up. The lone tree marks the highest spot on the ridge, on the Yorkist right flank. In 1461 the battlefield seems to have consisted of hedgeless open fields, with patches of woodland on both flanks, steep slopes down to the Cock Beck to the west and some marshy ground to the east.

*King Henry VI by an unknown
16th-century artist.*

In September 1460 Richard of York followed up the Yorkist victory at Northampton by entering the Palace of Westminster and claiming the throne of England. His actions were greeted with dismay by many of England's nobility who were quite prepared to see York as Protector and *de facto* ruler of the country but were not ready to overthrow Henry VI. Eventually a compromise was reached in an Act of Accord, which named Richard as Henry's heir. Henry's wife, Margaret of Anjou, still refusing to tolerate the disinheritance of their son, Edward, raised an army in the north to fight for the Lancastrian cause. At the end of December 1460, forces loyal to Margaret defeated and killed Richard at Wakefield, leaving Edward of March, his 18-year-old son, as the Yorkist claimant to the throne.

Margaret's army then marched south on London, defeating an attempt by the Earl of Warwick to stop them at St Albans on 17 February, and recapturing Margaret's husband, Henry VI. The Londoners, however, in 'mykel dread' of Margaret's northerners whose reputation for looting had preceded them, refused to let them into the city. As Margaret's forces fell back northwards, Edward of March, fresh from a victory over a force of Welsh Lancastrians at Mortimer's Cross, entered London where he was proclaimed King Edward IV. On 13 March, he left the city in pursuit of the Lancastrians, gathering together forces from the south, East Anglia and the Midlands and, by 27 March, his army had reached Pontefract. Planning to cross the River Aire the following day, Edward sent a detachment of his troops under Lord Fitzwalter to Ferrybridge to repair the river's bridge, which the retreating Lancastrians had destroyed.

Some very detailed and extremely exciting accounts of the ensuing events have been constructed over the years but the fact remains that no eyewitness description of the campaign has survived. For much of our information about the battle we have to rely on the contemporary but uncorroborated Burgundian chronicler, Jean de Waurin, and Edward Hall, writing 70 years after the battle. In these circumstances, it is very difficult to piece together what might have happened with any degree of certainty and what follows should be seen as a suggestion of what might have happened rather than as established fact.

We cannot even be sure about the size of the two opposing armies as accounts vary wildly. Contemporaries considered Towton to have been an exceptionally large battle, which is reflected in their estimates of the numbers involved. Some even claimed that Edward's force numbered 200,000 men, an impossibly large figure. Edward Hall is a little more measured, putting the combined strengths of the two armies at around 100,000 but even this seems far too high. Nevertheless, huge efforts had

A re-enactor wearing a sallet with visor. A complete suit of plate armour weighed little more than 27kg. Since the weight of the armour was spread evenly across the body a fit man could run, lie down or mount a horse with relative ease. But the lack of ventilation meant that it could become stiflingly hot and, wearing a helmet such as this, it was difficult to breath or even see. As a result helmets were often removed and visors raised, often with fatal consequences. At Shrewsbury both Harry Hotspur and Prince Henry were hit in the face by arrows, while at Towton Lord Dacre was shot and killed after removing his helmet in order to take a drink.

been made by both sides to muster as many troops as possible. Most of the major nobles of England were present with their retinues, so a figure of at least 25,000 Lancastrians and 20,000 Yorkists does not seem unreasonable and would still make this the largest battle on English soil until Flodden in 1513.

Early on 28 March, a detachment of Lancastrians under Lord Clifford surprised Fitzwalter's men at Ferrybridge, seized the crossing and once again destroyed the bridge. It seems that they beat off repeated Yorkist attempts to cross the river and only withdrew when another Yorkist force under Lord Fauconberg crossed the Aire elsewhere and outflanked them. Clifford and his men tried to reach the main Lancastrian army, which was camped in the vicinity of Towton, but were cut off and slaughtered at Dintingdale, just two miles from safety. The Yorkist army crossed the Aire and headed north, spending the night before the battle in the vicinity of Sherburn-in-Elmet.

The following day, the Yorkists, who were still waiting for the Duke of Norfolk's contingent to join them, passed through Saxton in bitterly cold weather and advanced up onto the high ground beyond it. As they did so, the Lancastrian army came into view, drawn up on a slight rise just south of Towton.

The Lancastrians' position was a strong one, with their left flank protected by marshland, their right by the steep slopes of the Cock Valley and with a slight incline to their front. The precise deployments of the two armies are not known, although both sides would have placed their archers in front of their main bodies of troops. It is just possible that the Lancastrians also placed an ambush party in Castle Hill wood on the Yorkist left flank but the evidence for this is extremely sketchy. The battle seems to have begun with an archery duel in which the Lancastrians came off worse. Hall takes up the story:

When each part perceived the other, they made a great shout, and at the same instant time, there fell a small sleet or snow, which by violence of the wind was driven into the faces of them, which were of King Henry's part, so that their sight was somewhat blemished and diminished. The Lord Fauconberg, which led the vanguard of King Edward's battle being a man of great policy, and of much experience in martial feats, caused every archer under his standard, to shoot one flight and then made them to stand still. The northern men, feeling the shot, but by reason of the snow, not well viewing the distance between them and their enemies, like hardy men shot their sheaf of arrows as fast as they might, but all their shot was lost and their labour vain for they came not near the southerners, by forty tailor's yards. When their shot was almost spent, the Lord Fauconberg marched forward with his archers, which not only shot their own whole sheaves, but also gathered the arrows of their enemies, and let a great

part of them of them fly against their own masters, and another part they let stand on the ground which sore annoyed the legs of the owners, when the battle was joined.

A modern painting by Graham Turner. The Yorkist men-at-arms move forward as Lord Fauconberg's archers loose their last arrows at the advancing Lancastrians. The man-at-arms in the left foreground is armed with a poleaxe.

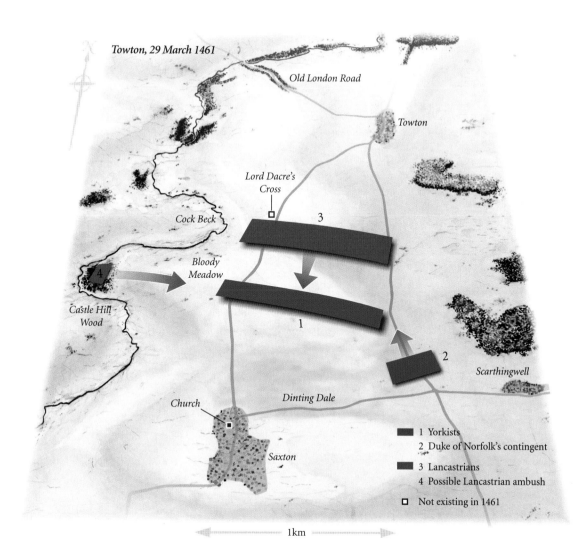

Towton, 29 March 1461

Old London Road

Towton

Lord Dacre's Cross

Cock Beck

3

Bloody Meadow

4

Castle Hill Wood

1

2

Scarthingwell

Dinting Dale

Church

Saxton

1 Yorkists
2 Duke of Norfolk's contingent
3 Lancastrians
4 Possible Lancastrian ambush

□ Not existing in 1461

1km

William Neville, Lord Fauconberg (d.1463)

Like Andrew Trollope – in many ways his opposite number on the Lancastrian side at Towton – the Yorkist leader Lord Fauconberg was a veteran of the French wars. Unlike Trollope, he was closely related to some of the most powerful men in the kingdom, for his father was Ralph Neville, first Earl of Westmorland, and his mother Joan Beaufort, daughter of John of Gaunt. Richard of York was a brother-in-law, the dukes of Somerset cousins and the Earl of Warwick a nephew. In 1436, the 35-year-old Fauconberg sailed to Normandy and for the next six and a half years played a leading part in the defence of the duchy. After service on the Scottish border he returned to France in 1448 but the following May he was seriously wounded and captured at Pont de l'Arche, remaining a prisoner of the French for over three years.

Upon his release, Fauconberg joined the royal council and remained at court, even after Richard of York and his brother the Earl of Salisbury had withdrawn, acting it seems as a go-between for the rival factions. He stayed at Henry VI's side at the first battle of St Albans, and it was only when Margaret of Anjou seized power in November 1458 and Fauconberg was dismissed from his office as Constable of Windsor Castle that he openly sided with the Yorkists. After their rout at Ludford,

Fauconberg successfully defended Calais against an attack by the Duke of Somerset and, when the Yorkists tried their luck again in June 1460, he seized Sandwich as a base for their landing. Fauconberg fought successfully at Northampton that July, and in the following March, his military expertise was to be a crucial factor in bringing Edward IV victory at Towton.

Fauconberg was well rewarded for his part in Edward's triumph at Towton, and in November 1461 he was created Earl of Kent. Towards the end of 1462, he travelled north to assist in the reduction of the remaining Lancastrian strongholds but he died in the January of the following year. He was one of 23 children and in order to secure an inheritance for him, his father had married him off in 1422 to Joan Fauconberg, the young heiress to a barony in Cleveland. While Joan gave him a title, land and three daughters the marriage was, even by medieval standards, hardly a love match; she had severe learning disabilities and was bluntly described in 1463 as 'an idiot from birth'. It is perhaps then hardly surprising that Fauconberg fathered at least two illegitimate sons. One of these, known as 'the Bastard of Fauconberg', rebelled against Edward IV in 1471 and was executed after an abortive attack on London.

Hall's account has to be treated with care because he was writing such a long time after the battle, and we do not know where he got his information. Hall's grandfather had fought in the campaign, however, and his description of how Fauconberg used the weather to his advantage is at least partially corroborated by the Yorkist Abbot of St Albans who wrote that, thanks to God, the wind suddenly changed direction and began to blow hard in the faces of the Lancastrians, to the disadvantage of their bowmen. Finally, although Hall was writing for a Tudor court and can thus be expected to hold a pro-Lancastrian bias, in his account of Towton at least he seems to have been quite balanced in his treatment of the two sides, acknowledging both the military skill of the Yorkist Fauconberg and the inspirational leadership of his king, Edward IV.

Archers in battle, deployed at the front of their respective armies. From a 15th-century French translation of Caesar's Commentaries.

Ev commence le vij.º liure qui contient en foy .xvij. chapi
tres parciaux, [ ] Ou premier il traite comment Cesar.
requist ayde a pompee pour la mentation nouuelle des
gaullois qui se rebellerent. Et comment il vainqui de re

With thousands of arrows falling on his men and casualties mounting by the minute, the Duke of Somerset, who seems to have been the Lancastrian commander on the day, had little option but to order an advance. The massed ranks of Lancastrians left their defensive position and headed off into the blizzard towards the Yorkists, shouting 'King Henry! King Henry!' This is Jean de Waurin's account of what happened next:

…Lord Rivers and his son with six or seven thousand Welshmen led by Andrew Trollope, and the Duke of Somerset with seven thousand more charged the Earl of March's cavalry, put them to flight and chased them for eleven miles, so that it appeared to them that they had won great booty, because they thought that the Earl of Northumberland had charged at the same time on the other flank, but he failed to attack soon enough…

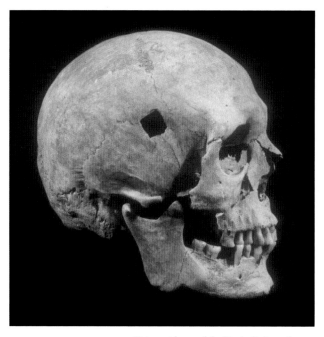

Grim evidence of the kind of injury that medieval weapons could inflict was uncovered in 1996, when a mass grave containing the remains of over 40 skeletons was unearthed by workmen digging the foundations for a garage at Towton Hall. All except one of the skulls examined showed evidence of head wounds, and many had been struck several times. As the grave pit is approximately a mile away from the area where the main fighting took place it seems likely that the bodies are those of Lancastrian soldiers, cut down as they attempted to flee. The large number of head wounds suggests that these men may have thrown away their helmets as they ran. Three of the skeletons had variations in the bones of arms and shoulders, suggesting that they were archers, while nine skulls showed evidence of previously healed wounds. The majority of the wounds seem to have been caused by edged weapons but the square hole in the skull of this unfortunate man was probably caused by the beak of a warhammer or the spike of a poleaxe.

At this time, 'cavalry' was a general term for men-at-arms whether mounted or dismounted, while in writing 'Welshmen' Waurin may have misunderstood the information given to him. His account implies that the Lancastrians made good progress on one flank but were held on the other. It has been suggested that Somerset advanced against the Yorkist left, and that if Lancastrian troops had indeed been placed in Castle Hill Wood, their intervention would have added to the pressure on the Yorkist line in that part of the battlefield.

Northumberland's lack of progress on the other flank may be explained by his tardiness but it is also worth remembering that his troops would have been attacking up the steepest part of the Yorkist position. As the snow continued to fall, the battle developed into a long, bitter hand-to-hand struggle, with men laying about each other with swords, bills, poleaxes and maces. Edward was fighting on foot in the midst of his men, and both de Waurin and Hall agree that his inspirational leadership helped to hold the beleaguered Yorkist line together. One chronicler claimed that 'the dead carcasses hindered those who fought', while Richard Beauchamp, the Yorkist Bishop of Salisbury, wrote that 'the result remained doubtful the whole day', and that victory came when 'almost all of our side despaired of it, so great was the strength and dash of our adversaries'.

The arrival of fresh troops in the form of the Duke of Norfolk's contingent eventually turned the tide in the Yorkists' favour. A Yorkist sympathiser later wrote:

Thus did the fight continue more than ten hours in equal balance, when at last King Henry espied the forces of his foes increase, and his own somewhat yield…

The Tudor historian Polydore Vergil is more specific:

About noon the aforesaid John Duke of Norfolk with a fresh band of good men of war came in, to the aid of the new elected King Edward.

As Norfolk's reinforcements had probably marched along the Ferrybridge–Tadcaster road, it is generally agreed that they joined the battle on the Yorkist right, and they may have forced the exhausted Lancastrians round so that they had their backs to Cock Beck. Faced with these fresh troops, the Lancastrian line slowly crumbled and eventually broke. Pursued by Yorkist horsemen, many Lancastrians slithered down the steep slopes of the Cock valley, only to be cut down as they struggled to cross the river. Some slipped in the water and were trampled underfoot. Others were trapped in Tadcaster where the bridge over the Wharfe had been destroyed. In a graphic description of the rout, Hall writes that the Lancastrians:

The Old London Road. In 1461 this was a major route, heading north-west out of Towton, crossing the Cock, then swinging north-east to Tadcaster. Large numbers of fleeing Lancastrians must have streamed along what is now little more than a track, with vengeful mounted Yorkists in hot pursuit. The point where it fords the Cock may well have been one of the places where 'men alive passed the river upon dead carcasses', as Hall graphically put it.

…fled toward Tadcaster bridge to save themselves; but in the mean way there is a little brook called Cock, not very broad, but of a great deepness, in the which, what for haste of escaping, and what for fear of followers, a great number were drenched and drowned, in so much that the common people there affirm, that men alive passed the river upon dead carcasses, and that the great river of Wharfe, which is the great sewer of the brook, and of all the water coming from Towton, was coloured with blood.

According to George Neville, one of Warwick's brothers, bodies were strewn over an area six miles long by three and a half miles across. It was reported at the time that the heralds had counted 28,000 dead while some contemporaries claimed the death toll was even higher. If the heralds had come up with such a figure, however, it must surely have been an estimated one, or based on reports sent to them. It is highly unlikely that they would have covered an area of 20 square miles in order to count the dead.

Given the contemporary propensity for exaggeration, the real total may have been considerably lower but, even so, the battle had been a disaster for the Lancastrians. Somerset and Exeter had escaped, along with King Henry and his queen, but five peers had fallen in two days, including Northumberland, Clifford and Dacre, while the Earl of Devon was captured the next day and beheaded in York. Dozens of Lancastrian knights had also fallen or been executed, among them Sir Andrew Trollope. Towton had been an enormous personal triumph for Edward. It had confirmed his kingship and, although the Lancastrians fought on in the north for a further three years, their cause had been fatally weakened.

The steep slopes down to Bloody Meadow and the Cock Beck. Many Lancastrians probably met their deaths here, as their line wheeled and crumbled following the intervention of the Duke of Norfolk's contingent.

Saxton Church with the tomb of Lord Dacre in the foreground.

Sir Andrew Trollope (d.1461)

With over 30 years' military experience, Sir Andrew Trollope was a key figure in the Lancastrian army. Born into a family of Durham dyers, he began his military career in the late 1420s as a mounted man-at-arms, and saw widespread service in France, notably under Sir John Fastolf. By 1440 he was a member of the Earl of Somerset's personal retinue, having taken part in the earl's raid into Picardy in February of that year, and Trollope was later appointed lieutenant of the fortress of Fresnay, which he was forced to surrender to the French in 1450. By 1455 he was Master Porter of Calais, the last surviving English possession in France, and continued to serve there when the Earl of Warwick was appointed captain of the town. In 1459, Trollope was chosen to lead a detachment of the Calais garrison – England's only official professional army at the time – to England to support Richard, Duke of York, in his quarrel with Henry VI and his Lancastrian supporters. However, at Ludford Bridge that October, unwilling to confront his sovereign in battle, Trollope deserted to the Lancastrians,

taking with him not only most of the Calais garrison but also the Yorkist plan of action. The Yorkist leaders were forced to flee and Trollope's defection earned him their lasting hatred.

The future Edward IV was also to have a more personal score to settle with the veteran soldier, for it seems that Trollope was the brains behind the Lancastrian victory at Wakefield, when Edward's father, Richard of York, was lured from his Sandal Castle stronghold, surrounded by superior forces, and killed. When Edward seized the throne from Henry VI in early March 1461, he exempted Trollope from the general pardon he had issued and put a price on his head.

Trollope may well have limped to his death at Towton; six weeks earlier at the second battle of St Albans, where he again played a prominent part in the Lancastrian victory and was knighted, he trod on a caltrop (a spiked device that was thrown on the ground to disable horses) and injured his foot.

The Rose of Rouen

For to save all England The Rose did his intent,
With Calais and with London with Essex and with Kent,
And all the south of England up to the water of Trent,
And when he saw the time best The Rose from London went.
Blessed be the time, that ever God spread that flower!

The way into the north country The Rose full fast he sought,
With him went The Ragged Staff that many men there brought,
So did The White Lion full worthily he wrought,
Almighty Jesus bless his soul that their armies taught.
Blessed be the time, that ever God spread that flower!

The Fish Hook came to the field in full eager mood,
So did the Cornish Chough and brought forth all her brood,
There was The Black Ragged Staff that is both true and good,
The Bridled Horse, The Water Bourget by The Horse stood.
Blessed be the time, that ever God spread that flower!

The Greyhound, The Hart's Head they quit them well that day,
So did The Harrow of Canterbury and Clinton with his Key,
The White Ship of Bristol he feared not the fray
The Black Ram of Coventry he said not one neigh.
Blessed be the time, that ever God spread that flower!

The Falcon and the Fetterlock was there that tide,
The Black Bull also himself would not hide,
The Dolphin came from Wales, Three Corbies by his side,
The proud Leopard of Salisbury gaped his eyes wide.
Blessed be the time, that ever God spread that flower!

The Wolf came from Worcester, full sore he thought to bite,
The Dragon came from Gloucester, he bent his tail to smite,
The Griffen came from Leicester, flying in as tight,
The George came from Nottingham, with spear for to fight.
Blessed be the time, that ever God spread that flower!

. . . The northern party made them strong with spear and with shield,
On Palm Sunday afternoon they met us in the field,
Within an hour they were right fayne to flee, and eke to yield,
Twenty seven thousand The Rose killed in the field,
Blessed be the time, that ever God spread that flower!

Sir Robert Wingfield (1432–93),
Comptroller of Edward IV's Household,
from a 15th-century stained-glass window
in East Harling Church, Norfolk.
Wingfield wears a tabard bearing his
family arms over his armour and a Yorkist
collar of suns and roses around his neck.

The Rose of Rouen is a contemporary Yorkist ballad, which celebrates Edward IV's victory at Towton. It clearly sees the battle in terms of a struggle between north and south, with the Lancastrians described as 'the northern party' and the Yorkists as coming from south of the River Trent.

Leading Yorkists are referred to in the poem by their livery badges, while towns that supplied troops for Edward are also listed. 'The Rose' is Edward IV himself, who was born in Rouen in 1442 and who used the rose as one of his badges. Other senior Yorkists who are mentioned in the ballad are: the Duke of Norfolk, 'The White Lion'; the Earl of Warwick, 'The Ragged Staff'; Viscount Bourchier, 'The Water Bourget'; Lord Fauconberg, 'The Fish Hook'; Lord Scrope, 'The Cornish Chough'; Lord Grey of Ruthin, 'The Black Ragged Staff'; Sir William Herbert, 'The Bridled Horse'; Sir Walter Devereux, 'The Greyhound'; and Sir William Hastings, 'The Black Bull'.

The effigy of Lionel, Lord Welles on his tomb in the Waterton Chapel in St Oswald's Church, Methley, West Yorkshire. Welles was a Lincolnshire Lancastrian who was a confidant of Henry VI and an ally of the Beauforts. He was killed at Towton; after the battle his body is said to have been spirited back to Methley in a sack, to be buried next to his first wife, Joan, in her family chapel.

The ballad shows just how few of the senior English nobility actually fought on the Yorkist side at Towton. A much higher proportion of the peerage turned out to fight for the Lancastrian Henry VI. After Towton, the victorious Yorkists passed an Act of Attainder listing the defeated Lancastrians to be deprived, sometimes posthumously, of their lands and titles. The list begins:

Henry Duke of Exeter, Henry Duke of Somerset, Thomas Courtenay, late Earl of Devonshire, Henry late Earl of Northumberland, William Viscount Beaumont, Thomas Lord Roos, John late Lord Clifford, Leo late Lord Welles, John late Lord Neville, Thomas Grey Knight, Lord Rugemond Grey, Randolph late Lord Dacre....

Although Edward clearly enjoyed a considerable measure of popular goodwill, particularly in the south and Midlands, his relatively conciliatory attitude towards the sons of many of his defeated Lancastrian enemies may well be explained by his desire to broaden his support amongst the nobility. Despite this, in the decade after Towton he remained dangerously dependent upon the support of one major family, the Nevilles, and one man in particular: the Earl of Warwick.

Reprisal and revenge

So followed a day of much slaying between the two sides, and for a long time no one knew to which side to give the victory, so furious was the battle and so great the killing: father did not spare son nor son his father.

The Burgundian chronicler Jean de Waurin was joined in his assessment of Towton by many contemporaries, who agreed that Towton was highly unusual in terms of the numbers involved, the intensity of the fighting and the casualties suffered. For the leaders of the two armies, Towton was the latest act in a bloody cycle of reprisal and revenge.

The bloodiness of the battle had its roots in the deaths, in 1455, of the fathers of the Lancastrian leaders Somerset, Northumberland and Clifford, who had all been slain by the Yorkists at the first battle of St Albans. Five years later, in December 1460, the Lancastrians had their revenge at Wakefield where they killed Richard of York, the father of the future Edward IV, and his second son, the 17-year-old Earl of Rutland. Soon after the Earl of Salisbury, the father of the Earl of Warwick, was executed. According to Edward Hall, Rutland died at the hands of Lord Clifford who, remembering his own father's death at St Albans, is said to have shouted, 'By God's blood, thy father slew mine, and so will I do thee and all your kin'. The heads of the defeated Yorkist leaders were then displayed on York's Micklegate Bar – Richard's adorned with a paper crown to mock his ambitions of kingship. It is perhaps hardly surprising that at Towton, with these events fresh in his mind, the young Edward IV was in the mood for revenge. Hall writes that 'he made proclamation that no prisoner should be taken, nor one enemy saved', and although we have no evidence, it seems highly probable that the Lancastrian leaders would have given the same instructions to their followers.

This murderous situation was exacerbated by some long-standing family rivalries. There was deep-rooted hatred, for example, between the Nevilles and the Percy Earls of Northumberland, and armies of their retainers had fought each other on at least one occasion in the years leading up to the outbreak of the Wars of the Roses.

By forbidding the taking of prisoners, the leaders of the two armies had undoubtedly raised the stakes for their followers. It was now literally a case of kill or be killed. However, something else almost certainly contributed to the savagery of the fighting at Towton – the regional origins of the two armies. Southerners regarded northerners with a mixture of contempt and fear, sneering at what they saw as their strange accents and regarding them as little more than uncivilised brigands. Writing at the time, the Abbot of St Albans claimed that when

A late 15th-century Swiss illustration showing bodies being collected and buried in mass grave pits. In 1461 similar scenes must have taken place along the banks of the Cock and Wharfe rivers.

northerners spoke it sounded like the barking of the hounds of hell and described them as 'faithless people, people prompt to rob'.

As the Lancastrian northern army headed south after its victory at Wakefield, its ranks swelled by a contingent of Scots, rumours began to circulate of wide-scale looting and pillaging. According to the Prior of Croyland, 'an execrable and abominable army' was heading south like 'a plague of locusts'. The trail of destruction was almost certainly exaggerated but, living off the land as they were, the Lancastrians would indeed have stripped the areas through which they marched of supplies, and their unpaid troops certainly sacked the Yorkist towns of Grantham, Stamford and Northampton.

The Earl of Warwick, an old hand at manipulating public opinion, was able to make the most of the situation. By exaggerating and embellishing the misdeeds of the northerners, he was able to portray Edward IV as the saviour of the south, thus boosting recruitment to the Yorkist cause. As a result, many of the Yorkist soldiers at Towton must have felt they had a score to settle with their northern enemies.

The scale of the losses at Towton can partly be attributed to the duration of the battle and the size of the armies involved. The fact that the retreating Lancastrians' escape route was obstructed by two rivers, enabling their Yorkist pursuers to catch up with them, must have contributed to the butcher's bill. It is clea, however, that personal, family and regional rivalries also played their part in making Towton one of the most bitterly fought battles in English history.

Lord Dacre's Cross, which stands just behind where the right wing of the Lancastrian army was deployed. The origins of this evocative monument are obscure. The base and the cross on the top seem to be medieval but it was only erected in its present form in 1929. Despite its name it has no known connection with Lord Dacre.

BATTLE OF
TOWTON
PALM SUNDAY
1461

The Fog of War
Barnet, 14 April 1471

Fought on a cold, misty day, the chaotic battle of Barnet appears to be an early example of 'friendly fire', as two parts of the Earl of Warwick's army fought one another by mistake. The battle quite literally embodied the 'fog of war' and demonstrated the difficulties troops sometimes have not only in locating the enemy but also in recognising friend from foe in the heat of battle.

The area north-east of Monken Hadley with the valley of the Monken Mead Brook running north-eastwards across the picture. If the battle confused its participants, it also continues to confuse historians and its exact location remains a subject of research and debate. It seems likely that this particular area saw heavy fighting during the battle. This may have been after the soldiers of the Yorkist right overlapped and pushed back their Lancastrian opponents. It is also possible, however, that it was in fact the centre of the battlefield, with the Yorkists initially deployed in the valley and the Lancastrians on the higher ground to the north-west. In 1471 this area was mainly unenclosed heathland.

A 15th-century handgunner re-enactor. A variety of foreign mercenaries plied their trade in England during the Wars of the Roses. These included Swiss, Flemish and German pikemen and specialist troops such as artillerymen and handgunners. A contingent of Burgundian handgunners fought for the Earl of Warwick at St Albans in 1461 and, 10 years later, 500 Flemish handgunners served with Edward IV. Gunpowder had made its first appearance on European battlefields over a century earlier but the relatively high cost and slow rate of fire of the handgun meant that the longbow remained the dominant missile weapon throughout the Wars of the Roses. This soldier's weapon consists of an iron tube with a small touch-hole at the breech. It was muzzle loaded, with the projectile and main charge being rammed down the barrel. The gun was fired by touching a piece of smouldering cord against some priming powder in the touch-hole, which ignited, setting off the main charge in the barrel.

In September 1470 the Earl of Warwick, now allied with his former enemy, Queen Margaret of Anjou had, with French support, seized power in England in the name of Henry VI, and Edward IV had been forced to flee the country. The following March, however, with support from Burgundy, the enemy of France, Edward set sail from Flushing with 2,000 men in a bid to regain his crown. On 4 March he landed in Yorkshire, after a planned landing in East Anglia had to be abandoned when it was clear that the area was hostile. Much of the area was old Lancastrian territory, and no doubt the events of Towton (*see* chapter 5) had not been forgotten. But, although few joined Edward's cause, nobody attacked him as he headed south.

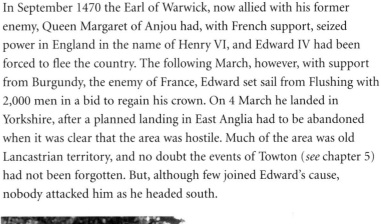

On 25 March, Edward crossed the Trent and reached Leicester where he was joined by 3,000 men, led by the retainers of Lord Hastings. On 29 March, he arrived outside Coventry where Warwick was based. It seems that Warwick intended to sit it out there until the forces of Montagu, Oxford, Exeter and Edward IV's brother George, Duke of Clarence, could join him. If this had happened, Edward would indeed have been hopelessly outnumbered, but Warwick's plan was wrecked when Clarence defected to his brother Edward's side, taking with him some 4,000 men. Edward decided to strike for London and by 10 April he had reached St Albans. Warwick hoped that London would refuse to admit Edward but the following day the city opened its gates to the Yorkist king and Edward's troops entered, led, one Londoner reported, by 500 of a 'black and smoky sort of Flemish gunners'.

Warwick, who had followed Edward south, drew up his army on high ground north of Barnet and, in a reversal of his previous

The Old Fold, a moated enclosure on the west side of Monken Hadley that was probably in existence at the time of the battle.

The battlefield monument at the north end of Monken Hadley at the junction of Kitts End Road (the old St Albans road) with the A1000.

policy, now offered battle. On 13 April, Edward, no doubt wishing to defeat his former ally before he could join forces with Queen Margaret, led his army back up the Great North Road in search of Warwick. Later that day, Edward's patrols found Warwick at Barnet, drove his patrols out of the village and located his main force north of the village.

Edward advanced through Barnet towards Warwick's army but as it was getting dark he decided to camp in order of battle ready for an attack in the morning. However, in the darkness he came up nearer to Warwick's force than he had intended and, as would become clear the following morning, his army had not drawn up exactly opposite to Warwick's. Each army's right flank overlapped its opponent's left, a configuration that was to have a major effect on the course of the battle the following day.

That night Warwick tried to make the most of his superiority in artillery

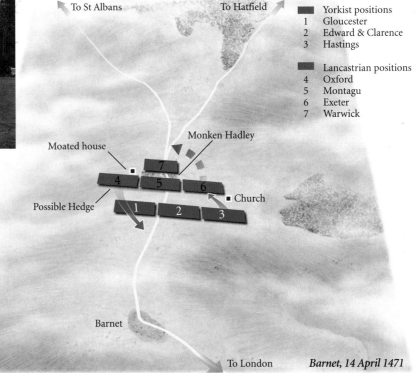

To St Albans
To Hatfield

Yorkist positions
1 Gloucester
2 Edward & Clarence
3 Hastings

Lancastrian positions
4 Oxford
5 Montagu
6 Exeter
7 Warwick

Monken Hadley

Moated house
7
4   5   6
Church
Possible Hedge
1   2   3

Barnet

To London

Barnet, 14 April 1471

1km

Edward IV (1442–83)

Edward was only 18 years old when the Yorkists proclaimed him king in March 1461 but he certainly looked the part. He was well over six feet tall, powerfully built and handsome. Indeed, in both appearance and character he is remarkably reminiscent of his more famous grandson, Henry VIII. He bore no resemblance whatsoever to his father, Richard of York, and doubts over his legitimacy were raised by opponents during his reign. These have often been dismissed as propaganda but it has recently been controversially claimed that Richard could not have been with his wife at the time of Edward's conception in Rouen as he was on campaign at Pontoise.

Edward was easygoing and affable and often extraordinarily forgiving towards his enemies, but he also had a ferocious temper and could be utterly ruthless when required. Crucially, while at first he probably relied heavily upon the advice of old hands like Lord Fauconberg (Warwick's uncle), he was an extremely skilled soldier and an inspirational commander, always in the thick of the action. Nowhere was this more apparent than at Towton, where his leadership was a major factor in the eventual Yorkist victory.

Even so, Edward knew that he would never have become king without the support of the Earl of Warwick and, initially at least, he was content to follow Warwick's advice. In 1464, however, Edward secretly married Elizabeth Woodville, a beautiful blonde Lancastrian widow. It was a humiliation for Warwick who had been trying to arrange Edward's marriage to a French princess, in order to cement an alliance with France. Warwick felt his influence slip further as the king heaped favours on his new wife's family, arranged profitable marriages for her siblings and favoured an alliance, not with France but with Burgundy.

Warwick's attempt to reassert his position in 1469 led to two years of chaos, which saw Edward imprisoned by Warwick then temporarily recover his power, only to be forced into exile when the Earl went over to the Lancastrian side, allied with his old enemy Margaret of Anjou, and returned to England with an army to rule in the name of Henry VI.

Edward's military skills had, however, not deserted him. With Burgundian help he returned to England in March 1471, raised an army and struck before Warwick and Margaret could join forces, killing the former at Barnet on 14 April. Three weeks later he captured Margaret at the battle of Tewkesbury and killed her son, the Prince of Wales. The Lancastrian cause was all but extinguished, and Edward made doubly sure by ordering the murder

King Edward IV by an unknown 16th-century artist.

of Henry VI, by now a pathetic prisoner in the Tower.

Edward was soon financially as well as politically secure. He invaded France in 1475 but allowed himself to be bought off without fighting. The annual subsidy which Louis XI agreed to pay him, coupled with a thorough reorganisation of the income derived from his extensive lands, enabled Edward to rule without resorting to heavy taxation. Edward had always been an enthusiastic womaniser. He had several mistresses, and an Italian at his court wrote that 'he was licentious in the extreme... He pursued with no discrimination the married and unmarried, the noble and lowly'. Edward grew fat in middle age, for he also enjoyed his food, and this may have contributed to his relatively early death in 1483.

by ordering a bombardment of Edward's position but, because the two armies were so close, Warwick's guns overshot the Yorkist army. Edward made sure that the Lancastrians were unaware of their error by ordering strict silence and forbidding his own gunners to return fire. The result was that Warwick's guns pounded away all night, to very little effect.

The following day was Easter Sunday. Edward had his troops ready for action before dawn. Although the precise positions of the two armies is still disputed, it seems that his army was deployed in the traditional three divisions or 'battles' across the Great North Road. Edward commanded the main body while the other two divisions were led by his brother, Richard of Gloucester, and Lord Hastings. Gloucester commanded the Yorkist vanguard. By custom the vanguard was deployed on the right of the line but the *Great Chronicle* says that the Earl of Oxford on the Lancastrian right defeated Gloucester's men, which would suggest that Gloucester was on the left and Hastings the right.

The Lancastrians were also deployed in three battles, with Warwick and his brother Montagu in the centre, Exeter on the left and Oxford on the right, possibly behind a hedge. Philippe de Commynes, a Burgundian writer of the period, claims that Montagu persuaded his brother to dismount and send away his horse. According to de Commynes, Warwick normally stayed on his horse during a battle so that he could escape if things were going badly but on this occasion he agreed to dismount so that his soldiers could see that he intended to remain at their side. It was very foggy that morning and the smoke from Warwick's guns, which had been firing all night, can only have made visibility even poorer. According to the *Great Chronicle*:

It happened to be so exceeding a mist that neither host could plainly see the other.

As Edward's troops moved forward to attack, neither they nor their opponents were thus aware that the two armies were not correctly aligned. As the *Historie of the Arrivall of King Edward IV* explains:

So it was, that the one ende of theyr batayle ovarrechyd th'end of the Kyngs battayle, and so, at that end, they were myche myghtyar than was the Kyngs bataile at the same [end] that ioyned with them, whiche was the west ende ... And, in lykewyse, at the est end, the Kyngs battaye, whan they cam to ioyninge, ovarrechyd theyr batayle, and so distresyd them theyr gretly...

As battle was joined, the troops on Edward's left found themselves outflanked by the Earl of Oxford's division, and soon broke and fled down the road to Barnet, with Oxford's men in hot pursuit. Some of the fugitives did not stop until they reached London, where they announced

A modern painting by Graham Turner. Richard of Gloucester and his standard bearer strain to make out Warwick's forces in the fog at Barnet.

Richard Neville (1428–71)

The son of the Earl of Salisbury, Neville was married to the nine-year-old Anne Beauchamp at the age of six. When his young wife inherited the earldom of Warwick in 1449, he became master of a vast inheritance that was vigorously contested by Anne's half-sisters and their husbands including the king's leading minister, the Duke of Somerset. Warwick's subsequent support of Richard of York in his bid to replace Somerset as Protector in 1453 was partly motivated by a desire to protect his inheritance and partly an expression of the traditional Neville hatred of the Percys whose leader, the Earl of Northumberland, was an ally of Somerset. In May 1455, factional rivalry spilled over into open warfare as York and the Nevilles attacked the court at St Albans, capturing Henry VI and killing both Somerset and Northumberland.

Warwick, now York's right-hand man, was appointed Captain of Calais. He kept the post when York was dismissed as Protector and was even appointed admiral to combat French raids on the south coast. For the next four years Warwick kept the Calais garrison paid and made himself a popular hero by plundering neutral shipping and defying Margaret of Anjou's government when it attempted to call him to account. Despite the collapse of the Yorkist rising at Ludford Bridge in 1459, Warwick managed to retain control of

Calais. His popularity in the south east enabled him to enter London the following year, raise an army and capture Henry once again – this time at Northampton. After Margaret's victory at Wakefield, where York and Warwick's father met their deaths, Warwick confronted her forces at St Albans only to be thoroughly outmanoeuvred and routed. When the Lancastrians retreated north, Warwick joined York's son, the newly proclaimed Edward IV, in their pursuit, raising more troops for him in the Midlands.

After his crushing victory at Towton, Edward heaped rewards upon Warwick, granting him land and appointing him Great Chamberlain of England, Warden of the Cinque Ports and Constable of Dover Castle, all for life. His captaincy of Calais was renewed, and he was made Admiral of England. Warwick, who had also inherited his father's estates after Wakefield, was now by far the most powerful subject in the realm and the young king's chief advisor.

After Edward's marriage to Elizabeth Woodville, Warwick became increasingly disenchanted with the king's policies. He felt denied the influence he believed was his right and resented the king's failure to find suitable matches for his daughters. In the late 1460s, he began plotting with Edward's younger brother, the Duke of Clarence, taking the first

Richard Neville, Earl of Warwick, from the late 15th-century Rous Roll. *The extraordinarily complicated coat of arms reflects the numerous Neville marriages that helped create his vast inheritance.*

steps along the road that was to lead to his death on a foggy Easter Sunday at Barnet.

'Warwick the Kingmaker' was no great general. His military reputation was based more on his exploits at sea and the huge resources he commanded than on any particular ability as a soldier. Although undoubtedly ambitious, his primary motivation seems to have been defensive – a desire to protect both his influence and his vast but precarious inheritance. Even so, his willingness to resort to arms whenever he felt his interests were threatened, and the ruthless way in which he treated his defeated enemies, are undeniable.

that Edward had been defeated. Oxford's men stopped in High Barnet where they set about looting both the village and the enemy's baggage:

> *...afftyr the Sunne was upp, eythir hoost approachid unto othir, But than it happid to be soo excedyng a myst that nowthir hoost cowde playnly see othir, soo that It happid therle of Oxynfford to sett upon the wyng or end of the duke of Glowcetirs people and afftyr sharp ffygth slew a certayn of theym and put the Remenant to fflygth, and anoon as they had a while chacid such as ffled, soom Retournyd and ffyll to Ryfelyng and soom of theym wenyng that all had been wonne, Rood In alle haast to london and there told that kyng Edward haddf lost the ffeeld ... Then afftyr this ffayt was doon by therle and he parceyvid well that he had erryd of his waye, he then wyth such as were abowth hym sett upon the Remenant of that hoost and held batayll wyth theym.*

A late 15th-century German visored sallet helmet. During the Wars of the Roses, the sallet seems to have been the helmet of choice for both mounted troops and foot soldiers.

In the centre, completely unaware of what had happened, the two sides battled away in the fog, with Edward, as usual, in the thick of the fighting. Further east, where they outflanked the Lancastrians, the Yorkist right pushed back their opponents and may have begun to put pressure on the Lancastrian centre. Meanwhile, the Earl of Oxford had gathered together as many of his victorious troops as he could and was returning to the fray with about 800 men. In the centre, peering into the fog, Warwick's men saw them coming. The line of advance of Oxford's men must have made them appear to be Yorkist reinforcements and, if the chronicle written by John Warkworth is to be believed, the situation was not helped by the fact that, in the mist, Oxford's livery badge – a star with streams – looked very similar to the sun-in-splendour badge of Edward IV. Thinking they were about to be attacked by a fresh party of Yorkists, Warwick's men loosed arrows into the advancing troops. No doubt thinking that Warwick's men had changed sides – it had, after all, happened before – some of Oxford's troops shot back while the rest, believing the day to be lost, fled the field shouting 'treason!'

In the ensuing chaos, the main Lancastrian line, already under pressure from the Yorkists on their left, began to crumble amid accusations of treachery. Finally, it broke, and it was probably now that Warwick's army suffered its heaviest casualties. Among them was the Earl of Warwick himself, captured and stabbed to death before Edward could prevent it. Warwick's brother Montagu was also killed, along with perhaps 1,000 Lancastrians. Exeter had been badly wounded but Oxford and his brothers managed to escape and reach the safety of Scotland.

The Yorkists had also suffered some notable casualties, including Lords Say and Cromwell and Sir William Blount. The battle was over before noon. According to the *Arrivall* it lasted just three hours, while Warkworth writes that the fighting ended at 10am. Edward returned to

Middleham Castle, North Yorkshire. The castle originally belonged to the Nevilles, and Edward IV was briefly held prisoner here following Warwick's seizure of power in 1469. After Warwick's death at Barnet, Middleham passed into the hands of Richard of Gloucester who used it as his power base in the north.

London and, striding into St Paul's while a service was taking place, he is said to have laid Warwick's banner on the altar. He ordered that the bodies of Warwick and Montagu should be displayed outside St Paul's Cathedral, so that rumours could not spread that they were still alive. Three days later, the bodies were taken for burial in the family vault at Bisham Abbey.

Edward's victory at Barnet and the deaths of Richard, Earl of Warwick, and his brother John, Marquis of Montagu, had broken the power of the Nevilles. Three weeks later he secured his crown by destroying Queen Margaret's army at Tewkesbury.

Badges of colour and confusion

It is ironic that Oxford's star badge seems to have caused so much confusion at Barnet, for one of the purposes of such livery badges was to offer an easy method of recognition. By the late Middle Ages, the coats of arms of the nobility were often so complicated that they were difficult to reproduce, expensive to carve, exhausting to embroider and, unless one was an expert in the field, impossible to recognise, especially in the heat of battle.

As a result nobles also adopted livery badges, which, like a modern logo, were simple and memorable, could be sewn onto clothes and even used to mark property. The symbols used for some of these badges included a crescent for the Percys, a ragged staff (or crooked billet) for their rivals, the Nevilles, and a portcullis for the Beauforts. In 1454, the Duke of Buckingham purchased 2,000 Stafford knot badges for his followers, and in 1483 Richard of Gloucester ordered 8,000 white boar badges 'wrought upon fustian' to be made for the coats of his supporters. Twenty-five years earlier, the white boar seems to have been a Lancastrian symbol, used by the Courtney Earls of Devon.

As these badges were so widely used they were much more familiar to people than a lord's arms and could therefore be a very handy method of telling friend from foe. On the battlefield men could be identified by

Livery badges. Clockwise from top left: Earl of Oxford; Earl of Oxford (conjectural); Beaufort family; Earl of Devon (1461) and Richard of Gloucester (1483); Edward IV; and Earl of Warwick.

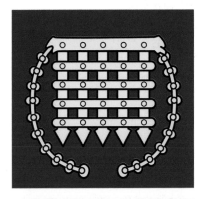

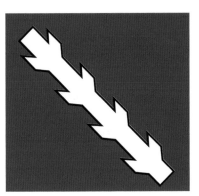
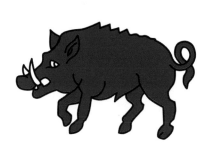

Some medieval livery badges are still in use today. This is a Percy crescent on an estate cottage in Albury, Surrey.

their livery coats and badges if they had them, and by the standard under which they fought. Nobles would gather around their lord's personal standard, a long pennant that featured his two livery colours, the cross of St George and the noble's badge and motto. The choice of livery colours was not governed by heraldic law and did not have to be linked to the tincture on a noble's coat of arms. So, for example, Edward IV's livery colours were azure and murrey (blue and dark mulberry red) and, although the Percys' tinctures were azure and *or* (blue and gold), their livery colours were russet, yellow and orange.

A noble's retainer might also wear a livery coat, the colours of which would be the same as those on his lord's standard. The Earl of Warwick's followers wore red coats with the ragged staff symbol on the front and rear, and Warkworth's account of the battle mentions that the Earl of Oxford's men wore his star badge 'both before and behind'. (Interestingly, the battle of Empingham in 1470 derives its alternative name, 'Losecoat Field', from the speed with which the defeated rebels discarded their livery coats in a bid to avoid detection.)

A star and sun with streams

But it hapenede so, that the Erle of Oxenfordes men hadde uppon them ther lordes lyvery, bothe before and
behynde, which was a sterre withe stremys, wiche [was] myche lyke Kynge Edwardes lyvery, the sunne with
stremys; and the myste was so thycke, that a manne myghte not profytely juge one thynge from anothere; so the Erle
of Warwikes menne schott and faughte ayens the Erle of Oxenfordes menne, wetynge and supposynge that thei
hade bene Kynge Edwardes menne; and anone the Erle of Oxenforde and his menne cryed "treasoune! treasoune!"
and fledde awaye from the felde withe viii c. menne

John Warkworth's *Chronicle of the First Thirteen Years of the Reign of King
Edward the Fourth* describes what may have been the decisive moment in
the battle of Barnet. The author of the chronicle was writing over five
years after Barnet and this story is not told in the other accounts of the
battle. Nevertheless, it seems entirely plausible and there must have been
an element of mutual suspicion between the followers of the diehard
Lancastrian Earl of Oxford and the former Yorkists of Warwick.

The Battle of Barnet portrayed in the
15th-century Ghent version of the
Historic of the Arrivall of Edward IV.

Treason and Plot?
Stoke, 16 June 1487

'You can easily invade if you win over one of the barons. There always exist malcontents and those who want a change… But subsequently when you want to maintain your rule, you will run into countless difficulties, as regards both those who have helped you and those you have subjugated. Nor is it enough for you to destroy the ruler's family because there still remain nobles to raise insurrections…' Machiavelli's analysis of the problems of holding onto newly acquired power could well be applied to Henry Tudor. Treachery had helped him win at Bosworth. Now, two years later, would it lead to his downfall?

Looking north towards Fiskerton, which is on the far bank of the River Trent. A ford existed there in 1487 and Lincoln's army may have used it to cross the Trent, although Molinet writes that the rebels crossed at Newark, then marched along the Fosse Way. It seems more likely that some of the routed rebels, having fled down Red Gutter, attempted to escape across the Trent by this route. Any medieval road from Fiskerton has disappeared, and the lane in the picture was laid out following parliamentary enclosure in the 18th century. At the time of the battle the fields here consisted of meadows and marshland.

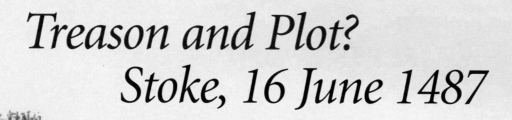

Although Henry Tudor had won the crown at Bosworth in August 1485, it was by no means certain at the time that he would be able to hold onto it. Enough disgruntled Yorkists remained, particularly in the north of England, to make rebellion a distinct possibility. Henry attempted to strengthen his claim to the throne by marrying Elizabeth of York, the daughter of Edward IV. He placed the 15-year-old Earl of Warwick, Edward's nephew and a potential Yorkist claimant to the throne, in 'protective custody' in the Tower of London. In 1486, Henry was indeed faced with two attempted rebellions – one in the West Midlands led by Humphrey Stafford and one in the north led by Richard III's old friend Francis, Viscount Lovell. But neither attracted much support; the risings soon collapsed and their leaders fled. Stafford was dragged from sanctuary in Colchester Abbey and, when the judges ruled that the right of sanctuary did not extend to traitors, he was hanged, drawn and quartered. Lovell, however, escaped to the Low Countries and made his way to the court of Margaret of York, the Dowager Duchess of Burgundy and sister of Richard III and Edward IV, where he was later joined by John de la Pole, Earl of Lincoln.

Margaret of York, the sister of Richard III and Edward IV and widow of Charles the Bold of Burgundy. She remained an implacable enemy of Henry VII despite the fact that he had combined the houses of Lancaster and York by marrying her niece, Elizabeth.

With Warwick locked up in the Tower, the Yorkist exiles believed that the lack of a royal Yorkist figurehead had been a major factor in the failure of their 1486 risings. An opportunity came their way in 1487, however, when an impostor turned up in Ireland and declared that *he* was the Earl of Warwick, lately escaped from the Tower. The impostor, who later turned out to be 'Lambert Simnel', an Oxford artisan's son who had been tutored in courtly manners by a local priest, may well have been planted on the Irish by Lincoln and Lovell. Nevertheless, the traditionally pro-Yorkist Irish lords were only too willing to recognise the youth as 'King Edward VI'. The exiled Yorkists had the figurehead they needed.

In May 1487, Lincoln and Lovell set sail for Dublin, with 2,000 Swiss and German mercenaries paid for by Margaret and commanded by Martin Schwarz, one of the most famous warriors of his age. An Augsburg shoemaker turned soldier, Schwarz had made his reputation fighting for Charles the Bold of Burgundy before entering the service of Maximilian,

Francis, Viscount Lovell (1454–?)

Francis Lovell was one of Richard III's closest friends and most trusted servants. The two men probably first met at Middleham Castle where Lovell, who was a ward of the Earl of Warwick, had been sent to begin his training as a knight. Following Warwick's death at the battle of Barnet in 1471, Lovell was made a ward of the Duke of Suffolk, the father of another future comrade-in-arms, John de la Pole, Earl of Lincoln.

In 1481, Lovell served under Richard of Gloucester in his campaign against the Scots, distinguished himself in the fighting and was knighted outside Berwick. When Richard became king in 1483, Lovell rapidly rose to become one of the most important men in the country. His appointment as the king's chamberlain is evidence of the two men's intimacy and, as one of the king's closest advisors, Lovell was one of those lampooned in William Collingbourne's famous couplet:

The Cat, the Rat and Lovell our Dog,
Rule all England under a Hog

The verse referred to Richard's chancellor, William Catesby; Sir Richard Ratcliffe, a north country soldier and a member of the king's council; Lovell, whose crest was a silver dog; and Richard himself, whose badge was a white boar.

It seems likely that Lovell fought at Bosworth in August 1485, for it was initially reported that he had been killed there but in fact he escaped and joined Humphrey and Thomas Stafford in sanctuary in Colchester Abbey. In the spring of 1486 Lovell and the Staffords broke out and tried unsuccessfully to lead risings against Henry Tudor. Lovell headed north but was unable to enlist much support, and when Henry VII offered a pardon to those who had taken up arms against him the rising fizzled out.

Lovell fled to the court of Margaret of York, the Dowager Duchess of Burgundy, where, the following year, Lovell and the Earl of Lincoln found support for their ill-fated invasion of England. After the debacle at Stoke, Lovell is said to have escaped by swimming his horse across the Trent. He seems to have fled north to Scotland where, in June 1488, James IV granted him safe conduct.

What happened to him next is a mystery. If he ever did return to England he would have had to do so in secrecy. Indeed, writing in the 17th century, Francis Bacon recounts a story that Lovell 'lived long after in a cave or vault.' Bearing this in mind, the fact that, in 1708, a skeleton is said to have been found in a hidden room at Lovell's Oxfordshire home might just be more than a coincidence.

The ruins of Minster Lovell Hall,
the Oxfordshire home of Francis,
Viscount Lovell.

the future Holy Roman Emperor. A hard drinker who loved ostentatious jewellery, Schwarz was nevertheless a highly professional soldier, and the boldness – and cruelty – of his men was legendary.

On their arrival in Ireland the Yorkists moved quickly. They crowned Lambert Simnel as King Edward VI on 24 May and, reinforced by 4,000 Irish troops under Thomas Fitzgerald, set sail for England in early June. On 4 June, they landed at Foudray in Lancashire where one of their supporters, Sir Thomas Broughton, had extensive holdings of land. They marched south and crossed the Pennines into Yorkshire where a few families, such as the Scropes of Masham and Bolton, joined their cause. However, despite the presence of their new 'king', they failed to gather as much support in the county as they had hoped. An attempt to enter York had to be abandoned when the citizens, reinforced by Lord Clifford and having been informed by the Earl of Northumberland that he was coming to their aid, declared their loyalty to Henry. According to Polydore Vergil:

The Earl of Lincoln meanwhile had entered Yorkshire with the other rebels, proceeding slowly and offering no harm to the local inhabitants, for he hoped some of the people would rally to his side. But when he saw his following was small he resolved none the less to try the fortunes of war, recalling that two years earlier Henry with a small number of soldiers had conquered the great army of king Richard.

It appears that Lincoln had also promised Martin Schwarz that large numbers of Englishmen would flock to their army, for the *Great Chronicle of London* notes that:

…Martin Schwarz was deceived, for when he took this voyage upon him he was comforted and promised by the Earl of Lincoln, that great strength of this land after their landing would have resorted unto the said Earl. But when he was far entered and saw no such resort, then he knew he was deceived, wherefore he said unto the Earl, Sir, now I see well that ye have deceived yourself and also me…

Yet all was not lost for the Yorkists. Richard III's defeat at Bosworth had shown that it was one thing to bring a large army into the field but quite another to persuade it to fight for you. The fortunes of war might yet favour them after all. The rebels duly headed south, heading for Newark. Northumberland and Clifford followed them but had only been gone for a matter of hours when the Scropes arrived outside York and launched an unsuccessful attack on the city. Whether this was a deliberate ploy to prevent Northumberland joining Henry is not clear but it certainly had that effect. Northumberland and Clifford turned their forces around and headed back north.

Meanwhile, Henry, who had initially been concentrating his forces at Kenilworth, had advanced north-eastward to Nottingham where he linked up with the forces of Lord Strange. With perhaps 15,000 men now under his command, Henry carried on in the direction of Newark and, on 15 June, camped near the Trent at Radcliffe. It is possible that morale was shaky in Henry's camp, for an anonymous herald who accompanied Henry's army and left an account of the campaign later wrote:

That evening there was a great scry, which caused many cowards to flee.

The following morning, however, the royal army continued its march north-eastward in search of the rebels. According to Henry's anonymous herald-chronicler, local guides showed them the way:

…the King had five good and true men of the village of Radcliffe, which showed his grace the best way for to conduct his host to Newark, which knew well the country, and showed where were marshes and where was the river of Trent, and where were villages or groves for bushments [ambushes], or straight ways, that the King might conduct his host the better.

Henry VII. A portrait painted 18 years after the battle of Stoke, in 1505.

The main road to Newark was the Fosse Way, which passes about two miles to the east of Newark, and it seems likely that at least some of the royal army would have used it if they could. On the other hand, the need for guides and the herald's mention of the River Trent suggests that Henry's men might have taken a different route. What is clear is that the Royalist order of march was in the traditional three divisions: the vanguard under the Earl of Oxford; the main body under the king; and the rearguard under Lord Strange.

Meanwhile the rebels had drawn up on some high ground near the village of Stoke. Exactly where they were or how they got there is not known for certain. Local tradition has it that they forded the River Trent

The ancient track of Humber Lane, leading up to the crest of the hill where the rebel army probably deployed. Running parallel with the Fosse Way, this was a major road from Nottingham to Newark in 1487.

(which was much wider and shallower than it is today) at Fiskerton, four miles south-west of Newark but the Burgundian chronicler, Jean de Molinet, writes that they crossed the river in the town itself and then followed the river south.

The rebel army, consisting of some 8,000 men, probably then deployed to the south-west of Stoke on some high ground known as Burnham Furlong. The core of the army was, without doubt, Martin Schwarz's 2,000 mercenaries, some of whom were equipped with pikes. Perhaps 2,000 English were also present but the rest of Lincoln's force was made up of Fitzgerald's Irish, whose lack of armour made them highly vulnerable to Henry's archers. According to de Molinet the entire rebel army was drawn up in a single body.

At about 9am Oxford's vanguard approached the rebel position. He may have had as many as 6,000 men, with two wings of cavalry flanking a body of infantry. Probably hoping to defeat Oxford before the rest of Henry's army could arrive, Lincoln led his troops down the hill in an all-out attack on the royal vanguard. It is clear that the battle was extremely hard fought, and Oxford's vanguard, which seems to have been the only part of Henry's army to take part in the fighting, was initially very hard

A late 15th-century Flemish illustration of an army deployed for battle, depicting pikemen and handgunners, with cavalry and archers on the flanks. The pike was probably carried by at least some of Schwarz's mercenaries at Stoke. Unlike the troops in this picture, however, the Irish levies that made up a substantial proportion of Lincoln's army did not enjoy the benefit of armour.

John de Vere, Earl of Oxford (1442–1513)

It is surprising that Oxford was still alive to fight for Henry Tudor, for despite Edward IV's relatively conciliatory attitude towards him, he had shown a stubborn loyalty to the Lancastrian cause and an unwavering hatred of the House of York. Edward had executed Oxford's father and elder brother for treason in 1462 but hoped, somewhat unrealistically, that he could make a supporter out of the young earl. As his father had not been attainted, Oxford was permitted to inherit his extensive East Anglian estates, and he was gradually brought back into court life. He was created a Knight of the Bath at the coronation of Elizabeth Woodville, Edward's wife, and married the youngest sister of the Earl of Warwick. Nevertheless, in 1468, he was imprisoned in the Tower of London where he confessed to having been plotting with fellow Lancastrians.

Remarkably, the king pardoned him but the following year Oxford joined his brother-in-law, the Earl of Warwick, in opposition to Edward. In 1470, he carried the sword of state at the 'recrowning' of the restored Henry VI and presided over the trial of John Tiptoft, Earl of Worcester, Edward's cultured but brutal enforcer. After the Lancastrian defeat at Barnet, Oxford fled to Scotland and eventually reached France. Funded by the French, he raided Calais, attempted a landing in Essex and carried out a successful campaign of piracy, before seizing St Michael's Mount in September 1473. Besieged there by Edward's forces, he held out until the following February when, deserted by most of his men and wounded in the face by an arrow, he was forced to surrender.

He was to spend the next 10 years of his life in Calais as a prisoner in Hammes Castle. Despite an escape (or, perhaps, suicide) attempt in 1478, when Oxford climbed the castle walls and jumped into the moat, Edward refrained from taking the easy way out by having him killed.

In 1484 Richard III ordered his transfer to England but Oxford escaped with the aid of his jailer and joined Henry Tudor at Montargis on the Loire. Henry, whose followers included plenty of disgruntled former Yorkists but precious few true Lancastrians, was delighted to have such a stalwart Lancastrian on his side.

After Bosworth, where he commanded the Tudor vanguard, Oxford reaped the rewards for his support for Henry. He was made Admiral of England, Constable of the Tower of London and was given extensive estates, particularly in East Anglia. Oxford was the new king's most trusted lieutenant. As well as winning the battle of Stoke for Henry, he led the vanguard of Henry's army on the invasion of France in 1492 and began the attack on the Cornish rebels at Blackheath in 1497.

He was frequently visited by Henry VII, but the oft-repeated story that the king fined him heavily for illegally keeping retainers appears to be without substance. Oxford died in March 1513. Six months later the Earl of Surrey, his old adversary at Bosworth, would be leading a Tudor army to victory over the Scots at Flodden.

Hedingham Castle , Essex. Family seat of the de Veres.

pressed. Vergil writes that, 'both sides fought with the bitterest energy' and comments on the fighting prowess of Schwarz's mercenaries:

Those rugged men of the mountains, the Germans, so practised in warfare, were in the forefront of the battle and yielded little to the English in valour.

However, just as he had done at Bosworth, Oxford put up a stiff resistance. His bowmen took a terrible toll of Fitzgerald's Irishmen who, according to Molinet:

…could not withstand the shooting of the English archers…and, although they displayed great bravery… they were routed and defeated, shot through and full of arrows like hedgehogs.

As Lincoln's advance began to run out of steam, Oxford ordered a counter-attack of his own and the rebels broke, some fleeing through Stoke and others making for the ford at Fiskerton. Local tradition has it that the Red Gutter, a steep gully leading down from Burnham Furlong to the flood plain of the Trent, was used by some of the fleeing men, and human remains are said to have been found there. Mass graves have been found in the vicinity of Stoke village, which suggests that many of the rebels retreated in that direction. Many of the rebel casualties must have occurred during the rout, especially as the royal vanguard included a large contingent of mounted troops, ideally suited for a pursuit.

Looking south-east up Red Gutter to the top of Burnham Furlong, the high ground where Lincoln's forces are believed to have deployed. Some of the defeated rebels may have fled down this valley, which at the time was not heavily wooded. Richard Brooke, who visited the battlefield in 1825, noted in his pamphlet on the battle that 'human bones and other indicia of slaughter' had been found in Red Gutter.

Of the rebel leaders, only Lovell escaped. Lincoln, Schwarz and Fitzgerald were all killed along with as many as 4,000 of their troops. Lambert Simnel was captured but Henry spared his life, making him a turnspit in the royal kitchens. Eventually he rose to be trainer of the king's hawks.

Stoke was the final battle of the Wars of the Roses. Henry's victory strengthened his grip on the crown, and although he had to deal with other rebellions and face another pretender in Perkin Warbeck between 1495 and 1497, he never had to take the field against a rival again.

Treachery on the battlefield

Fear of betrayal was a common feature of the Wars of the Roses. At Ludford Bridge, Northampton and Bosworth, commanders had changed sides with disastrous results for their former allies, while at both Tewkesbury and Barnet (*see* chapter 6) the Lancastrian armies had disintegrated amongst bitter accusations of treachery.

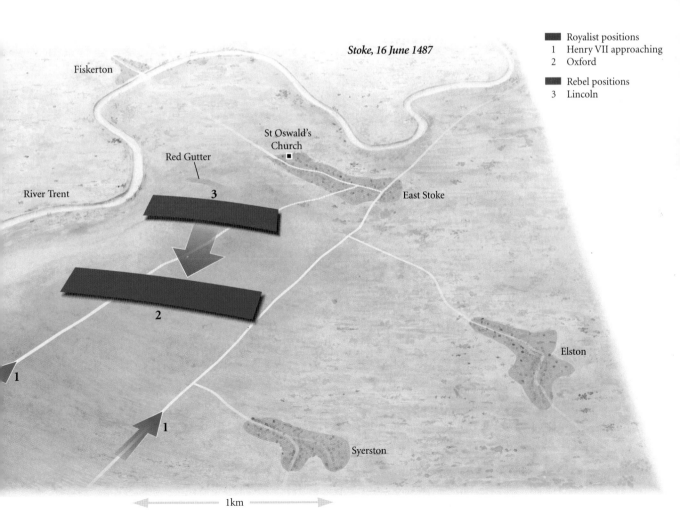

Stoke, 16 June 1487

Royalist positions
1 Henry VII approaching
2 Oxford

Rebel positions
3 Lincoln

Fiskerton

St Oswald's Church

Red Gutter

River Trent

3

East Stoke

2

1

Elston

1

Syerston

1km

Many military leaders dismounted and fought on foot, partly to become less conspicuous targets to the enemy but also to show their determination not to desert their men but to stay and fight, and, if necessary, die beside them. Edward IV claimed to have won nine battles in this manner. Henry VII's actions in the build-up to the battle of Stoke, however, did nothing to calm the nerves of his followers. On more than one occasion he rode away from his army, without explaining what he was doing or where he was going, giving rise to rumours that he had fled the field. The rebels seem to have played on this uncertainty. According to the *Great Chronicle of London*:

…men were set between the place of the field and many of the king's subjects which were coming toward his Grace, showing unto them that the King had lost the field and was fled. By such subtle means and report many a true man to the king turned back again, and some men of fear rode unto sanctuary, and tarried there till to them was brought better tidings.

The garter stall plate with its silver dog crest of Francis Lovell 'our dog' in St George's Chapel, Windsor.

Henry had assembled a formidable force with which to confront the rebels at Stoke but this was no guarantee of victory. There was always the danger that some of his supporters might hold back and await the course of events or, even worse, change sides. Only two years earlier, at Bosworth, Richard III's army had been far larger than that of Henry Tudor but many of his so-called supporters had let him down. Northumberland failed to commit his troops to the fight, while the Stanleys eventually changed sides altogether.

Was the Earl of Lincoln hoping for something similar to happen at Stoke? Clearly Henry feared some kind of conspiracy against him, for he ordered the Earl of Oxford to place the Marquess of Dorset under arrest before he could join the royal army.

It is worth noting that Henry was beside himself with rage when he learned that Lincoln had been killed in the battle, for he had ordered that the Earl should be taken alive. Henry had hoped to 'question' Lincoln in order to extract the names of any nobles with whom he had been plotting. However, as Polydore Vergil put it:

'…it is said that the soldiers declined to spare the earl, fearful lest by chance it would happen that the sparing of one man's life would lead to the loss of many…'

Dead men tell no tales.

An Italian writes English history

We have already heard from one chronicler several times in the above account of the battle of Stoke. Polydore Vergil was born near Urbino, Italy, in about 1470 and came to England in 1502 as a papal tax collector. He had already established a reputation as a scholar, and, in 1505, Henry VII commissioned him to compile a history of England. His initial draft, which covered events up to 1513, was completed that year and published in 1534.

Vergil's work aroused considerable nationalistic fury at the time, for he dismissed Geoffrey of Monmouth's claim that Britain had been settled by Brutus, a refugee from Troy, and also denied the historical existence of King Arthur. Vergil continues to cause fury today – amongst members of the Richard III Society – for he did a thorough job of blackening the name of their hero in his ostensibly impartial history.

In spite of his undeniable role as a Tudor propagandist, however, when it comes to the battle of Stoke, Vergil makes no attempt to exaggerate Henry VII's role in the battle, and he seems to have tried to produce as objective an account as possible. Although he was writing 20 years after the event, Vergil's court connections did mean that he was able to speak with people who had taken part in the events of 1487.

Effigy of Sir John Cheney in Salisbury Cathedral. A giant of a man, Cheney was one of a number of experienced soldiers who rallied to Henry's cause in 1487. He had joined Henry in France in 1483 and fought at Bosworth where he was unhorsed by Richard III in person.

His details of the battle itself – the role played by Henry's vanguard led by the Earl of Oxford, the fierceness of the struggle, the heavy casualties suffered by the unarmoured Irish – are all corroborated in other accounts. Vergil's geography does let him down in an earlier section, where he has Henry's army approaching Stoke from the wrong direction but the other main accounts of the battle are also not without their problems: Jean de Molinet confuses the royal vanguard and rearguard and describes the Irish as Germans, while the only account by someone who was present at Stoke, the unknown herald in Henry's army, describes the actual battle in a single sentence!

Vergil's account in his *History of England* is somewhat fuller:

The following day the King, having formed his whole force into three columns, marched to the village of Stoke, halted before the

Earl's camp and, on the level ground there, offered battle. Accepting the chance, the Earl led forward his troops and, at a given signal, gave battle. Both sides fought with the bitterest energy. Those rugged men of the mountains, the Germans, so practised in warfare, were in the forefront of the battle and yielded little to the English in valour; while Martin Schwarz their leader was not inferior to many in his courage and resolution. On the other hand the Irish, though they fought most spiritedly, were nevertheless (in the tradition of their country) unprotected by body armour and, more than the other troops engaged, suffered heavy casualties, their slaughter striking no little terror into the other combatants. For some time the struggle was fought with no advantage to either side, but at last the first line of the King's army (which was alone committed to the fray and sustained the struggle) charged the enemy with such vigour that it at once crushed those of the hostile leaders who were still resisting. Thereupon the remaining enemy troops turned to flight, and while fleeing were either captured or killed. Indeed it was only then, when the battle was over, that it was fully apparent how rash had been the spirit inspiring the enemy soldiers: for of their leaders John Earl of Lincoln, Francis Lord Lovell, Thomas Broughton, the most bold Martin Schwarz and the Irish captain Thomas Geraldine were slain in that place. . . Lambert the false boy king was indeed captured, with his mentor Richard: but each was granted his life - the innocent lad because he was himself too young to have committed any offence, the tutor because he was a priest. Lambert is still alive to this very day, having been promoted trainer of the King's hawks; before that for some time he was a turnspit and did other menial jobs in the royal kitchen.

The tomb of Sir John Savage in the Church of St Michael, Macclesfield. Savage had commanded the left wing of Henry's army at Bosworth and led the cavalry on the left wing of Oxford's vanguard at Stoke. He was killed five years later at the siege of Boulogne.

An excellent portrayal of a late 15th-century foot soldier. He is armed with a glaive – a cutting weapon comprising a long blade attached to a six foot staff. At this time the glaive may well have been as common a weapon as the better-known bill. For protection he wears a jack, a quilted doublet consisting of layers of fabric stuffed with tow. Some soldiers wore a brigandine, a form of body armour consisting of small overlapping iron plates riveted inside a jack. It seems that even some of the country's richest nobles may have preferred a brigandine to conventional plate armour. According to the will of John de Vere, Earl of Oxford, his armoury contained sallets, brigandines, arm and leg armour but no complete suit of steel plate.

Old versus New Flodden, 9 September 1513

New weapons can sometimes give an army an edge in battle but it can take time to learn how and where to use them effectively. The soldiers of James IV took the field at Flodden equipped with a brand-new weapon – the pike – but inadequate training and unsuitable terrain saw them slaughtered by Surrey's English troops wielding their tried-and-tested bills.

The monument on Piper's Hill to the dead of both nations.

When Henry VIII invaded France in May 1513, Louis XII asked James IV of Scotland to attack England under the terms of the defensive alliance they had signed in 1512. He sent money, arms and experienced soldiers to help James train and fit out an army. Henry was expecting such an attack. He knew that Louis had been equipping the Scots and, as the Tudor historian Edward Hall put it:

he and hys counsayll forgat not the olde Prankes of the Scottes which is ever to invade England when the kynge is oute...

An English billman. Essentially an agricultural implement adapted for military use, the bill could be used to cut, pull or stab and was a highly effective weapon in individual, close-quarter combat. Whereas the pike, with which the Scots took the field at Flodden, required new skills to use effectively, the bill was a tried and tested weapon. It was ideally suited for use by the labourers who made up a substantial proportion of Surrey's army. As many spent much of their working lives chopping, scything, mowing and threshing, wielding a bill would have come naturally to them.

As a precaution, Henry only took troops from the south and the Midlands to France and left his northern levies under the command of his lieutenant-general in the north, Thomas Howard, Earl of Surrey. On 22 August, James crossed the River Tweed with the largest and best-equipped army ever to leave Scotland, numbering perhaps as many as 40,000 men, and set about reducing the English border strongholds with his powerful train of artillery. As soon as he heard the news of the Scottish invasion, Surrey headed north from Pontefract, gathering men as he went. By 4 September, he was at Alnwick with around 26,000 men from the seven northern counties: Yorkshire, Lancashire, Cheshire, Durham, Northumberland, Cumbria and Westmorland.

Surrey was desperate to fight James as soon as possible. He knew that if James fell back, undefeated, over the border, lack of supplies would soon force the English army to disband, leaving the Scots free to raid at will throughout the winter. Surrey therefore decided to appeal to James's well-known sense of chivalry and sent Rouge-Croix, his herald, to challenge him formally to give battle by 9 September. Some commentators have seen this as evidence of a certain old-fashioned naïveté on his part but Surrey, whose experiences during the Wars of the Roses must have rendered him anything but naïve, was merely trying every means at his disposal to bring James to battle. Rouge-Croix also delivered the Scottish king a threatening and insulting letter from Surrey's son, Thomas Howard, designed to goad James into action. To refuse to fight after receiving such a letter would have been seen as a humiliating climb-down.

James duly accepted Surrey's challenge but had a trick of his own up his sleeve. Instead of allowing the English herald to return to Surrey with his reply and, of course, information about the dispositions of the Scottish army, James detained Rouge-Croix and instead sent a herald of his own with the news that he would fight. Anticipating a battle on level ground somewhere on the Milfield plain, Surrey advanced north but when Rouge-Croix finally returned to his master on 7 September, he brought with him the news that:

The King of Scots did lie with his army upon a high hill in the edge of Cheviot… there was no passage or entry unto him but one way where was laid marvellous and great ordnance of guns…

James had moved his army to Flodden Edge, a mile-long hill that rose to over 150 metres above the Milfield Plain. With his troops secure in an entrenched encampment, and gun emplacements protecting his front and flanks, James was in an impregnable position. Realising that any attempt to attack the Scots was thus doomed to failure, Surrey once again tried appealing to James's sense of chivalry, sending him a reproachful letter asking him to fight on equal ground. Not surprisingly, James was unmoved and took the opportunity to put Surrey in his place, sending a letter saying that he would:

Twizel Bridge, which the English vanguard used to cross the Till on the morning of the battle. Completed in about 1500, this 27m single-arch bridge was at the time the largest of its kind in England. Its parapets were repaired in the 19th century.

take and choose his ground and field at his own pleasure and not at the assigning of the Earl of Surrey.

Faced with James's curt refusal to quit his hillside stronghold, Surrey took a bold decision. If he could not shift James by persuasion, then he would do so by manoeuvre. On 8 September the English broke camp, crossed the River Till near Wooler and, in pouring rain, marched round the eastern flank of the Scottish position. The Scots were puzzled by this new turn of events. Unsure whether Surrey was planning a counter-invasion of Scotland or simply trying to lure him from Flodden Edge, James watched and waited. Attacking the English as they marched past was not an option, for Surrey's flank was protected by the River Till. In any case he was unwilling to abandon his superb defensive position unless compelled to do so.

On the morning of 9 September Surrey's intentions became clear. News reached James that Surrey's army had recrossed the Till and were approaching the Scots from the north. Faced with the fact that the English now stood between his forces and the route back to Scotland, James turned his army around and marched to Branxton Hill, one mile away on the northern edge of the Flodden

Thomas Howard, Earl of Surrey (1443–1524)

Thomas Howard, Earl of Surrey. By surmise, in his Camp, at Berner Wood near Twysulford, on the Morning of the Battle of Flodden Sepr 5th (sic), 1513. *From a drawing in a late 16th-century book of heraldry.*

Surrey was the eldest son of John Howard, a relative of the Mowbray dukes of Norfolk, whose intervention had been a decisive factor in the Yorkist victory at Towton (see chapter 5). He followed his father in the service of Edward IV, fighting for him at Barnet (see chapter 6), where he was wounded, and accompanying him on his invasion of France in 1475. However, the marriage of Edward's second son, Richard, to Anne Mowbray in 1478 scuppered the Howards' hopes of inheriting the Mowbray titles and estates; this may explain their support for Richard III's usurpation in 1483.

Richard made John the Duke of Norfolk and his son, Thomas, Earl of Surrey. He granted them extensive lands, making them the most powerful noble family in south-east England.

Both Howards fought for Richard at Bosworth where Norfolk was killed and Surrey wounded and captured. After three years as a prisoner in the Tower of London, Surrey was released and gradually earned back his confiscated estates by proving his loyalty and usefulness to Henry VII.

In 1489, Howard crushed a rebellion in Yorkshire and, in 1497, repelled a Scottish attack on Norham Castle, following up this success with a raid into Scotland of his own. In 1499, he was recalled to court, was made Lord Treasurer of England in 1501, and took part in the negotiations for Prince Arthur's marriage to Catherine of Aragon. He had already played an important role in the negotiations leading up to the treaty of perpetual peace with Scotland, and, in 1503, he accompanied Princess Margaret, Henry VII's daughter, to Scotland for her wedding to James IV, with whom Surrey appears to have got on extremely well.

After the accession of Henry VIII in 1509, Surrey seems to have hoped to have become the young king's leading minister but was supplanted by Thomas Wolsey. Further

disappointment was to follow in 1513 when, instead of accompanying the king on his invasion of France, the doughty old warrior was left behind to guard the north against a Scottish invasion. Surrey was not at all pleased. According to Edward Hall he said of James:

Sorry may I see him ere I die, that is the cause of my abiding behind, and if ever he and I meet, I shall do that in me lieth to make him as sorry if I can.

As it turned out, while Henry conducted a fairly meaningless campaign in northern France, Surrey was to win one of England's greatest ever military victories at Flodden. He received the Dukedom of Norfolk as a reward, together with grants of land, and the Howard arms were augmented with a Scottish lion – shot in the mouth by an arrow. By 1521, he was nearly 80 years old, and looking to retire from court but he had one last duty to perform for his king. As Lord High Steward he presided over the trial of his cousin Edward Stafford, Duke of Buckingham, whose wealth and royal blood had aroused the paranoia of Henry VIII. It is said that tears ran down the old man's face as he read out the death sentence. Finally, in 1523, Thomas Howard retired to his castle at Framlingham, where he died the following May.

A Tudor drawing of an English army on campaign, possibly Henry VIII's expedition to France in 1513. The army, which is screened by cavalry, is accompanied by guns, baggage wagons, camp followers, one or two troublesome dogs and herds of cattle and sheep, which will be slaughtered to feed the soldiers. Whereas Surrey's army at Flodden primarily consisted of archers and billmen, this is a more modern force. As well as archers, the troops depicted include handgunners, halberdiers and German mercenary landsknecht *pikemen.*

feature. Burning the rubbish around their camp to create a smokescreen to mask their movements, the Scots reached the hill before the English, who had been slowed down by the need to wade across an expanse of marshy ground around the Pallinsburn beck.

As the English vanguard under Thomas Howard approached Branxton Hill, they saw the Scots deployed in four divisions, or battles, on its crest. The Scottish left was composed of border pikemen and more lightly armed highlanders under Lord Home and the Earl of Huntly; next were the pikemen of the earls of Errol, Montrose and Crawford; to their right was the king's main battle, again equipped with pikes; finally, on the far right, were more highlanders under the Earls of Argyll and Lennox. It is possible that a fifth battle, under the Earl of Bothwell, stood in reserve.

The English army eventually mirrored this deployment, with Surrey's younger son, Edmund Howard, commanding the right-hand battle, Thomas Howard the centre-right on Piper's Hill and Surrey himself the centre-left in front of Branxton village. As they were last in the line of march, the left-hand division, under Sir Edward Stanley, had not yet arrived when the battle began. Finally, 1,500 border horsemen under Lord Thomas Dacre were deployed as a reserve.

Thomas Howard had been concerned that the Scots might come crashing down the hill before the English were properly formed up but, initially at least, the Scots were content to wait, for it seems that James wanted a set piece battle in which he could use his guns to goad Surrey's men into an uphill attack, before using his pike columns to sweep them away. Finally, at about four o'clock in the afternoon, the action began with the first ever artillery duel in a British battle: a duel that the English won, as their lighter guns outshot the cumbersome Scottish artillery. According to Edward Hall:

The Master Gunner of the English part slew the master Gunner of Scotland and beat all his men from their ordnance…

In fact, Robert Borthwick, the Scottish Master Gunner, survived the day but the Scottish artillery gradually fell silent, enabling the English to turn their attention onto the closely packed ranks of Scottish pikemen. With mounting casualties, James was forced to change his plans and order an all-out assault. As Hall put it:

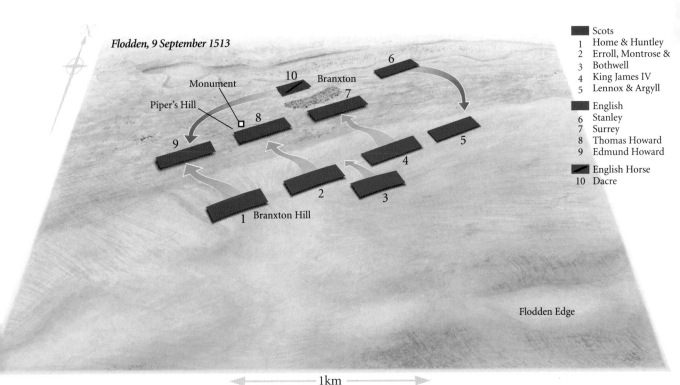

Flodden, 9 September 1513

Monument

Piper's Hill

10   Branxton

9

8

7

6

5

4

2

3

1   Branxton Hill

Flodden Edge

◄———— 1km ————►

Scots
1   Home & Huntley
2   Erroll, Montrose &
3   Bothwell
4   King James IV
5   Lennox & Argyll

English
6   Stanley
7   Surrey
8   Thomas Howard
9   Edmund Howard

English Horse
10 Dacre

Looking down from Branxton Hill to the English lines along Piper's Hill. It is likely that some of the lower land was used for arable farming in 1513 but it is not known whether the crops had been harvested at the time of the battle. The terrain would have been hedgeless in 1513. The battlefield cross marks the position of Thomas Howard's battle. Branxton Church, which served as a mortuary after the battle, can be seen to the right.

'the Englishmen's artillery shot in the midst of the King's battle and slew many persons, which seeing the King of Scots and his noblemen made the more haste to come to joining, and so all the four battles in manner descended the hill at once.'

True to form, James insisted on leading his troops from the front:

His captains did what they could by words to remove him from his purpose, declaring to him the duty of a prince; which is not rashly to enter the fight but to provide and see that everything be done in order: and whereas coming to try the matter by hand blows, he can do no more than another man; yet by keeping his place as appertained to his person, he may be worth many thousands of others.

But James was having none of it. Writing home in 1497 the Spanish ambassador had said of him:

James IV (1473–1513)

James IV was a man of considerable personal charm. Athletic and brave, he was attractive to women and admired by men. He came to the throne in 1488 following the murder of his father, James III, but successfully dealt with the political disruption that inevitably followed. Unlike his father, he avoided relying on a small group of favourites, and broadened his support by including supporters of his late father in his government. Evidence of his generally conciliatory attitude can be seen in his treatment of Archibald Douglas, Earl of Angus, who led an unsuccessful rebellion against the young king in 1491. Not only did James make him his chancellor, he even later shared one of his mistresses with him. In the 1490s, he extended and strengthened his authority over Scotland, subduing the Highlands and extending his rule to the Western Isles.

James was a notable patron of education, literature and the arts, developed Scotland's civil courts and in 1507 he licensed the country's first printing press. However, these solid achievements were to be fatally undermined by his unrealistic determination to play a leading role on the international stage.

In his later years as king, James undertook a programme of massive military expenditure, spending a small fortune on fortifications, expanding his navy and developing a siege train that was the envy of Europe. While this undoubtedly added to his prestige as a monarch, however, such a policy was financially beyond his means as the ruler of a small and relatively poor country. The treasure he had inherited from his father was soon spent and, despite extensive financial manoeuvring, he was eventually reduced to pawning valuables and melting down jewellery.

Although James had supported the pretender Perkin Warbeck against Henry VII, in 1502 he agreed a treaty of 'perpetual peace' with England, cementing it in the following year by marrying Henry's daughter, Margaret. The treaty was underwritten by the papacy, and one of its clauses stated that if either king broke the treaty he would be excommunicated. It was perhaps inevitable that the alliance James later concluded with Louis XII of France would lead to trouble. When Henry VIII invaded France in 1513, Louis called on James, whom he had been supplying with money and arms, for help. Notwithstanding the terms of the treaty of perpetual peace, James duly invaded England

James IV

only to meet with disaster at Flodden where he and a large section of the Scottish nobility met their deaths.

As he had now been excommunicated, James never received a funeral, and his remains were bundled off to England, first to Berwick and then to Richmond Palace. Fifty years later some workmen found his body, dumped in the back of a storeroom. James's French alliance had dragged him into a pointless war with England from which Scotland had little to gain. Although his defeat and death at Flodden was by no means a foregone conclusion, his overspending might well have led to disaster for Scotland, even if he had survived the battle.

The dominating Scottish position on Branxton Hill, viewed from the English lines. In 1513 the upper parts of the hill would probably have been rough pasture used for sheep and cattle grazing. They were only enclosed in the late 1700s.

He is courageous, even more than a King should be… He said to me that his subjects serve him with their persons and goods, in just and unjust quarrel, exactly as he likes, and that therefore he does not think it right to begin any warlike undertaking without being the first in danger.

James seized a pike and took his place at the front of his column. The Scots probably attacked with their columns in echelon with Home and Huntly leading on the left, followed by Errol, Crawford and Montrose and finally James's own division. As the Scots came into range, Surrey's archers loosed their arrows but for once the dreaded longbow had little effect, for 'there was great wind and sodden rain, all contrary to our bows and archers'. Furthermore, as the Bishop of Durham pointed out:

The Scots were so surely harnessed with complete harness, German jacks, rivets, splints, pavises and other habiliments, that shot of arrows in regard did them no harm.

Home and Huntly on the Scottish left were first to come into contact with the English. The relatively even slope down which they had advanced had probably allowed Home's pikemen to maintain their formation and, with Huntly's highland swordsmen alongside them, they bore down on Edmund Howard's division. Heavily outnumbered and unnerved by the approaching phalanx of pikes:

…the Cheshire and Lancashire men never abode stroke and few of the gentlemen of Yorkshire abode but fled.

A contemporary poem suggested that the reason for their flight was their resentment at having to serve under a Howard for 'they were want at all wars to wait upon the Stanleys.'

Stained-glass window at St Leonard's Church, Middleton, Lancashire. Installed by Sir Richard Assheton, it commemorates the local archers who fought with him at Flodden. Each one wears a blue livery coat and carries a sheaf of arrows and a bow, with his name inscribed beside it.

However, not all of Edmund Howard's men had fled: small groups of Englishmen stood their ground and fought on desperately. Howard's standard-bearer was hacked to pieces while Howard himself was knocked to the ground three times by Scots wanting to capture him for ransom. But help was at hand in the form of Lord Dacre and his border horsemen who charged into the disorganised Scotsmen, many of whom

were now busy looting the dead. Howard was rescued by the splendidly named John Bastard Heron, an English border ruffian who was wanted by the Scots for murder, and together they cut their way back to safety. Eventually the fighting died down and the two sides drew apart. Home's borderers could advance no further and Dacre's horsemen contented themselves with guarding the English flank. The fighting on the English right had ended in stalemate.

Meanwhile, the other two Scottish battles were having a much tougher time, for the uneven ground and the presence of a boggy stream at the foot of Branxton hill robbed them of their momentum and disorganised their ranks. The Scottish pikemen lost cohesion as they struggled up the slopes around Piper's Hill, with the result that the English billmen were able to break in amongst them. And in hand-to-hand combat the Scots' 18-foot pikes were little more than a liability. The English, with their lighter and handier bills, could easily dodge the cumbersome pikes and hack, stab and slice at the pikemen. One observer wrote:

'Veritas Vincit' (The truth prevails) banner carried at Flodden, believed to be that of William Keith, Earl Marischal of Scotland, who was killed in the battle.

Our bills…disappointed the Scots of their long spears wherein was their greatest trust…

The only thing the Scots could do was to cast aside their now useless pikes and draw their swords. According to an Italian poem:

…you saw so many weapons lowered that it seemed as if a wood were falling down.

But now the English had the advantage of reach and:

though the Scots fought sore and valiantly with their swords… they could not resist the bills that lighted so thick and so sore upon them.

Erroll, Montrose and Crawford's battle was steadily cut to pieces by Thomas Howard's men, and although King James's battle had initially pushed Surrey's men back, its advance was soon brought to a halt. It is said that James got to within a spear's length of the Earl of Surrey before being cut down and killed but, in the heat of battle, his death went unnoticed. Meanwhile, on James's right, the Highlanders of Lennox and Argyle were about to intervene in the battle when they were surprised by the troops of Sir Edward Stanley who seems to have climbed the north eastern slopes of Branxton Hill without being spotted. Stanley's archers are said to have taken a heavy toll of the unarmoured Highlanders before his billmen charged and broke them. At least some of Stanley's men must have worked their way round the Highlanders' right flank for, according to Edward Hall, when the Scots fled:

…Sir Edward and his people followed them over the same ground where the earl's battle first joined…

Attacked from all sides, James's battle gradually disintegrated. Few prisoners were taken, and when nightfall finally brought an end to the slaughter at least 9,000 Scots and as many as 5,000 English lay dead on the field. Scotland had lost its king and a large proportion of its nobility. The accession of a minor to the throne was to lead to yet another period of political instability in Scotland.

An English bill (left), and two 16th-century European pike heads.

Weapons and tactics: the bill and the pike

The English victory at Flodden has sometimes been cited as evidence of the bill's superiority over the pike but the reality is a little more complex. Pikes had been used to devastating effect by the Swiss since the mid-15th century: they could outreach polearms and swords; horses would shy away from them; and a well-delivered attack by pike-armed troops could steamroller enemy infantry. However, the weapon's effectiveness depended entirely upon the cohesion of those carrying it. Any disorder in the ranks of a column of pikemen could provide a gap into which enemy soldiers could pour and, as the Scots were to discover, in individual hand-to-hand combat the pike was little more than a liability.

The Swiss achieved their success with the pike through long experience, savage discipline and, crucially, thorough training. Although Louis XII sent 40 French captains under the Chevalier D'Aussi to train the Scots in the use of their new weapon, they had only just started this task when the invasion of England began. Furthermore, the Swiss used a combination of halberdiers, handgunners and crossbowmen to protect and support their pikemen. Although the ship that carried the French captains to Scotland also brought 1,000 firearms, these never reached James's army in time for the campaign. James had his pikes but had not spent sufficient time training his troops how to use them and had failed to obtain the weapons needed to support them.

These deficiencies, together with the difficult terrain over which the pikemen had to operate, ultimately led to disaster for the Scots at Flodden. It is worth noting, however, that on the Scottish left, where Home's borderers were supported by troops with other weapons and had easier ground over which to march, the pike, initially at least, lived up to James's expectations.

Although Henry VIII had hired 6,000 German pikemen for his campaign

Etal Castle. Etal's thin walls would have been no match for James's artillery and the castle rapidly surrendered to the invading Scots. Captured Scottish guns were secured here after the battle and signs of the hole knocked in the wall of the main tower to enable them to be stored in the basement can still be seen.

Early 16th-century woodcut from John Skelton's Ballade of the Scottyshe Kynge. *While the knight on the left wears plate armour and a sallet, the figure on the right wears an open helmet and a studded brigandine over what appears to be a mail shirt. Many of Dacre's borderers would have been equipped in this manner at Flodden.*

in France, his northern army was still relying on the tried and trusted combination of bills and bows. Originally an agricultural hedging tool, the bill was an 8-foot-long polearm that had found its way into the English army as an improvised weapon carried by peasant levies. It was soon improved by the addition of a spike and a hook at the end and could be used to batter away at armour, stab and cut at unprotected parts of the body, pull opponents off balance, or rip the tendons behind the knee. It was the ideal weapon for the particular kind of fighting that developed at Flodden. However, the action at Flodden also underlined the fact that, while the longbow could still be devastating against troops like Lennox and Argyle's highlanders, it was relatively ineffective against the plate armour of the period.

Weapons and tactics: artillery

The Scottish siege train that James IV took with him to England in 1513 was one of the finest in Europe. His 15 large pieces included seven heavy guns taken from Edinburgh Castle known, somewhat predictably, as 'the Seven Sisters.' The largest of these behemoths fired a 60-pound shot and required 36 oxen to drag it along. They battered Norham Castle into submission within a week and led to the rapid surrender of the smaller castles of Etal, Ford and Wark. However, although these guns were devastating against fortifications, they were simply not suited for use on the battlefield. Their huge size made loading them a lengthy job; their massive recoils meant they had to be hauled laboriously back into position after every shot; and any major repositioning was virtually impossible once battle was joined.

The guns in Surrey's army, however, were perfect for the task in hand. Henry had taken his heavy artillery with him to France with the result that Surrey was left with 18 falcons, which fired a 2-pound shot, and five serpentines, which fired a 4-pound shot, all mounted on light carriages. Their manoeuvrability meant that when the English marched round the Scottish flank on 8 September, they were able to take their guns with them, and use them at the very start of the battle. Anything larger would still have been on the move. Surrey's guns had a much higher rate of fire than those of the Scots, and while a 2-pound ball would have had very little impact upon a castle wall, the effect it could have on a body of men drawn up in close order could be devastating.

A near-contemporary engraving of the battle of Flodden by Hans Burgkmair. James IV lies dead in the foreground as his Scottish pikemen retreat in disorder before the English, many of whom are carrying bills.

The crosier and the sword

The Scots lacked nothing necessary for the wars but only the grace of God, for of elect men, harness, ordnance and victuals they had such plenty that never the like has been heard of in these parts, and I assure you all England could not have victualled our host as they were victualled, everything considered… The said Scots were so surely harnessed with complete harness, German jacks, rivets, splents, pavises, and other habilments, that shot of arrows in regard did them no harm; and when it came to hand strokes of bills and halberds, they were so mighty, large, strong, and great men that they would not fall when four or five bills struck on one of them at once. Howbeit our bills quitted them very well, and did more good that day than bows, for they shortly disappointed the Scots of their long spears wherein was their greatest trust; and when they came to hand stroke, though the Scots fought sore and valiantly with their swords, yet they could not resist the bills that lighted so thick and sore upon them.

This description of the action at Flodden is taken from a letter written by Thomas Ruthal, Bishop of Durham, to Thomas Wolsey, 20 September 1513, 11 days after the battle. Ruthal's letter offers a remarkable insight not only into the Flodden campaign but also into the duties of a late medieval Bishop of Durham, for he shows an interest in and a knowledge of warfare that might seem unusual for a churchman. The Bishop of Durham was no ordinary cleric, for his was a unique combination of spiritual and temporal responsibilities. To differentiate his ecclesiastical and civil functions, the bishop used two seals: the almond-shaped seal of a bishop and the oval seal of a nobleman, while the arms of the diocese were set against a crosier and a sword instead of the usual two crosiers.

Because Durham was so far from London, its bishop was given a wide range of devolved powers and duties in order that the king's government could function there on a day-to-day basis. One such duty was the defence of the border with Scotland, and to that end he was given both the power to raise troops and the possession of the vital border fortress of Norham. Ruthall had spent a large sum of money strengthening the castle, and he was devastated when James's artillery battered it into submission in just six days.

The English Civil War

The English Civil War, as it is usually known, should really be seen as a British conflict, as few areas of the British Isles were not in some way affected. Indeed, many of the events that propelled the nation into civil war took place outside England.

The constitutional and financial stresses caused by Charles I's rule without parliament, and his support of Archbishop Laud's religious reforms were brought to a head in 1639 when he attempted to impose the English Prayer book on Scotland. The Scottish Covenanters made short work of Charles's armies, and the king was forced to recall parliament in order to raise the money needed to pay them off. Parliament took the opportunity to put right what most saw as the abuses of Charles's personal rule, forcing him to make a number of constitutional and religious concessions. However, some MPs, under the leadership of John Pym, pushed for further reforms, driving more conservative MPs into royalism.

The flashpoint arose in 1641 when an army was needed to put down a Catholic rebellion in Ireland. It was the king's prerogative to raise an army but many in parliament feared that he might use such an army against his own subjects in England. In the event, both sides issued orders to raise troops and the nation stumbled into Civil War.

The first major battle, at Edgehill in October 1642, proved indecisive, and the war developed into a series of essentially regional conflicts. The king, based at Oxford, controlled Cornwall, Wales, part of the Midlands, and much of the north, while Parliament was strongest in the South and the East. For much of 1643 the king held the strategic initiative, with Sir Ralph Hopton making good progress in the south west, defeating Sir William Waller at Roundway Down, and capturing the valuable port of Bristol. Meanwhile, the Marquis of Newcastle's northern Royalists defeated the Parliamentarians at Adwalton Moor and pushed south into Lincolnshire.

However, the Royalist advance stalled before the ports of Hull and Gloucester. In September 1643 the Parliamentarian Earl of Essex led an army from London to relieve Gloucester and, returning to the capital, fought off a Royalist attempt to intercept him at Newbury as he returned to the capital. As 1643 drew to a close, both sides sought reinforcements from outside England. In Ireland the Royalists signed an armistice with the Irish rebels, freeing up the English troops serving there for service against parliament. At the same time parliament entered into an alliance with the Scots who agreed to provide an army in exchange for money and the imposition of Presbyterianism in England.

Sir John Byron soon lost many of the king's reinforcements when his attempt to conquer Cheshire was crushed by Sir Thomas Fairfax at Nantwich. There was further bad news for the king in the South, where Hopton was defeated by Waller at Cheriton in March 1644. But the biggest blow to the king was to come in July 1644 when, in the largest battle of the war, an Anglo-Scottish army crushed the Royalists at Marston Moor. The defeat lost Charles most of the north. By now the strategic balance had shifted in favour of Parliament but, even so, the king's main army proved remarkably resilient. The main Royalist army had already defeated Waller at Cropredy Bridge in June, followed this up by destroying an army under Essex at Lostwithiel in September, and avoided an attempt by the combined forces of Essex, Waller and Manchester to trap it at Newbury in late October.

Although Parliament had far greater resources and manpower at its disposal, localised interests and internal rivalries had hindered its war effort. Its response was to carry out a thorough reform of its armed forces, removing army commanders and combining many of its troops into a national force – the New Model Army. In the spring of 1645 the new army took the field, commanded by Sir Thomas Fairfax, with Oliver Cromwell as its general of horse. Even so, a

Parliamentarian victory was still far from certain. In the Scottish highlands a Royalist army under Montrose had won a number of success against the Covenanters. As for the New Model, while its horse were of a high quality, many of its foot soldiers were untested, and many were former Royalist prisoners of war.

The decisive moment came in June 1645 when Fairfax utterly destroyed the king's smaller but more experienced army at Naseby. The loss of their main field army made it increasingly difficult for the Royalists to extract supplies, troops and money from the shrinking territory they controlled and, without an army to relieve them, their strongholds fell like ninepins. In July the New Model defeated the king's western forces at Langport and in September the Royalists were defeated at Rowton outside Chester; 11 days earlier Montrose's shrunken army had been destroyed at Philipaugh. In early 1646 the Parliamentarians stormed through Devon, and in March 1646 the last Royalist army surrendered at Stow-on-the-Wold.

Although defeated militarily, Charles was still able to exploit divisions between Parliament, the army and the Scots. In 1648, many of those who had fought against him in 1642 now believed that parliament was now acting in a far more arbitrary and unconstitutional way than the king ever had, thus enabling Charles to cobble

together an alliance of Scots and local forces. But Cromwell defeated an invading Scottish army at Preston, and the New Model crushed local risings in Kent, Essex and South Wales.

After the execution of Charles in January 1649, Cromwell turned his attention to Ireland, building on Michael Jones's victory over the Irish Royalists at Rathmines by storming Drogheda and Wexford. Cromwell returned to England, leaving the final defeat of the Royalists and their Catholic allies to his subordinates. In 1650 the young

Charles II enlisted Scottish help in his bid to regain the throne but in September Cromwell defeated them at Dunbar. Charles and the Scots rallied, and invaded England the following year. However, they attracted little English support and Cromwell crushed them again at Worcester. The wars had begun a decade earlier with rebellion in Ireland and armed opposition in Scotland. They ended with England for the first time ever in almost complete control of the entire British Isles.

English Civil War battles and garrisons.

The steeps slopes at the west end of Roundway Down where many of Waller's defeated cavalry crashed to their deaths. The area at the bottom of the hill is still known today as Bloody Ditch. The old Bristol road runs along the horizon and Oliver's Castle, an Iron Age hill fort, is on the right.

Cut and Thrust
Roundway Down, 13 July 1643

In July 1643 a Parliamentarian army had succeeded in bottling up their Royalist opponents in Devizes. The Roundheads seemed on the point of victory but at Roundway Down their cavalry was suddenly swept from the field by a Royalist relief force. Success had turned to utter failure in the space of a couple of hours.

By July 1643 the focus of the Civil War in the west had shifted to the area around Bath and Bristol, where a Royalist army under the Marquis of Hertford and Sir Ralph Hopton was faced by a Parliamentarian force under Sir William Waller and Sir Arthur Hesilrige.

On 5 July, intending to capture Bath by advancing along Lansdown Hill, the Royalists approached from the north, only to find that Waller had got there first and had strengthened what was already a formidable natural defensive position by constructing breastworks along the summit. As the Royalists prepared to withdraw, Waller sent a force of cavalry to attack their rear but, after routing some of the Royalist horse, the Parliamentarians were themselves driven back by Hopton's Cornish infantry who then clamoured to be allowed to storm the hill. Hopton agreed and ordered flanking attacks to be made by parties of musketeers, while the central thrust was made by Sir Bevil Grenville's Cornish pikemen, supported by some bodies of horse.

St John's Churchyard, Devizes. In the background is the tower of a 19th-century castellated mansion that was built on the site of a medieval castle in which the Royalists stored their ordnance. It was captured by Cromwell in 1645 and demolished three years later.

Despite the steepness of the hill, the heavy fire poured into them and the loss of their leader, who was mortally wounded, the Cornish struggled to the crest of the hill and fought off a number of counter-attacks. As more Royalists reached the summit, Waller pulled his troops back to the cover of a dry stone wall – that still exists today – and the battle petered out into a musketry duel. That night Waller retired to Bath, while the Royalists, who had suffered heavy casualties in storming the hill and were desperately short of ammunition, prepared to retire as well.

Things were to get worse for the Royalists. The following day, the accidental explosion of a powder cart severely wounded Hopton and further reduced the Royalist reserves of ammunition. Pursued now by Waller, who had heard what had happened, the Royalists carried out a fighting retreat to Devizes, which they reached on 9 July. The town had no defences but the Royalists improvised, placing their guns in the remains of the castle and barricading the town's narrow streets with tree trunks, carts and anything else they could find.

Waller placed his guns on Coatefield Hill from where they could bombard the town. Yet Waller did not have enough men to surround Devizes completely, and on the evening of 10 July, a Royalist Council of War agreed that their remaining cavalry, who were of limited use in a siege environment anyway, should break out of the town and ride to the king's capital, Oxford, to seek help. At midnight, the Royalist horse formed up in the market square and galloped out of the town, first heading south-east to avoid their pursuers, before turning north for Oxford.

The next day some of Waller's cavalry intercepted a Royalist cavalry force under the Earl of Crawford, which was approaching Devizes from the north-east with supplies, ammunition and reinforcements. The Parliamentarians dealt with them easily enough and captured the ammunition, but Waller was concerned at the ease with which the Royalists could reach Devizes. He urged the Earl of Essex, whose army was watching Oxford, to prevent any further excursions of this kind.

From the outset of the campaign, Waller had been strong in cavalry but weak in infantry, which he would need if he was going to fight his way into Devizes. Wanting to avoid having to attack the town, and knowing that the Royalists were running out of ammunition, he offered them terms of surrender. The Royalists refused but not until they had spun out the negotiations for as long as possible to buy time for a relief force to arrive.

The following day Waller launched an attack on the town. Fighting their way down Morris Lane, his men got within sight of St John's Church, which still bears the scars of battle, before being repulsed.

St John's Alley, Devizes. During the siege the Royalists rapidly began to run out of ammunition, particularly match. Faced with this crisis, Hopton ordered his men to go from house to house in the town and gather up all the bed cord they could find, then beat it and boil it in resin. This ingenious piece of improvisation may have ruined the beds of Devizes but it supplied the Royalists with fifteen hundredweight of much-needed match.

St John's Church, Devizes. The Royalists barricaded the town's narrow streets and Waller's assaults made little progress. Nevertheless, one Parliamentarian attack, from the east down Morris Lane, nearly reached the church, the west wall of which is still peppered with bullet marks.

Sir John Byron (1599–1652)

Sir John Byron was one of seven brothers, all of whom fought for the king in the Civil War. Born in Nottinghamshire, he sat in James I's last parliament and the first two parliaments of Charles I. He was High Sheriff of Nottinghamshire in 1634 and served in the Scots War of 1640. In 1642 he briefly held the Lieutenancy of the Tower of London, much to the dismay of many MPs who feared his Royalist sympathies.

Byron was one of the first men to raise a regiment of horse for the king. He fought at Powick Bridge and at Edgehill, where his regiment formed the second line of the right wing under Prince Rupert. Rupert routed all the cavalry in front of him and, had Byron been a little less headstrong, he might have held back his regiment as a reserve or led them against the Parliamentarian foot to his left. Instead, he joined in the pursuit, effectively leaving the king with no cavalry. What Byron seemed to like was a good charge. He certainly got one at Roundway Down, where he routed Waller's horse and played a major part in the Royalist victory.

After distinguishing himself at the first battle of Newbury in September 1643, Byron was given command in November that year of the Royalist forces in Worcestershire, Shropshire, Cheshire, Lancashire and north

Sir John Byron. The scar on his cheek was caused by a Parliamentarian halberd during a skirmish at Burford in January 1643.

Wales. Reinforced by regiments released for home service by the truce in Ireland, he swept through Cheshire until only Nantwich defied him. He laid siege to the town but was defeated by a Parliamentarian relief force led by Sir Thomas Fairfax on 25 January 1644. On 26 December 1643, he had stormed Barthomley Church in Cheshire, smoking out and massacring some villagers who had taken refuge in the tower. The Parliamentarians nicknamed him the 'Bloody Braggadocio' after claiming to have intercepted a letter to the Marquis of Newcastle in which he boasted about the incident, saying 'I put them all to the sword which I find to be the best

way to proceed with these kind of people for mercy to them is cruelty.'

At Marston Moor in July 1644, Byron's headstrong nature seems to have got the better of him once again. He is said to have led his cavalry out to meet Cromwell, masking the fire of the Royalist musketeers. His troops were routed.

By the end of the Civil War Byron was governor of Chester, which he defended with great determination. As supplies began to run short, some of the City Corporation urged him to surrender. He invited them to dinner and served up what he had been living on – boiled wheat and spring water. When he was eventually obliged to surrender the city he got good terms from the enemy and held out in Caernarvon until June 1646.

In 1648, after failing in an attempt to raise north Wales for the king Byron left the country and spent the rest of his life in exile. He was a soldier through and through. Proud, ruthless, brave and headstrong, he was the ideal man to lead a charge or defend a breach but he lacked the finer tactical skill needed in a battlefield commander.

On 13 July, the Parliamentarians decided to try one of Waller's specialities – a night attack. During the morning, however, news arrived that a large body of Royalist horse was approaching from the direction of Oxford. For the Royalists in Devizes, help was at hand in the form of two brigades of cavalry under Lord Wilmot and Sir John Byron. The relief force paused in Marlborough to allow others to join them, including Crawford's defeated troopers, then moved onto Roundway Down, firing two signal guns to announce their arrival to the defenders of Devizes. Faced with this new threat, Waller pulled his troops back from the town and deployed his army at the south-western end of the down on Roundway Hill, between Devizes and the relief force. In his account of the campaign Hopton later wrote:

…there was notice brought to Sir Ralph Hopton in to his lodging that the enemy drew off, and upon inquiry finding that he drew off towards the downs he presently concluded, that the expected succour from Oxford was at hand, and gave order to have all the soldiers in their quarters in readiness to march out.

However, Hopton's council of officers suspected a trap. It would have been typical of Waller to feign a retreat in order to draw them out of Devizes, so they urged Hopton to wait and see how things developed. As Hopton put it:

Sir Ralph Hopton, calling the principal Officers to him propounded to draw out with the forces they had, the enemy being by that time drawn into Battalio 3 miles from them upon the top of a hill… But the major part of the principal officers apprehending, reasonably enough, that all that was seen might be but a stratagem of Sir Wm Waller's to get the forces out of the Towne, prevailed with him to delay.

Up on Roundway Down, Wilmot and Byron were preparing to advance against Waller, who had drawn up his army in the traditional manner. He had 2,500 infantry in the centre, 1,200 or so cavalry and dragoons on each flank and seven guns to the front.

Marks of shot in the west wall of St John's Church, Devizes.

The two Royalist commanders agreed that initially only their brigades should attack. Byron wrote:

… my Lord Wilmot very discreetly ordered it, that only his brigade and mine should charge (which both together made not above 1200 horse), and that the other troops, (because they had lately taken an affright and had been put to the worse by Waller's men), should only stand as a reserve, and not be employed till it should please God to renew their courage with our success, as we marched towards the rebels.

In theory, at least, a well-protected Civil War horseman would be supplied with a buff coat, helmet, back and breast plates, and an iron gauntlet for his bridle hand but, in practice, few commanders could afford to equip their men so lavishly. This re-enactor wears a buff coat, a typical three-barred helmet, a gorget to protect his neck and carries a wheel-lock pistol. Although there were a few exceptions, like the 'Lobsters' of Sir Arthur Hesilrige, both sides' cavalry were dressed virtually identically. They distinguished friend from foe by means of coloured sashes (normally red for the Royalists and tawny for the Parliamentarians), or 'field signs', such as a sprig of foliage attached to the hat or helmet. This system was obviously open to subterfuge. At Newbury in 1643 some of the Royalist horse attempted to gain an advantage by adopting the Parliamentarian field sign. One Roundhead later recalled '…one regiment of their Horse had got green boughs, and rode up to our regiments crying, 'Friends, friends'; but we let fly at them…'

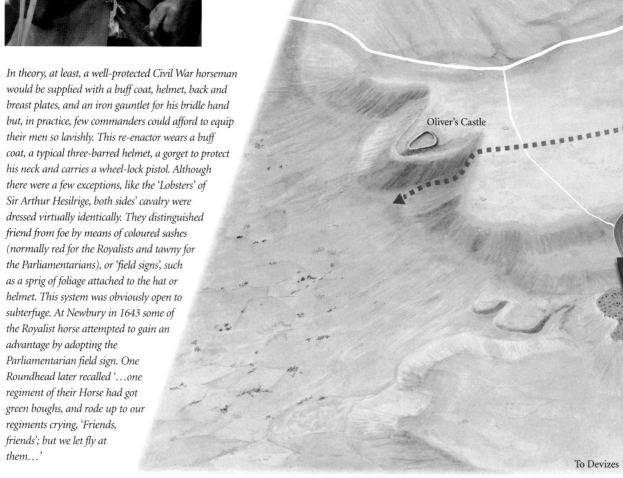

Heddington

Oliver's Castle

To Devizes

Both sides sent out 'folorn hopes': advanced parties of troops whose job was to test the ground, skirmish in front of the main armies and try to disorganise the enemy. As the Royalists gained the upper hand, the other Parliamentarian commander, Sir Arthur Hesilrige, decided to intervene. Byron describes what happened:

…they sent down some troops towards us, which were gallantly encountered by Sgt Major Paul Smith (who led our forlorn hope, consisting of 300 commanded men), and forced them to turn their backs. Sir Arthur Hazelrig seconded these with his formidable regiment of lobsters, I mean his cuirassiers whom the Lieut. General intermyned with his brigade, and forced them to retreat, not so, but that they rallied themselves again and charged the second

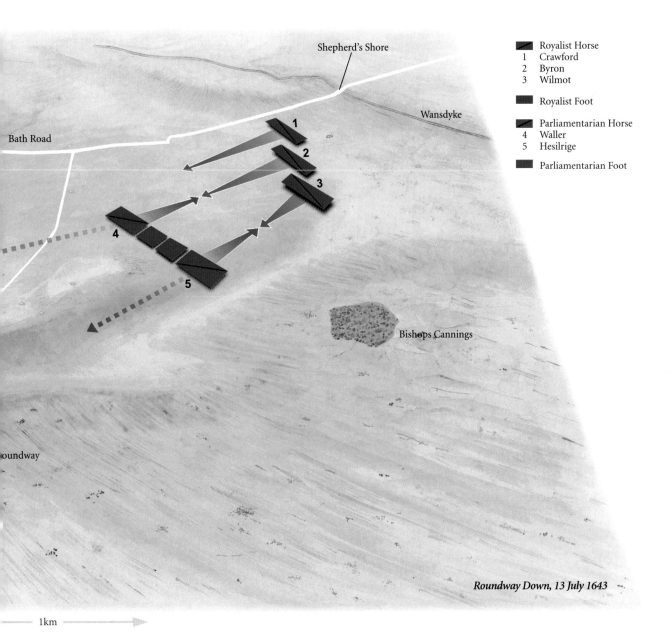

Roundway Down, 13 July 1643

time, but with worse success; for then my brigade being drawn up to second my Ld. Wilmot,
they all ran away that could, and from that time Sir A.H. appeared no more in the battle.

Richard Atkyns who participated in the battle noted that although
Hesilrige's troopers had the advantage of numbers, their tightly packed
six-deep line was overlapped by the Royalists:

I cannot better compare the figure of both armies than to the map of the fight at sea, between
the English and the Spanish Armadas, (only there was no half moon) for though they were
above twice our numbers; they being six deep, in close order and we but three deep, and open
(by reason of our sudden charge) we were without them at both ends.

As Hesilrige's troopers retreated, Waller advanced with the rest of the
Roundhead cavalry. It would soon be the turn of Byron's brigade to

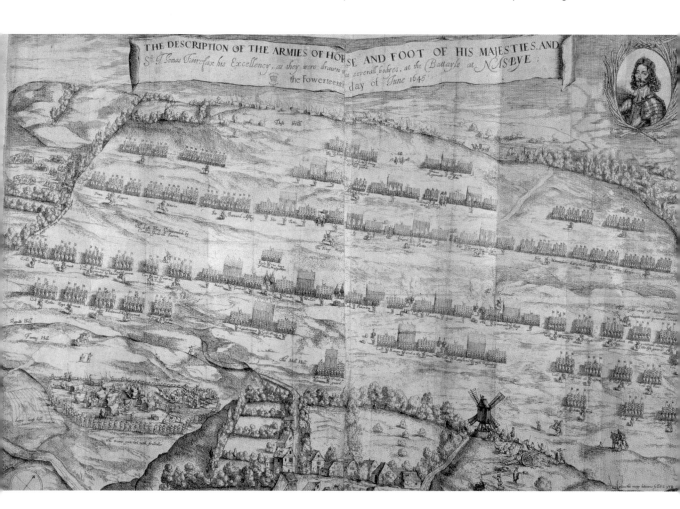

A near-contemporary plan of the battle of Naseby, 14 June 1645. The two armies (Royalist top, Parliamentarian bottom) are drawn up
in the conventional 17th-century manner, with infantry in the centre and cavalry on the flanks. Waller deployed his army in this way at
Roundway Down but his infantry, initially at least, were left with no one to fight.

Present and give Fire.

From John Cruso's Militarie Instructions for the Cavallerie, *originally published in 1632. (top) Cuirassier giving fire, turning his wheel-lock pistol to ensure that its priming powder stays in contact with the sparking wheel; (bottom) Cuirassier loading his pistol, putting the ball in his mouth until he is ready to insert it in the barrel.*

Lade with Bullet and Ramhome

charge, and its commander just had time to shout out last-minute instructions to his men:

The command I gave my men was, that not a man should discharge his pistol till the enemy had spent all his shot, which was punctually observed, so that first they gave us a volley of their carbines, then of their pistols, and then we fell in with them, and gave them ours in their teeth, yet they would not quit their ground, but stood pushing for it a pretty space, till it pleased God, (I thinke) to put new spirit into our tired horse as well as into our men, so that though it were up the hill, and that a steep one, we overbore them, and with that violence, that we forced them to fall foul upon other reserves of horse that stood behind to second them, and so swept their whole body of horse out of the field and left their foot naked and pursued them near 3m., over the downs in Bristol way till they came to a precipice, where their fear

The old Bristol Road looking east. The Royalists pursued Waller's broken cavalry westwards, across the fields on the right.

made them so valiant that they galloped as if it had been plain ground, and many of them brake both their own and their horses' necks.

Waller's infantry, who had been mere spectators up to this point, were now completely isolated. Even so, their pikemen managed to keep the Royalist cavalry at bay for an hour and a half, until Hopton's Cornish infantry finally emerged from Devizes and marched up onto the down. The Parliamentarians attempted to march away in good order but the retreat rapidly became a rout. According to Byron:

…our horse fell in amongst them and killed 600 of them, and hurt many more, and took 800 prisoners and all their colours…

Sir Arthur Hesilrige (1601–61)

A man of disobliging carriage, sour and morose of temper, liable to be transported with passion, and to whom liberality seemed to be a vice.

This was fellow republican Edmund Ludlow's assessment of Sir Arthur Hesilrige. The Royalist Earl of Clarendon was more succinct, dismissing the Leicestershire baronet as having 'more will than wit'. Yet whatever contemporaries thought of Hesilrige as a man, he was impossible to ignore. Whether on the battlefield or in the debating chamber, he always seemed to create a stir.

A fierce critic of Charles I's personal rule in the 1630s, Hesilrige was elected MP for Leicestershire in both the Short and Long Parliaments. As a close supporter of John Pym he soon made a name for himself as one of Charles's most outspoken opponents. In the spring of 1641 he was one of the prime movers in the attainder of the king's chief minister, the Earl of Strafford.

Hesilrige was an uncompromising opponent of Archbishop Laud, and when a bill to exclude bishops from the House of Lords was defeated, he was one of those who called for their abolition altogether. Finally, in December 1641, it was Hesilrige who introduced into the Commons the Militia Bill, which sought to transfer the right to raise an army from crown to parliament. With a track record such as this, it is hardly

surprising that Hesilrige was one of the five MPs whom Charles I tried to arrest for treason in January 1642.

After commanding a troop of Parliamentarian horse at Edgehill in October 1642, Hesilrige set about raising probably the most extraordinary cavalry regiment of the entire Civil War. Most leaders would have been more than happy to see their troopers equipped with helmets and stout leather buff coats but Hesilrige extravagantly clad his men in three-quarter armour, earning them the nickname of the 'lobsters' and the respect of the Royalist cavalry who found them extremely tough opponents.

Serving as second-in-command in Waller's southern army Hesilrige was seriously wounded at Roundway Down but recovered in time to take part in the Parliamentarian victory at Cheriton in March 1644. As a leading member of the 'war' party in parliament, Hesilrige sought to impose a settlement on the king by winning a military victory. He supported the creation of the New Model Army and the Self-Denying Ordnance, which obliged MPs to resign their military commissions.

Following parliament's victory in the First Civil War, Hesilrige was appointed governor of Newcastle and amassed a considerable fortune by buying up confiscated

Sir Arthur Hesilrige, 1640. While it was fashionable to be portrayed in armour, Hesilrige also wore his on the battlefield.

Royalist and Church land. He took up military command once more during the Second Civil War, bloodily storming the Royalist-held Tynemouth Castle.

His duties in the north enabled Hesilrige to avoid taking part in the trial of the king or signing his death warrant. Nevertheless, after the execution of the king he became a leading member of the new Republic's Council of State. Enraged by Cromwell's dissolution of the Rump Parliament in 1653, he became an implacable opponent of the Protectorate. Hesilrige helped to engineer the overthrow of Richard Cromwell in 1659 but, in doing so, unwittingly set in motion a chain of events that ultimately led to the restoration of Charles II and his own imprisonment in the Tower of London, where he died in 1660.

However, a colonel in Waller's army put the Roundhead losses at 50 horse and no more than 200 common soldiers killed or taken prisoner. Perhaps the truth is somewhere between the two.

It could not be denied, though, that this extraordinary and unexpected Royalist victory had destroyed Waller's army as a fighting force. It also led to the capture of Bristol later in the month, for Waller had taken a substantial proportion of its garrison to bolster his army before Roundway Down. The Royalists were triumphant. The Earl of Clarendon later wrote:

This glorious day, for it was a day of triumph, redeemed the king's whole affairs, so that all clouds that shadowed them seemed to be dispelled, and a bright light of success to shine over the whole kingdom.

The beaten Parliamentarians were bemused and depressed. A campaign that had been going so well had fallen apart in the space of little more than an hour. One officer wrote:

We must look upon this as the hand of God mightily against us, for 'twas He only that made us fly.

A clash of cavalry tactics

The battle of Roundway Down was not just a case of Roundhead against Royalist; it was also a clash between two very different doctrines of cavalry tactics. During the Civil War, those used by the Royalist cavalry were heavily influenced by Prince Rupert, the king's nephew. An experienced commander who had read widely on the subject, Rupert introduced the Swedish system into the Royalist army. This called for cavalry to form up three deep and to charge to contact. At Edgehill he had formed his cavalry in three ranks, and told his men to:

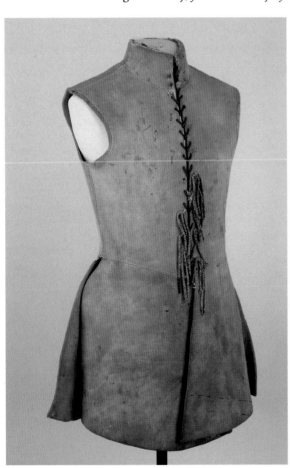

A sleeveless leather buff coat of the Civil War period. Buff coats were often worn by those horsemen who could afford them as an alternative to body armour.

…march as close as possible, keeping their ranks with sword in hand, to receive the enemy's shot without firing either carbine or pistol till we broke in amongst the enemy, and then to make use of our firearms as need should require.

These words of advice are very similar to the instructions that Byron gave to his soldiers before they charged Waller's horse at Roundway Down (*see* quote page 137).

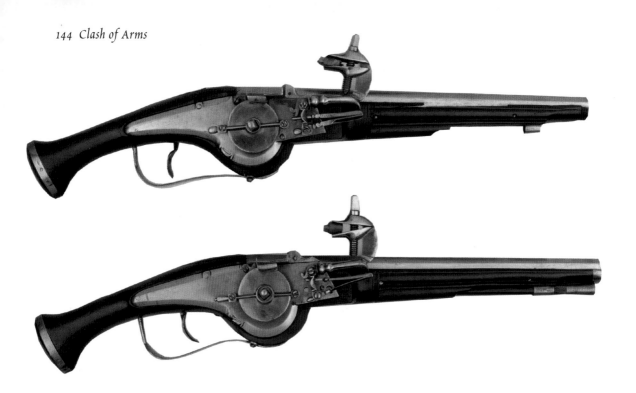

A pair of wheel-lock pistols. A wheel-lock consisted of a clamp containing a piece of iron pyrites, pressed against a spring-loaded metal wheel, which was wound up with a spanner. When the pistol's trigger was depressed, the wheel was released and span rapidly, scraping against the pyrites and creating a shower of sparks. These fell into the pistol's pan, igniting the powder there and then the main charge in the barrel. Wheel-lock pistols were expensive, complicated, and rather temperamental, as the Parliamentarian commander Edmund Ludlow discovered in 1644 at the siege of Old Wardour. He later wrote, 'My pistols being wheellocks and wound up all night, I could not get to fire'.

In the early part of the war at least, the Parliamentarians favoured a completely different system, based on the teachings of the Dutch army, which had enjoyed considerable success at the start of the century. This older system relied on firepower to break up an enemy formation and called for cavalry to be deployed six deep. In an attack, one rank after the other would ride forward to fire their pistols at the enemy and then wheel away to the rear until sufficient casualties had been caused for the rest of the unit to charge home. Given that the Royalists' aim was to charge as soon as possible, however, the Parliamentarians had little chance to use this leisurely tactic. In defence, the enemy's charge was received at the stand in the hope that weight of fire would break up the attack. Both Hesilrige and Waller seem to have used this Dutch system at Roundway Down. Byron's account makes it clear that Waller's troopers attempted to drive his men off by carbine pistol fire, and as Atkyns later wrote:

we advanced at a full trot and kept in order; the enemy kept their station and their right wing of horse being cuirassiers were I'm sure five if not six deep, in so close order that Punchinello himself had he been there could not have gotten into them.

It seems that although the Dutch system could be used to good effect to drive off hesitant enemies, it was of little use against a determined charge by well-trained horsemen. If the defenders failed to stop the attackers with their fire, they found themselves faced with troops who had lots of momentum…and a pair of loaded pistols.

Hand-to-hand combat

Twas my fortune in a direct line to charge their general of horse, which I supposed to be so by his place; he discharged his carbine first, but at a distance not to hurt us, and afterwards one of his pistols, before I came up to him, and missed with both: I then immediately struck into him, and touched him before I discharged mine; and I'm sure I hit him, for he staggered, and presently wheeled off from his party and ran. When he wheeled off, I pursued him, and had not gone twenty yards after him, but I heard a voice saying, 'Tis Sir Arthur Haslerigge follow him'; but from which party the voice came I knew not they being joined, nor never did know till about seven years since, but follow him I did, and in six score yards I came up to him, and discharged the other pistol at him, and I'm sure I hit his head, for I touched it before I gave fire, and it amazed him at that present, but he was too well armed all over for a pistol bullet to do him any hurt, having a coat of mail over his arms and a headpiece (I am confident) musket proof, his sword had two edged and a ridge in the middle, and mine [was] a strong tuck; after I had slackened my pace a little, he was gone twenty yards from me, riding three quarters speed, and down the side of a hill, his posture was waving his sword on the right and left hand of his horse, not looking back [to see] whether he were pursued or not, (as I conceive) to daunt any horse that should come up to him; [in] about six score more I came up to him again (having a very swift horse that Corner Washnage gave me) and stuck by him a good while, and tried him from head to the saddle, and could not penetrate him, nor do him any hurt; but in this attempt he cut my horse's nose, that you might put your finger in the wound, and gave me such a blow on the inside of my arm amongst the veins that I could hardly hold my sword; he went on as before, and I slackened my pace again, and found my horse drop blood, and not so bold as before; but about eight score more I got up to him again, thinking to have pulled him off his horse; but he having now found the way, struck my horse upon the cheek, and cut off half the headstall of my bridle, but falling off from him, I ran his horse into the body and resolved to attempt nothing further than to kill his horse; all this time we were together hand to fist.

In this nick of time came up Mr Holmes to my assistance (who never failed me in time of danger) and went up to him with great resolution, and felt him before he discharged his pistol, and though I saw him hit him, 'twas but a flea-biting to him; whilst he charged him, I employed myself in killing his horse, and ran him into several places, and upon the faltering of his horse his headpiece opened behind, and I gave him a prick in the neck and I had run him through the head if my horse had not stumbled at the same place; then came in Captain Buck a gentleman of my troop, and discharged his pistol upon him also, but with the same success as before, and being a very strong man, and charging with a mighty hanger, stormed him and amazed him, but fell off again; by this time his horse began to be faint with bleeding, and fell off from his rate, at which Sir Arthur, 'What good will it do you to kill a poor man?' said I 'Take quarter then', with that he stopped his horse, and I came up to him, and bid him deliver his sword, which he was loathe to do; and being tied twice about his wrist, he was fumbling a great while before he would part with it; but before he delivered it, there was a runaway troop of theirs that had espied him in hold; says one of them 'My Lord General is taken prisoner'; says another, 'Sir Arthur Haslerigge is taken prisoner, face about and charge', with that they rallied and charged us, and rescued him; wherein I received a shot with a pistol, which only took off the skin upon the blade bone of my shoulder.

Published in the 1660s, Richard Atkyns' account of his struggle with Sir Arthur Hesilrige during the battle of Roundway Down is one of the most graphic descriptions of hand-to-hand combat that we have from the Civil War. It is worth remembering that although Hesilrige was one of the leading politicians of the age, unless Atkyns had met him before he

would have had no idea what he actually looked like. Atkyns identifies the person he is fighting by his position on the battlefield and only later hears his name. It is quite possible that he was not able to see Hesilrige's face anyway, as the Parliamentarian commander was wearing a headpiece, perhaps some form of closed helm, that Atkyns considered to be musket proof.

After Hesilrige misses him at long range with a carbine and a pistol, Atkyns actually touches Hesilrige with his pistol before pulling the trigger. Although Hesilrige appears to have been wounded by Atkyns' first shot, his heavy cuirassier armour saves his life. Two more Cavaliers join in the struggle to kill Sir Arthur but they too are thwarted by the strength of his armour, and Atkyns is reduced to attempting to kill his horse. As his horse begins to weaken Hesilrige is about to surrender when he is suddenly rescued by a party of Roundheads. When Charles I heard about this extraordinary encounter, he made possibly his only recorded joke, saying:

Had he been victualled as well as fortified, he might have endured a siege of seven years.

Dutch Cuirassier armour c.1630.

Oliver Cromwell (1599–1658)

Fame came late to Oliver Cromwell. A minor East Anglian gentleman of modest means, he spent the first two-thirds of his life as a relative nonentity and was in late middle age when war broke out in 1642. As an MP he had been a vocal opponent of royal policies in the parliaments of 1640–2 but the fact that he was not one of the five MPs singled out for arrest by Charles I in January 1642 suggests that the king did not consider him to be one of his leading opponents at that time.

Cromwell began the Civil War as a captain of a troop of horse and over the next two years was propelled into prominence by his success as a soldier. Despite the fact that he had no pre-war military experience whatsoever, Cromwell took to warfare like a duck to water. Personally brave – he was unhorsed at Winceby and wounded at Marston Moor – he relished the thrill of combat and was a natural leader. The units he commanded were well recruited, well disciplined and well motivated. Serving in parliament's Eastern Association Army he won a series of impressive victories, culminating in July 1644 with Marston Moor where he commanded the cavalry on the Parliamentarian left.

Cromwell was a supporter of the 'war party' in parliament, committed to imposing a settlement on the king through military victory. Frustrated by the failure of parliament's leading commanders to follow up their victory at Marston Moor, he backed the establishment of the New Model Army, a new central army in which he initially served as second-in-command under Sir Thomas Fairfax.

In June 1645 Cromwell played a key role at the battle of Naseby, where his ability to keep his troops under control and maintain a reserve were major factors in the Parliamentarian victory. He was then heavily involved in the mopping-up operations that followed. In 1647 he saw off attempts by parliament to limit the power of the army, while at the same time suppressing the more radical elements within it. The following year, shocked by an outbreak of Royalist uprisings and a Scottish invasion, which he defeated at Preston, Cromwell supported the purging of parliament's more moderate members and the trial and execution of the king. In 1649 he ruthlessly crushed resistance in Ireland before returning to defeat a

new Scottish Royalist army at Dunbar on 3 September 1650 and again at Worcester exactly a year later.

Worcester was Cromwell's last battle, his 'crowning mercy' as he called it. His remaining years saw him drawn into military dictatorship as he tried to pursue two conflicting aims – 'Healing and Settling' the nation and promoting 'Godly Reformation'. In 1653, angered by parliament's failure to make much progress with either, he dissolved it by force, and replaced it with a Nominated Assembly of 'godly' men, nicknamed the 'Barebones Parliament' after one of its more radical members. Indeed, the radicalism of this minority alarmed the conservative majority who quickly surrendered their power. Cromwell then accepted the Army's 'Instrument of Government'. England's first written constitution, it called for triennial parliaments, and appointed Cromwell Lord Protector for life. Three years later Cromwell rejected the offer of the crown but became king in all but name. He died in 1658, on the seventh anniversary of his triumph at Worcester.

Surprise Attack
Alton, 13 December 1643

Sir William Waller's surprise attack on Alton was the finest operation of its kind in the entire Civil War. Waller showed outstanding qualities of leadership as he pulled together a dispirited and mutinous Parliamentarian army and led it on a hazardous, cross-country night march to surprise and overwhelm a Royalist outpost.

St Lawrence's Church and churchyard, showing the original site of the west door. The Parliamentarians broke into the churchyard from the right.

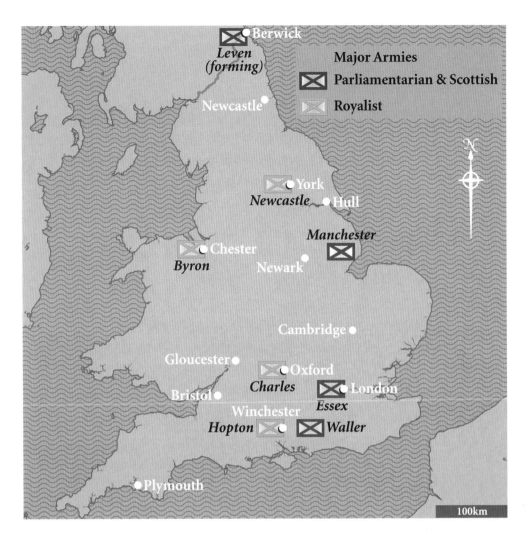

England, December 1643

At the end of September 1643, Sir Ralph Hopton had been given command of a small Royalist army with a paper strength of about 3,500 men. He was ordered to push on through Dorset, Wiltshire and Hampshire, and make as much progress as he could towards London. Once again he found himself pitted against his old friend, Sir William Waller (*see* chapter 9) who had been appointed parliament's commander in the south-east. Hopton soon received much-needed reinforcements. Two experienced English regiments of foot, each about 500 strong, arrived in Bristol from Ireland, where they had been fighting against the rebellion. Hopton described them as:

…bold, hardy men, and excellently well officer'd, but the common-men verie mutinous and shrewdly infected with the rebellious humour of England, being brought over merely by the vertue, and loyalty of theire officers…

One of the regiments did indeed mutiny shortly after its arrival in England but Hopton brought it into line by executing two or three of the ringleaders.

Waller's army included a brigade of troops from London, who were to prove even more troublesome. The Green Auxiliaries, the Yellow Auxiliaries and the Westminster Liberty, or Red Regiment took their names from the colours they carried and had been chosen by lot to serve with Waller. Their training and discipline left much to be desired, as Waller was to find out almost immediately. On 6 November Waller's army laid siege to Basing House, the powerful Hampshire stronghold of the Royalist Marquis of Winchester. Lieutenant Archer of the Yellow Auxiliaries describes what happened when the Westminster Regiment tried to launch an attack:

… either throgh want of courag or discretion I know not, but their Front fired before it was possible they could doe any execution, and for want of intervals to turne away speedily the second and third wranks, fired upon their owne Front, and slew and wounded many of their owne men…'

Waller was also faced with mutiny amongst the Londoners. Most had not wanted to leave the capital in the first place and, as the weather deteriorated, their morale plummeted and many began to desert. After nine frustrating days, Waller received news that a substantial Royalist force was marching to the relief of Basing. He initially considered marching to meet them but, as he later described in a letter to the Speaker of the Commons:

When the regiments were drawn out, as I was riding about to give orders, I was saluted with a mutinous cry among the citty regiments of 'Home, Home.' So that I was forced to threaten to pistol any of them that should use that base language…

Waller abandoned the siege and fell back to his headquarters at Farnham, where he immediately set about urging parliament to send him reinforcements. On 27 November, Hopton's army moved against Farnham. Waller drew up his forces in the park beneath his headquarters in Farnham Castle, but refused to be drawn into battle. Instead, he used his guns to fire on the Royalists from their positions in the castle. Waller later wrote:

The enemy drew up in a full body before us upon the heath… and after a while advanced into the Park to us with their foot and some horse within musket shot, but we gave them such entertainment with our pieces that they thought it their best course to retire to the heath again.

Farnham Castle. Stormed by the Parliamentarians in 1642, it served as Waller's headquarters in late 1643.

Realising that they were not going to be able to shift Waller from such a strong position, the Royalists fell back to their headquarters at Odiham. Reviewing the situation at a Council of War, Hopton and his officers decided that there was little that could be done until the following spring, and took the fateful decision to disperse their army into winter quarters. Hopton divided his troops into four brigades, each of horse and foot, and quartered them in Winchester, Alresford, Petersfield and Alton, which was only 10 miles from Waller's army at Farnham. Not everyone was happy with this decision, though. Colonel Joseph Bamfield, who was at the meeting later wrote:

One present at the Councel, declared his opinion, that it was dangerous to divide the Army into so many open quarters, whilest Sir William Wallers remained in one entire Bodie, since he could in one night (as his custome was to march) force any of the nearest to him, before the others could be advertised, joine, and succour the quarter attacqued; this coming from a verry young man was neglected as of no moment…

Sir Ralph Hopton (1596–1652)

The son of a wealthy Somerset landowner, and MP for Wells in the Long Parliament, Sir Ralph Hopton was initially an opponent of Charles I's government, and a critic of his ministers. Alarmed by its more radical moves, however, he began to believe that parliament represented a greater threat to the liberties of England than the king, and by January 1642 he was sliding towards Royalism.

As war broke out he returned to Wells and, with the Marquess of Hertford, tried to raise troops there for the king. Popular opinion was against them, however, and Hopton was forced to flee the county, ending up in Cornwall, where he managed to recruit a Royalist army of about 5,000 men. Hopton was no stranger to military affairs – as a young man he had volunteered to serve Queen Elizabeth of Bohemia. After the battle of the White Mountain he is said to have carried her to safety on the back of his horse.

For six months there was something of a stalemate. Hopton's army repelled every Parliamentarian invasion of Cornwall but was driven back every time it tried to advance into Devon. Finally, in May 1643, Hopton crushed the Earl of Stamford's army at Stratton, near Bude, enabling him to move into Devon. The following month he joined forces again with the Marquess of Hertford and advanced into Somerset, where he came up against his old friend and comrade from the Thirty Years War, Sir William Waller. Waller rapidly exposed Hopton's limitations as a general. As the two armies manoeuvred around Bath in July 1643, Hopton was sucked into a pointless and costly attack at Lansdown and was forced to take refuge in Devizes. His army was only rescued when a Royalist relief force arrived from Oxford and unexpectedly routed Waller at Roundway Down (see chapter 9). Hopton took little part in that action for he had been badly burned and temporarily blinded by the explosion of a powder wagon after Lansdown.

After a brief spell as Lieutenant-Governor of Bristol, Hopton was appointed commander of the Royalist forces in the south and was ordered to push on into Sussex. At the end of 1643 he managed to seize Arundel Castle but made the mistake of dispersing his army into winter quarters, and Waller's forces picked off his outposts at Romsey and Alton and soon recaptured Arundel. In March 1644, reinforced by troops under the Earl of Forth who became nominal commander of the army, Hopton once again took the field only to be defeated by Waller at Cheriton near Winchester. After this defeat, the king abandoned operations in the south east and Hopton's troops were absorbed into the main Royalist army.

Hopton took part in the defeat of the Earl of Essex at Lostwithiel and was later made the king's General of Ordnance. He was again given an independent command in January 1646, when he was made general of the remaining Royalist forces in the west but by now the Royalist cause was lost. In February, the New Model Army crushed his forces at Great Torrington, and in April he followed the Prince of Wales into exile, dying at Bruges in 1652.

Hopton seems to have avoided the infighting that plagued the Royalist high command through much of the Civil War, and nobody seems to have had a bad word to say about him. Nevertheless, the number of times he lost control of his troops or was surprised or outmanoeuvred suggests that he was perhaps not as talented a general as he is sometimes made out to be. He was certainly not of the same calibre as his great friend and rival Sir William Waller. The best assessment of Hopton's character and ability is probably that of the Royalist historian, the Earl of Clarendon, who described Hopton as:

… a man of great honour, integrity and piety, of great courage and industry, and an excellent officer… for any command but the supreme, to which he was not equal.

Sir Ralph Hopton.

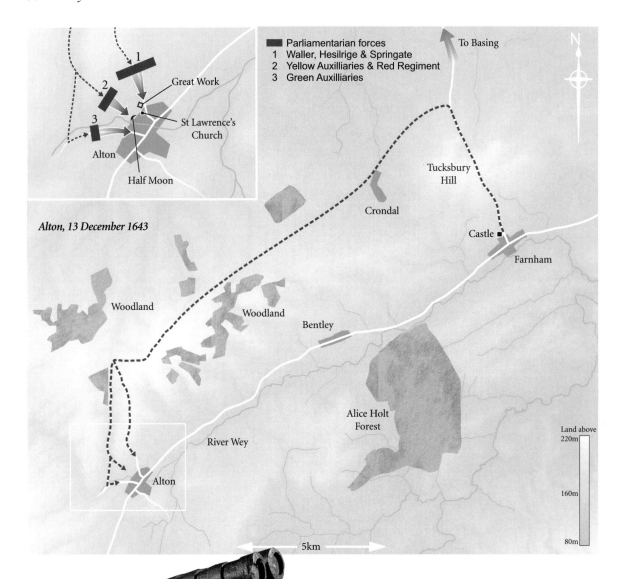

Alton, 13 December 1643

Parliamentarian forces
1   Waller, Hesilrige & Springate
2   Yellow Auxilliaries & Red Regiment
3   Green Auxilliaries

To Basing

Tucksbury Hill

Crondal

Castle

Farnham

Woodland

Woodland

Bentley

Alice Holt Forest

River Wey

Alton

Great Work

St Lawrence's Church

Alton

Half Moon

Land above
220m

160m

80m

5km

A Scottish double-
barrelled leather gun, probably
manufactured by James Wemyss, who
supplied Waller with his guns for the
Alton raid.

When Waller heard news of what the Royalists had done, he sensed an opportunity. By now he had been reinforced with some reliable troops, together with a number of highly mobile leather guns, and he knew that if he could surprise the outpost at Alton, the other Royalist brigades would be too far away to help. By 12 December he was ready to move but first he had to deal with the London Brigade, who were due to return to the capital the following day. That evening he drew up his foot in Farnham Park and addressed the Londoners. He thanked them for their service and told them that if they were determined to leave he would let them go the following day. However, he pointed out that they had hardly covered themselves with glory in the campaign so far, and that there was now a real opportunity to go home with honour if they would stay with him for just a few more days.

According to Lieutenant Archer:

…we considering gave our full consent to stay, for which he gave us many thanks, in a very joyfull expression advising us presently to prepare for the service because delaies are dangerous. Whereupon most of our men went presently into the Towne to refresh and prepare themselves for the service (where although they before gave their general consent) many of them stayed behinde and went not with their Colours.

17th-century map of Alton in 1666. St Lawrence's Church can be seen at the top of the map. The regiments of Waller, Springate and Hesilrige attacked from the north and north-west, while the London brigade probably approached along Lenten Lane (E). Soldiers from the Yellow and Red Regiments then pushed on up St Lawrence Lane (I) and eventually broke into the churchyard from Holy Lane (K).

Waller must have known that many men would not join him in the fight but by offering to send the troops away, he could at least ensure that those who returned were committed to the task in hand. Futhermore, by leaving things to the last minute, he had made it very difficult for any Royalist sympathisers to slip away to warn the Alton garrison.

Waller knew full well that the main roads into Alton would be guarded by the Royalists. Indeed, when Hopton received news of Waller's

reinforcements, he suspected that his opponent was planning something 'nimble'. He warned his men to be extra vigilant and, at the slightest sign of any movement by Waller, to pull back to Winchester. But Waller was not planning to take the main roads. In order to throw any observers off the scent, Waller first led his army northwards out of Farnham, in the direction of Basing House. It was about seven o'clock in the evening.

Waller's infantry, upon whom the main burden of fighting would fall, consisted of his own regiment, the London Brigade, part of the green-coated Farnham Castle garrison, and five companies each of Sir William Springate's whitecoats and Sir Arthur Hesilrige's bluecoats, the latter under the command of Colonel John Birch. Ten miles away in Alton, unaware of what was in store for them, was a Royalist brigade of about 1,100 footsoldiers, drawn from a number of regiments, under the command of Colonel Richard Bolles, and about 300 horse under Lord Crawford.

After marching perhaps two miles towards Basing, Waller's army wheeled left and headed south towards Alton. Hopton later wrote:

Sir Wm Waller had verie politiquely and souldier-like taken advantage of the woodines of that Country, and drawen his men, and his light leather-gunnes into the woods, and with pioneers, made his way through them, without comeing into any of the high-waies.

Waller was helped by the fact that the weather was extremely frosty, enabling his men to march across the hard ground without too much difficulty. At about nine o'clock in the morning his army arrived at Alton, to the north-west of the town. It had been an extraordinary achievement. Waller had marched an army of 5,000 men in the middle of the night to within half a mile of Alton without getting lost or being spotted.

Eventually, the alarm was raised and, as the true nature of their predicament dawned on them, the Royalists decided that Lord Crawford should ride with his cavalry to seek help, while Bolles held on as best he could in Alton. He set off down the Winchester road only to be driven back into the town by Waller's horse. Crawford eventually escaped by heading south but the prospect of his bringing back a relief force in time to save Bolles had now disappeared. As a Parliamentarian newspaper gloatingly reported, Waller's horse:

… were immediately appointed to make good all passages, so that the Enemy could not have the benefit of their accustomed running away…

Bolles and his men were trapped. The battle for Alton now unfolded. The Royalist defences centred on St Lawrence's Church, which stood on

The original west doorway of St Lawrence's Church.

the north-west edge of the town, surrounded by a number of buildings. The regiments of Waller Hesilrige and Springate approached from the north and north-west but had to wait until the soldiers of the London Brigade, who had further to march, could join them on their right. Lieutenant Archer recalls how the Royalists:

…bent all their force against those three Regiments, and lined divers houses with musqueteers, especially one great brick house neere the Church was full, out of which windows they fired very fast, and might have done great prejudice to those men, but that when our Traine of artillery came towards the foote of the hill, they made certaine shot which took place upon that house and so forced them to forsake it.

Waller's leather guns had proved their worth. Meanwhile, the London Brigade had launched its attack. Supported by the greencoats of the Farnham Castle garrison, the Red Regiment advanced into the town from the west, only to be held up by some heavy fire from Royalist troops in a defensive earthwork known as a Half Moon. On this occasion, however, the Londoners showed a lot more determination than they had at Basing House. Under cover of the smoke from a thatched cottage that they had set alight, the Green Auxiliaries outflanked the Half Moon and fired on it from the rear, forcing its defenders to fall back to the church. Under pressure from virtually all sides, Bolles pulled his troops back into the churchyard. Some of his troops lined its stone wall, others occupied a 'great worke' they had dug to the north of St Lawrence's while the rest occupied the church itself, where scaffolding had been erected to enable them to shoot out of the windows.

The Royalists kept up a heavy fire for nearly two hours but eventually the superior Parliamentarian numbers began to tell. At the south-east corner of the churchyard, where the Yellow Auxiliaries and Red Regiment had been pressing hard, the Royalist fire suddenly stopped. The Parliamentarians, who could still see the muzzles of muskets sticking up behind the churchyard wall, suspected at first that the Royalists had decided to lie in ambush. After a time, they came to the conclusion that as nobody was actually using the muskets, the enemy must have fled. A sergeant from the Yellow Auxiliaries edged forward to the gate of the churchyard and peered inside. Down to his left the Royalists were still

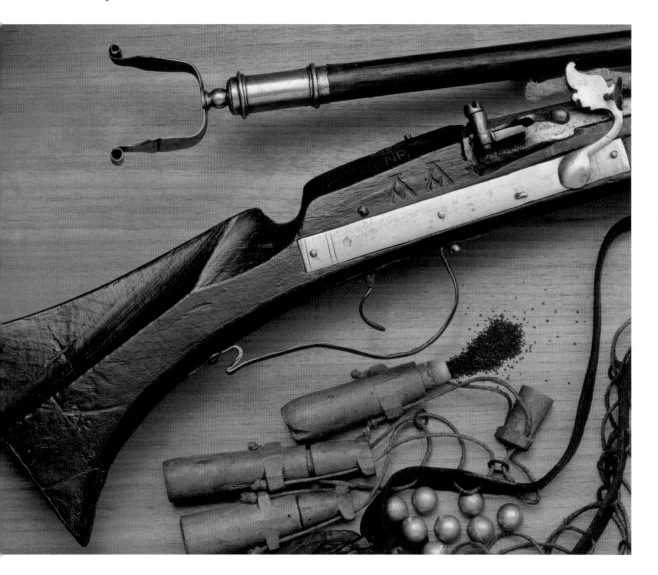

A musketeer's equipment – matchlock musket with rest, musket balls and a bandolier of wooden tubes, each containing sufficient powder for a single shot. A matchlock musket was fired by depressing its trigger, bringing the match (a length of slow-burning cord) into contact with the gunpowder in the musket's priming pan. Misfires were common, especially in wet weather. As musketeers needed to keep their match burning so as to be ready for action, they used up large quantities of it whether they fired their muskets or not. Needless to say, it was extremely dangerous to have burning match in the vicinity of gunpowder, as numerous musketeers discovered to their cost.

firing but this part of the churchyard was deserted. According to Archer, the sergeant looked behind for the men who were supposed to have been following him to find that there was only one man with him!

Nevertheless he flourishing his sword, told them if they would come, the Church-yarde was our owne…

Scars of battle on the old west door of St Lawrence's Church, now hanging in the south porch.

Finally, parties of musketeers from both London regiments came forward and rushed into the churchyard, attacking the Royalists from the rear. Archer describes the chaotic scene that followed. As the Royalists made a dash for the relative safety of the church:

…our men followed them so close with their Halberts, Swords, and Musquet-stocks that they drove them beyond the Church doore, and slew ten or twelve of them, and forced the rest to a very distracted retreat, which when the others saw who were in the great worke on the North side of the Church-yard, they left the worke and came thinking to helpe their fellows, and coming in a disorderly manner to the South-west corner of the Church with their Pikes in the Reare…their front was forced back upon their owne Pikes, which hurt and wounded many of the men, and brake the pike in pieces. By this time the Church-yard was full of our men, laying about them stoutly, with Halberts, Swords, and Musquet-stocks, while some threw hand-granadoes in the Church windowes…'

Still hoping that he might be rescued, Bolles refused to surrender and held out in the church with the remains of his men, reputedly directing its defence from the pulpit. However, it seems that the Royalists had not been able to secure the church door and the Roundheads forced it open. Colonel Birch's secretary describes the scene inside:

Nay, at the opening of that church, dreadful to see, the enemy… with their pikes and muskets, the horses slaine in the allies, of which the enemy made breastworks, the churchyard as well as the church being covered with dead and wounded…

The interior of St Lawrence's Church, scene of the Royalists' last stand. According to one Parliamentarian account the Royalists used dead horses to barricade the aisles.

As the Parliamentarians stormed into the church, Bolles still fought on. According to Archer, he swore 'God damne his Soule if he did not run his Sword through the heart of him which first called for quarter' before being killed in the melee. At this point most of the defenders lost heart and surrendered although a few 'desperate villains', as Archer called them, spurned quarter and fought to the death.

Waller's raid had been a brilliant success. Over 900 prisoners had been taken and 60 Royalists killed. Reporting the battle, a Parliamentarian newspaper claimed that 'there were not above five of our men slaine, and about six wounded, and about six scorched with powder, by reason of their own negligence.' This may have been an understatement but it is clear that Parliamentarian losses had been slight. Waller set the prisoners to work clearing up the mess and burying the dead before sending them to Farnham where many subsequently re-enlisted in his army.

The defeat had seriously weakened Hopton's army and was a tremendous blow to his morale and reputation. When reinforcements arrived the following March, they came under the command of the Earl of Forth, an officer much senior to Hopton.

Places of worship and warfare

Since most Civil War soldiers believed that God was on their side, they had few qualms about using His houses for military purposes. A church might well be the only stone building in a village, and its thick walls offered a ready-made strongpoint in the event of attack. Many had stone towers, ideal for use as observation posts, or had churchyards enclosed by stone walls which could be lined with musketeers.

The 17th-century pulpit of St Lawrence's Church, Alton. The pulpit, which originally stood in the centre of the church, is said to be the place where Colonel Richard Bolles met his death.

St Lawrence's Church at Alton was not the only church to be used for a last stand. After their defeat at Nantwich in Cheshire in January 1644, many Royalist officers barricaded themselves into St Mary's Church at Acton, before they were eventually forced to surrender. Among the prisoners that day was George Monck, who later agreed to serve in parliament's army, and in 1660 marched south from Coldstream to bring about the restoration of Charles II.

Churches were sometimes chosen as long-term military strongholds. The Parliamentarian garrison at Farndon in Cheshire used St Chad's Church as their headquarters. Perched on a low cliff, it dominated the 14th-century bridge that led the River Dee to the Royalist-controlled village of

Sir William Waller (1597–1668)

William Waller was born at Knole House in Kent into an extremely well-connected upper-gentry family. He had prospered during the reign of Charles I, and in many ways he seems an ideal candidate to become a Royalist. Perhaps the key to his decision to support parliament can be found in his memoirs, which reveal him to be an ardent believer in providence. Waller believed that everything that happened to him in his life was the will of God. His memoirs are full of amazing escapes from danger, which Waller saw as evidence of God's active intervention on his behalf. In 1617, he fought with the Venetians, narrowly avoiding being hit by a 'near shott', and in 1620, served alongside his friend, Ralph Hopton, in Bohemia, narrowly avoiding being captured by some Cossacks after the battle of the White Mountain.

Waller was no revolutionary. He wrote that he went to war in 1642 in order that 'God might have his fear; the King his honour; the Houses of Parliament their privileges; the people of the kingdom their liberties'. Despite an unhappy time at Edgehill where his regiment of horse was routed with much of the rest of the Parliamentarian cavalry, Waller turned out to be an able soldier. He was described as being particularly skilled in choosing ground, and his ability to use darkness to his advantage gained him the nickname of 'the Night Owl'.

Sir William Waller.

In the early months of the Civil War he captured Portsmouth, Farnham, Winchester and Arundel, helping establish Parliamentarian control in central southern England and earning himself a second nickname, William the Conqueror. In the summer of 1643 he campaigned in the West Country against Sir Ralph Hopton, running rings round his old friend and bottling him up in Devizes. However, his cavalry were no match for a Royalist relief force from Oxford, and his army was destroyed at Roundway Down. Nevertheless, Waller was given a new army and once again took the field against Hopton, inflicting a number of setbacks upon him at the end of the year, then defeating him at Cheriton in March 1644.

Waller's final campaigns were beset by mutinous troops and a shortage of cash. He was quite happy to hand over his command in 1645 under the terms of parliament's Self-Denying Ordinance, which required MPs to resign their commissions.

As time went on, Waller became deeply unhappy about the route the revolution was taking. He was one of the many moderate MPs purged from parliament by the Army in 1648, he opposed the execution of Charles I and was imprisoned without trial for three years. Although he was released in 1652, he was regarded with suspicion by the government and, in 1658, he was arrested and brought before his old subordinate, Oliver Cromwell. Waller wrote that Cromwell was polite but examined him 'as a stranger, not as one whom he had aforetime…obeyed'.

In the end, Waller saw the return of the monarchy as the only solution to the divisions within the country and he was active in the negotiations for the return of Charles II. As his plans came to fruition he was re-admitted to parliament in 1660 but, as he and his allies entered Westminster Hall in triumph, William Prynne's 'long sword ranne between Sir W Waller's short legs and threw him down, which caused laughter'. No doubt Waller would have seen this as a warning by God against the sin of pride.

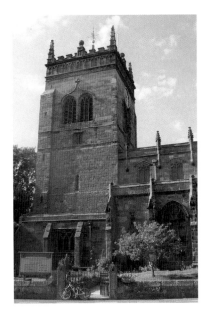

St Mary's Church, Acton, Cheshire. In January 1644 a number of Royalist officers briefly held out here following their defeat at Nantwich. Shot marks can still be seen on the south aisle wall.

Holt in Wales. In Hampshire, All Saints Church at Crondall guarded the western approaches to Farnham and was used by Lieutenant-Colonel Birch as a base for his reconnaissance patrols in the days leading up to Waller's raid on Alton. At Clun, in Herefordshire, the Royalists abandoned the old ruined castle and garrisoned the church instead. It was better situated and in better repair.

Sometimes churches were employed in sieges as improvised gun emplacements. Artillery pieces could be mounted on a church roof to improve their field of fire. In 1643, William Waller used St Nicholas's Church as a base from which to bombard Arundel Castle in Sussex, and in 1645, William Brereton occupied St John's Church in Chester, bombarding the nearby city wall from its tower.

Churches could also serve as prisons. After his victory at Alton, Waller sent his prisoners, tied together in pairs with match, to Farnham, where they were detained in the parish church. During the battle of Torrington in February 1646, Thomas Fairfax kept the prisoners he had taken in the town church. Unfortunately it was also being used as a gunpowder store, and a stray spark led to a tremendous explosion which killed 200 prisoners as well as their guards. In May 1649, after crushing the Army mutiny at Burford, Fairfax and Cromwell briefly imprisoned the rebellious troops in St John's Church. Its font still bears an inscription: 'Anthony Sedley 1649 Prisner'.

Detail from a 17th-century window in St Chad's Church, Farndon, Cheshire, depicting the Royalist Colonel Sir Francis Gamul with musketeer's equipment, pikeman's armour, staff weapons, a civil-war colour and a drum. Note the mould for casting bullets.

'A nimble execution'

And so the Lo: Hopton retyr'd to Petersfield where having the dangerous quarter of Alton continually in his care, he went thither the next day to visit it, and there to confer with the E. of Craford, and Coll: Bolles. (Sir Jacob Ashley having some few dayes before desired leave to returne to Reading for awhile). There the Lo: Hopton, weiwing the large extent and unsecurity of that quarter, left expresse order with the E. of Craford and Coll.Bowles, to keepe as good guards and intelligence upon the Enemy as possibly they could, and that, if ever he found that the Enemy moved out of Farnham with a body, they should presently quitt that quarter, and retreate to him. . .

. . . that night Sir Hum. Benet shewed him a letter, which he just then received from a friend, that advertised him out of the Enemye's quarters, that Sir Wm Waller had gotten a recrewt of men from London, and some Leather-gunnes, which gave cause to suspect that he had some present designe that requir'd a nimble execution; The Lo: Hopton presently suspected Alton, and forthwith writt, and dispatc'd a messenger on horse-back thither to the E. of Craford, with a letter wherein he sent him a transcript of that intelligence, and desir'd him instantly to send out scouts and parties every way, and that, if he found but the least suspition, that the Enemy marched with a body, he should presently drawe off from those quarters, and retire to him with all that he had with him. This leter the E. of Craford received before 11 of the clock, as he himselfe afterwards acknowlid, and I am confident will allwaies acknowledge, and presently, as he was ordered, sent out parties upon all the wayes towards Farnham; But Sir Wm Waller had verie politiquely and souldier-like taken advantage of the woodines of that Country, and drawen his men, and his light leather-gunnes into the woods, and with pioneers, made his way through them, without comeing into any of the high-waies; And so, notwithstanding the advertisement and orders the Lo: Hopton had given, and all the diligences of the officers upon those orders, Sir Wm Waller was drawn out the next morning with his Ordinance, and all his forces into the next field to Alton, before they had the least notice of his moveing, and at the sane instant sent severall parties of horse and dragoons to beate up theire horse quarters that were without, and fell upon theire foot with his horse and cannon.

Pikemen on the march. In 1643 about a third of a regiment of foot consisted of pikemen. Equipped with long iron-headed ash spears, their job was to protect their regiment against enemy cavalry, and to provide the forward impetus in hand-to-hand combat. The pike was less useful when it came to fighting in confined areas, as the Royalists discovered at Alton. In these circumstances a musketeer swinging his weapon like a club was far more effective. Regiments were usually clad in a uniform colour. The colour itself depended on the availability of cloth, however, and the whim of the colonel. There was no army uniformity until 1645 when red coats were ordered en masse by parliament for its New Model Army. As a result, for the first 30 months of the war both armies were made up of regiments in a variety of coat colours. At Alton for example, Hesilrige's foot wore blue, the Farnham garrison green and Springate's probably white. In these circumstances, the infantry, used field signs to distinguish one army from another. Both armies also adopted a 'field word', a simple battle cry, which served as a rudimentary password.

Entitled *Bellum Civile*, Ralph Hopton's memoirs cover his Civil War service from 1642 to 1644, and were written while he was in exile after the war. He seems to have written them for the benefit of his old friend the Earl of Clarendon, who was writing a history of the Civil War. Alton was a bad defeat for Hopton, and in this passage he tries to ensure that neither he nor his subordinates are held to blame, in effect saying that he and Crawford had done all they could but were undone by Waller's brilliant generalship. In the 17th century, 'presently' meant immediately.

The leather guns referred to in the account were made of toughened leather bound with iron hoops. As Hopton himself put it, they were ideal for any operation requiring 'nimble execution' since they were light enough to be pulled by a single horse and could be dragged across country or along a muddy lane without too much difficulty. Each gun fired a shot weighing about a pound and a half and could be used about seven or eight times before its barrel became unserviceable.

Assault from the Sea
Tresco, 17–18 April 1651

Frequently overlooked by military historians, Admiral Blake's capture of
Tresco for the Parliamentarians is a fascinating example of an opposed beach
landing. Although it was ultimately successful, this 17th-century D-Day did
not initially go to plan, leading to arguments and bitter recriminations
between the soldiers and seamen of Blake's force.

*The old Tudor blockhouse in the distance
overlooking Old Grimsby beach on the east side of
Tresco, the site of the Parliamentarian landings.*

The English Civil War finally caught up with the Isles of Scilly in March 1646. With Royalist resistance collapsing on the mainland, the Prince of Wales arrived on St Mary's with a few followers, and stayed for six weeks before leaving for Jersey. Some months later the islands surrendered to a Roundhead flotilla under Sir George Ayscue. However, during the Second Civil War of 1648, Prince Charles took advantage of a mutiny amongst the Scilly garrison and appointed the 20-year-old Sir John Grenville as his governor of the islands.

A sea fight between the English and the Dutch off the coast of Ter Heyde, 1653, from the painting by J Abraham Beerstraten. A major reason behind the Parliamentarian expedition against Scilly was the fear that the islands might otherwise fall into the hands of England's commercial and maritime rivals, the Dutch. Just over a year after the recapture of the islands, war broke out between England and Holland. The war, the first of three fought against the Dutch in the 17th century, lasted until 1654.

By the time Grenville arrived on the islands the Royalists had been defeated on the mainland and Charles I executed. Nevertheless, reinforced by troops from Ireland and joined by other die-hard Royalists, he turned Scilly into a base for privateers who made a thorough nuisance of themselves, preying on all passing shipping, regardless of nationality. The Dutch, who had sheltered the Royalist navy during the recent war and were giving asylum to the new king, were especially annoyed by these attacks, and, in 1651, Admiral Tromp sailed to Scilly to demand compensation. When the representative he sent ashore at St Mary's was rebuffed by the Royalists, Tromp tried another tack. He sailed to the mainland with the message that he had 'declared war' on this nest of pirates, and that if the Parliamentarians were unable to evict them, then he was prepared to do the job himself.

Sir John Grenville (1628–1701)

The Grenville arms above the door to the family chapel at St James Church, Kilkhampton.

John Grenville was the eldest surviving son of Sir Bevil Grenville, the head of one of Cornwall's leading families. He was only 20 when he was appointed Governor of Scilly but he was already no stranger to military service. In July 1643, at the age of 14, he had fought at the battle of Lansdown, where he was hoisted onto the horse of his mortally wounded father, so that the Cornish infantry would still have a Grenville at their head. Knighted after the Royalists captured Bristol, he was badly wounded the following year at the second battle of Newbury. In 1645, he was made a Gentleman of the Bedchamber to the Prince of Wales, the future Charles II, whom he was to serve faithfully for the next 40 years.

After surrendering Scilly in May 1651, Grenville was given the opportunity to join Charles in exile but chose to remain in England, secretly supplying the exiled king with money and carrying messages to his supporters. As the Republic began to disintegrate following the death of Oliver Cromwell, Grenville acted as a middleman between Charles and General George Monck, whose armed intervention in November 1659 ultimately led to the Restoration of Charles II. Charles heaped rewards on Grenville, appointing him Groom of the Stool (an important court position reserved for one of the king's closest confidants), Keeper of St James's Palace, Steward of the Duchy of Cornwall, Warden of the Stannaries (the West Country tin-producing towns), Lord Lieutenant of Cornwall, Governor of Plymouth and Earl of Bath.

Grenville remained close to Charles to the very end and was one of only two peers present at the king's deathbed conversion to Catholicism. As one of the king's most important servants in the West Country, he had worked hard to secure the Duke of York's succession to the throne as James II in 1685 and also helped to suppress Monmouth's rebellion later that year. However, he avoided opposing William of Orange after his landing at Torbay in 1688, and, as a result, retained his offices after James's fall. Indeed, he was initially granted further honours by the new king, who made him Lord Lieutenant of Devon and, 40 years after he first took up the post, once again Governor of Scilly. Grenville was now at the height of

his power and influence but his final years were to be marred by disappointment and financial problems. In the mid-1690s, William pressurised him into resigning many of his offices. An expensive legal case following his unsuccessful attempt to secure the dukedom of Albermarle, together with heavy spending on the family home at Stow, left him seriously in debt. Grenville died on 22 August 1701. Within two weeks his son, allegedly overwhelmed by the scale of debts he had inherited, committed suicide. Both were buried on the 22 September in the family vault at Kilkhampton, north Cornwall.

Sir Bevil Grenville's memorial on the battlefield of Lansdown. It marks the spot where John Grenville's father was mortally wounded.

This was serious news for the English government. Although the Dutch were not yet an enemy of the English Republic, relations with them were decidedly shaky. Francis Godolphin, Governor of Scilly under Elizabeth I, had stressed the strategic importance of the islands, adding:

… there are good roads [anchorages] and convenient harbours and it would be mischievous for the enemy to take them. There was now a real risk that they might end up under Dutch control.

To prevent this calamity, Admiral Blake was given command of a small fleet with 1,100 newly recruited soldiers under Lieutenant-Colonel John Clarke and ordered to recapture the islands. He set sail on 12 April, supported by a force of seven ships (which had originally been assembled for the capture of Barbados) under Sir George Ayscue.

Star Castle, St Mary's. Built 1593–4, the castle (which is now a hotel) served as the Royalist headquarters on the Isles of Scilly. The future Charles II had briefly stayed there in March 1646 before leaving for Jersey.

Ayscue, who was familiar with the islands, advised Blake that although the Royalists had their headquarters at Star Castle on St Mary's, the key to victory was the capture of Tresco, for this would enable the Parliamentarians to blockade the approaches to St Mary's harbour. Starved of supplies, the Royalists would be forced to surrender without the need for a costly seaborne attack. Furthermore, the capture of Tresco would give Blake shelter for his ships – essential given the unpredictable nature of the waters around Scilly.

The Parliamentarian fleet arrived off Scilly on 13 April with Blake aboard the *Phoenix* and Ayscue, the *Rainbow*. Seeing that Grenville had covered the main, western approach to Tresco with two large frigates, the *St Michael* and the *Peter*, Blake and Ayscue decided to attack from the east. Unfavourable winds delayed the assault for three days but, on 17 April, 40 large rowing boats, each with a brass gun charged with case shot in the bows, set off from their fleet. Packed with soldiers, their objectives were the sandy beach in front of the Old Blockhouse at Old Grimsby and a second, stonier beach further to the west. Blake's ships fired on Tresco in support of the attack, and a Parliamentarian newspaper later reported that the bombardment could be heard at Land's End.

The terrain behind the Old Blockhouse.

But things went badly wrong for the men in the boats. The tide was so strong that the proposed landing on the western beach had to be abandoned, and all the boats were forced to make for the beach in front of the Old Blockhouse where the Royalists were waiting for them. Furthermore, the soldiers were unaccustomed to rowing, and their boats soon became scattered. Some ran aground on rocks, while others, misdirected, perhaps deliberately by local pilots, landed by mistake on Northwethel Island. The rest, packed with increasingly seasick soldiers, were forced to remain offshore in choppy water till the other boats could join them.

When a landing was finally attempted it was an utter failure. From behind the cover of rocks on the beaches, the Royalists unleashed a fusillade of fire on the Parliamentarians who were so tightly crammed in their boats that most were unable to use their weapons.

Northwethel Island viewed from Gimble Porth. Approaching from the far side, some of the Parliamentarians mistook Northwethel for Tresco and landed there by mistake. St Martin's Island is in the distance.

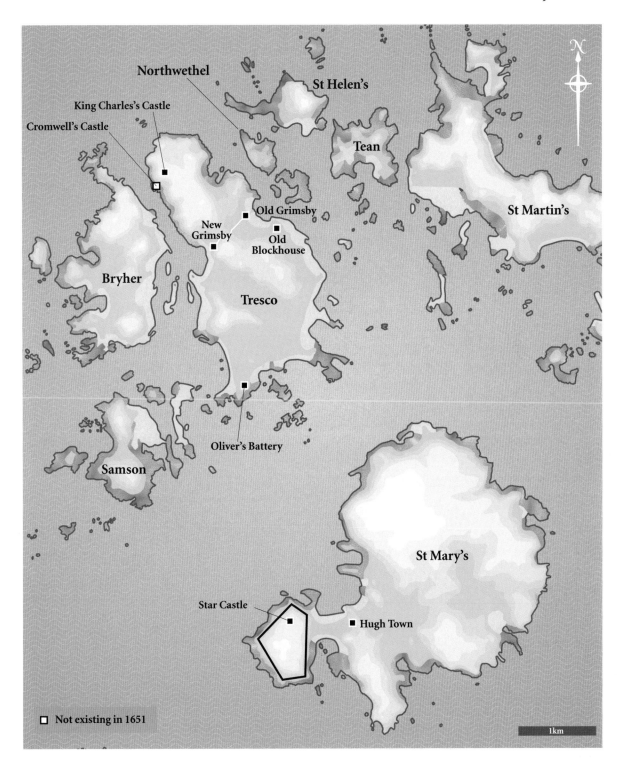

Tresco, 17–18 April 1651

Sir George Ayscue (c.1616–72)

While Robert Blake is credited with the capture of the Isles of Scilly in 1651, it seems certain that Sir George Ayscue's local knowledge proved crucial in the eventual success of the campaign. The plan to render St Mary's indefensible by capturing Tresco seems to have been devised by him.

Ayscue was born into a distinguished Lincolnshire family. His father was Gentleman of the Privy Chamber to Charles I, and he was a godson of George Abbot, Archbishop of Canterbury.

Despite his royal connections, Ayscue fought for parliament during the Civil War, commanding the *Expedition* at the siege of Pendennis Castle in 1646, and briefly served as governor of the Isles of Scilly. In January 1647, he returned to sea as captain of the *Antelope*. When a number of ships mutinied and joined the Royalists in 1648, Ayscue played a leading part in keeping most of the fleet loyal to parliament. In August that year he commanded part of the force that blockaded the Royalists in Hevloetslutys. He then served in the Irish Sea, keeping the sea route open to Dublin, which was beseiged by Royalists.

In 1650 Ayscue was ordered to recapture Barbados but before he could set sail he was diverted to assist Admiral Blake in the

Sir George Ayscue.

reconquest of Scilly. He eventually sailed for Barbados in August 1651, arriving in October with seven warships and 1,000 men. The island was held by Lord Willoughby with 7,000 men but, as it had done in the Scillies, Ayscue's indirect approach to the problem paid off. Denying the Royalists supplies by blockading the islands he set about undermining Willoughby's authority, informing the islanders that their leaders 'are altogether unable to give you protection without which this island can no way subsist'. He opened negotiations with Thomas Modyford, one of Barbados's leading planters and future patron of the buccaneer Henry Morgan. Having persuaded Modyford to join him with a thousand men, Ayscue landed on the south of the island where Willoughby marched to confront him but heavy rain prevented any fighting. Faced with further desertions, Willoughby was forced to surrender in January 1652.

Returning to England in May, Ayscue fought in the First Dutch War. He harassed Dutch shipping in the Channel fairly successfully but his performance as a commander in set-piece sea battles seems to have been rather mediocre. After a confused action off Plymouth in August he resigned his command, blaming ill-health. This may well have been the case, given the time he had spent in the West Indies but he also may have been unhappy about fighting fellow Protestants. He retired to his Chertsey home, which a contemporary described as standing 'environed with ponds, moats and water, like a ship at sea'.

In 1658 Ayscue served as a naval adviser in Sweden and, after the Restoration, he was appointed admiral in King Charles II's navy. He fought in the Second Dutch War but during the Four Days Battle of June 1666 his ship ran aground on a sandbank and his crew panicked and struck her colours. Although Ayscue was captured by the Dutch and paraded through the streets of The Hague, their attempts to interrogate him were hampered by their inability to understand his broad Lincolnshire accent. Released the following year, Ayscue was given yet another command when the Third Dutch War broke out but he died before he could take up the appointment.

Joseph Lereck, a Parliamentarian soldier describes the scene:

Now to be plain, when the boats drew somewhat near, and the great, small and case shot flew about to some purpose, and danger must be looked in the face, (for I believe we endured about 70 great shot, besides muskets in abundance) many of the boats, instead of rowing forward into the bay, turned the helm, and rowed backward, and aside, from the business.

Clarke, who had been doing his best to encourage his men, was finally forced to accept the inevitable and call off the attack. Three companies of his soldiers were left on Northwethel, 'to keep the enemy busy', while the rest landed on Tean Island, where they spent an uncomfortable night. As Joseph Lereck put it:

The place yielded but little fresh water, which, through the number of our men, was soon troubled, and made unfit to drink, which together with the want of provisions and the raw

View out to sea from King Charles's Castle. Despite its name, this small artillery fort was built in the reign of King Edward VI. It was intended to protect the narrow strait between Bryher and Tresco but turned out to be poorly sited – its guns could not be depressed sufficiently to fire on ships below. After the fall of Tresco in 1651 it was replaced by Cromwell's Castle, which was built just above the waterline and therefore in a far more effective position. The Royalists occupied King Charles's Castle in 1651 and strengthened its landward side with earthworks, traces of which can still be seen today.

constitution of our men newly come onshore, made this night's lodging the more irksome and comfortless.

Casualties had been surprisingly light in the attack – only six men had been killed – and although the Royalist guns opened fire on Tean the next morning, they merely succeeded in damaging some tents. However, the Parliamentarian leaders realised that time was now of the essence. Lereck wrote:

We thought it necessary to deal with the enemy speedily, while the weather was seasonable, for should it have proved otherwise, and our ships have been forced off to sea, we must either have perished, or have given ourselves up to the enemy for a morsel of bread. Upon consultation we resolved… to storm the enemy by night, and to that end had in this day time carefully observed how to direct our course up to the place we intended for landing (which was about a mile, and interrupted with many rocks in the way) for now we became our own pilots.

This time, however, the assault parties were strengthened by a detachment of 200 sailors, for it was felt that they would be better able to manage the boats and be less prone to seasickness. They were led by Captain Lewis Morris, a Barbados planter who was accompanying Ayscue on his interrupted expedition to recapture the West Indian island.

Blake's men set off at about midnight, the leading boats filled with sailors. Although the Parliamentarians had lit fires on Tean in an attempt to fool their enemies into thinking they were still camped there, the Royalists soon realised what was happening. As the Parliamentarians waded ashore holding their bandoliers in their mouths in a bid to keep their powder dry, they rushed to meet them with clubbed muskets. In desperate hand-to-hand fighting the Parliamentarians were temporarily forced back but as more boats arrived the Royalists were overwhelmed. About 120 of the defenders got to their boats and reached the safety of St Mary's but about 15 had been killed and the rest, 167 in all, were captured.

The island had been captured for the loss of only four men killed and 15 wounded on the Parliamentarian side. And not a moment too soon, for the following day the weather turned foul and no landings of any kind were possible for three days. With Tresco in their hands the Parliamentarians erected a battery at Carn Near on the extreme south of the island and mounted three large guns there to bombard St Mary's harbour. In a letter back to London, George Ayscue wrote:

…the gaining of the two islands [Tresco and its neighbour, Bryher] will render St Mary's useless to the enemy for we now have command of the Road as well as they, and enjoy a harbour which they have not.

Some 100 people had assembled to watch the bombardment, when the largest gun blew up, killing two, wounding nine and narrowly missing Blake and Ayscue. Nevertheless, the Royalists were now in a hopeless position. They were running short of food and there was no prospect of relief. Wanting to avoid a costly assault on St Mary's, Blake had offered them extremely generous terms of surrender, which, after some debate, were eventually accepted. The surrender document was signed on 23 May and, on 3 June, the Royalist garrison marched out of Star Castle. The Isles of Scilly were once again under Parliamentarian control.

Grenville returned to England, where he continued to serve the king, albeit in more clandestine ways. Clarke eventually became an MP, sitting in all of Cromwell's parliaments. Ayscue captured Barbados, and Morris returned to his plantation there, moving to New York in 1668. Morris's great nephew became Governor of New Jersey and his great-great nephew signed the US Declaration of Independence. Robert Blake went on to become one of Britain's greatest admirals.

Terms of surrender

Negotiating a surrender was one of the trickiest aspects of 17th-century warfare. An attacking army would normally 'summon' a town or fortress, offering the defenders certain terms if they would surrender quickly. These tended to vary according to circumstance. In order to bring things to a rapid conclusion, the attackers might offer to allow the defenders to march out with all their arms and equipment and join their main army.

But if the siege had dragged on, casualties had been heavy or the besiegers felt confident of success, the defenders might have to surrender without any conditions at all. Indeed, according to the 'laws of war' of the period, if the defenders forced the attackers to storm a place, then their lives were forfeit if it fell. Wholesale massacres were thankfully rare during the English Civil War but the slaughter of defenders in the heat of the moment certainly took place on numerous occasions.

Whether the defenders accepted the terms offered to them also depended on the particular circumstances. Any governor who surrendered too quickly risked being court-martialled and shot, so at least some show of resistance was required. If, however, there was no prospect of relief, or the garrison was starving a governor would normally seek to obtain the best terms he could.

Although the Royalists on St Mary's had absolutely no prospect of relief or supply, Blake realised how costly an assault on the island could be. Never losing sight of the fact that his objective was to recapture the

Robert Blake. A 19th-century engraving after the painting by Henry Briggs.

islands, not destroy the Royalist forces, Blake offered Grenville some particularly generous terms of surrender. Grenville's men were to be allowed to depart with their weapons and property, the Irish to Ireland, the English to join Prince Charles in Scotland. Blake would supply a vessel to help the Royalists carry away their supplies. Grenville himself was to go free and was even to receive financial compensation for some guns he had bought but would have to leave behind!

General Blake summoned this Island, offering reasonable terms of peace, if they might be accepted of in time. Our Governor presented his letter at a Council of War, and albeit they all acknowledged the place not to be tenable with less than 2,000 men and some horse (we having now not 500 able to do duty) in regard that there are some 16 bays of sand upon this Isle where boats may land, yet did they resolve rather to die every man than to quit this place. Here I confess I told them that, if these Islands could be preserved for the King with the loss of all our lives and be useful for his service (which now this place cannot be, they having got our best harbours and surrounded us about that we can take no more prizes), that then I should commend their resolution to die in His Majesty's service; but since the place cannot long be maintained, in regard we have no hopes of relief and that our few men will decrease daily, they being on continual duty, and that the enemy may have fresh supplies from land when he pleaseth, it were better upon honourable terms to quit the place and preserve their lives to do His Majesty's service in another place. For this advice I am reputed here a coward…

The writer of this letter was Henry Leslie, the 70-year-old Bishop of Down, who had recently joined the Royalists on Scilly. He was canny enough to realise that Blake's offer was a particularly good one, and his frustration at being shouted down by the young hotheads of the St Mary's garrison is evident. Nevertheless, common sense eventually prevailed§ and Blake's terms were grudgingly accepted.

Cromwell's Castle and the island of Brhyer from King Charles's Castle. The round tower of Cromwell's Castle was built shortly after Blake's recapture of Scilly to defend the western approach to Tresco and the castle was extended in the 18th century. In April 1651 two Royalist frigates were anchored in these waters.

Rival claims for glory

For as much as some men have taken upon them to write and report very falsely, and indeed scandalously, traducing the unspotted reputation of faithful instruments in managing the late reduction of the Isles of Scilly I hope 'twill be accounted no transgression, if I take leave to represent an honest and true account of the service done there.

I shall not venture, as some have unworthily done, to say ought upon bare hearsay, but shall write upon better knowledge, being actually in the service from first to last, and an eyewitness of what was done.

And why I may not with more reason expect to win credit upon that account than those who have written and reported swelling words of vanity and yet never hazarded their carcasses within cannon shot of danger in the service, I see not.

'Tis to be feared, I wish it be not so, that greediness of honour have prompted some to prepossess the world with their own worth above what was meet; and not only so, but thereby detracting from others have, with too much affectation, attempted to pin the honour of the work upon their own sleeves…

…what reason there is for some to write and report 'that the Seamen did all the work, that they alone gained the landing places, that they did the main, the work, that the work was undertaken by etc' undervaluing and declaiming the service of the soldiery, let all men judge.

A TRUE
ACCOMPT
of the late
REDUCEMENT
OF THE
Iſles of Scilly
Publiſhed;

In regard of the many falſe and
Scandalous reports, touching that
SERVICE.

July 24 LONDON,
Printed by *J. M.* for *Giles Calvert*, at the black ſpred
Eagle at the Weſt end of *Pauls.* 1651.

Front page of Joseph Lereck's account of the capture of Tresco.

Truly I would not detract a hair's breadth from their worth, nor would I write one word that might provoke emulation or stir up animosity. I love the girdle of amity and unity; the seamen did good service, and the soldiers did no less. But the main work, or gaining the landing place, was as some have too largely written and reported solely performed by them, I must deny as untrue. For although the seamen were in the second or third headmost boats (as I conceive, in reason they should, in regard of their better experience for guidance of the rest through that rocky passage in the night, and greater skill and acquaintance with marine service, and besides having under them the choicest and best accomplished boats for that purpose) yet had not the rest of the boats been carefully kept on together with them and, as it were, in the nick of time, put to the shore and the soldiers immediately grappled with the enemy (who to give them their due, sternly opposed), without doubt the seamen . . . must needs have perished.

In many ways, the reduction of Scilly had been a model operation. The plan of attack had been well conceived, and the Parliamentarians had rapidly recovered from the temporary setback of 17 April to capture Tresco with the minimum of casualties. By cutting off the Royalists on St Mary's, then offering them generous terms of surrender, Blake had succeeded in evicting them from the islands without the loss of a single ship. But human nature being what it is, bickering soon broke out between soldiers and seamen about who should take the credit for the victory. Annoyed by what he saw as claims that the sailors had done all the work, one soldier, Joseph Lereck, produced a long and detailed account of the campaign that was intended to put the record straight. In doing so he has provided us with a fascinating insight into some of the problems involved in mounting a 17th-century amphibious landing.

It seems that this inter-service enmity lingered on, for on 14 June it was reported from Plymouth that:

'we had that night a great quarrel between the seamen and soldiers, much harm had likely to have ensued, only it was timely prevented; there were many bloody pates, and one or two dangerously wounded, but none slain; the soldiers with the butt ends of muskets and swords, and the seamen with oars and poles; after a few broken pates the quarrel was taken up and all made friends.'

Perhaps someone had mentioned Tresco!

The Fortunes of War
Sedgemoor, 6 July 1685

'Is he lucky?' Napoleon is supposed to have enquired when asked to promote a deserving officer. Sometimes written off as a hare-brained scheme with little chance of success, Monmouth's daring plan to catch the royal army unawares at Sedgemoor by attacking at night from an unexpected direction came within a whisker of success. But, at a crucial moment, the fortunes of war intervened, and he ran out of luck.

Looking north-east along Langmoor Drove (which did not exist in 1685) towards the battle monument, which is near to the large tree. Feversham's infantry deployed from left to right about half way to the modern hedgeline, behind the Bussex Rhyne. Although the Bussex Rhyne, which played such an important part in the battle, has now vanished, its course has been established with the aid of aerial photography. Improvements in drainage have led to the disappearance or alteration of many of the old rhynes and the arrival of new watercourses but the character of the battlefield remains essentially unchanged.

Lyme Regis, Dorset. Monmouth arrived here on 11 June 1685 with three small ships and fewer than 300 followers. Twelve local men were later executed for their part in the Rising.

When the Duke of York succeeded to the throne as James II in 1685, some of his old opponents still believed it feasible to replace him with the Duke of Monmouth and that a rising in the name of Protestantism would attract enough support to enable them to overthrow the new Catholic monarch. Eventually, Monmouth agreed to the plan and while the Earl of Argyll set off to raise a rebellion in Scotland, Monmouth sailed for England with three ships and 300 followers, landing at Lyme Regis on 11 June 1685.

Monmouth and his rebels reached Taunton on 18 June, where he had himself declared king. By this time his army was more than 5,000 strong but, remembering the rapturous reception he received when he visited the West Country five years earlier, Monmouth had been hoping for many more. Even more worrying was the fact that very few gentry and only one peer, Lord Grey, had joined his cause. Monmouth's rising has gone down in history as 'the pitchfork rebellion' but in fact many of his recruits were artisans – cloth-makers and weavers – who had recently been hard hit by economic depression. A substantial number were Nonconformists who had been increasingly persecuted under the Stuarts.

Monmouth's next objective was Bristol. He hoped to obtain reinforcements there as well as arms and supplies for his ill-equipped men but he found that Lord Feversham, the commander of the royal army, had arrived there first with a force of cavalry. Monmouth decided not to attack the city and moved on to Bath instead. Bath also refused to surrender, and although his forces got the better of the advance guard of the royal army in a skirmish at Norton St Philip on 27 June, Monmouth felt unable to follow up his success.

The following day, devastating news reached the rebel camp. Argyll's Scottish rebellion had been crushed and the earl himself had been executed. Monmouth's men were on their own. As morale plummeted, men began to desert, taking advantage of the amnesty that King James had offered to those who went home immediately. A dispirited Monmouth pulled his army back to Bridgwater, where it was rumoured that a large body of peasants had gathered to support him. But when he arrived in the town on 3 July, their numbers were found to be disappointingly small. By now Lord Feversham's royal army was closing in and, on 5 July, it arrived at the village of Westonzoyland, just three miles away. Unwilling to face a siege in Bridgwater and knowing that his makeshift army would be no match for Feversham's regulars, Monmouth decided to risk all in a surprise night attack.

A number of excellent contemporary accounts and plans of Sedgemoor survive, from which we are able to reconstruct the course of the battle with a reasonable degree of certainty. Monmouth's rebel army consisted of about 3,000 foot, which were organised into five regiments, each named after a colour, 600 horse and four light guns. Although they were to outnumber the royal forces, they were poorly trained and ill-equipped. Some men had neither pike nor musket, and were equipped with nothing more than scythes, which would have been of little use in a conventional 17th-century battle. That said, a scythe could well have been a devastating weapon in the confused night fighting that Monmouth was going to try to initiate.

The church tower at Westonzoyland. The church served as a temporary prison for nearly 300 captured rebels after the battle, and later had to be thoroughly cleaned and fumigated.

Percy Kirke (c.1646–91)

Amongst Feversham's senior officers at Sedgemoor was Percy Kirke, a hard-bitten professional soldier who seems to have combined brutality and cynical self-interest in equal measure during his colourful 25-year military career. He joined Charles II's army as an ensign in 1666 and later received a commission in the regiment of horse commanded by his brother-in-law, the Earl of Oxford. In 1673, he served under the Duke of Monmouth, then fighting for the French in Flanders, and distinguished himself at the battle of Enzheim in October 1674 where he was wounded.

Further promotions followed and in 1680, he was given command of Lord Plymouth's regiment and posted to Tangier. Within months he had gained a notable victory over the Moors who were threatening the colony. The following year he was appointed governor of Tangier, a post he held until August 1683, and colonel of the 1st Tangier Regiment. By that time, however, the government had decided to abandon the colony, for it was proving an unendurable drain on resources and an expedition was sent under Lord Dartmouth to oversee the evacuation of the outpost and the destruction of its defences. Amongst Dartmouth's party was Samuel Pepys who, true to form, kept a diary of the expedition. Pepys, himself no prude, was scandalised by the behaviour of Kirke and his fellow officers, noting with horror Kirke's high-handedness, corruption, foul language and bawdy table talk. 'The tyranny and vice of Kirke in his way is stupendous', he wrote.

In early 1684, Kirke duly returned to England with his regiment, renamed the Queen's Regiment but nicknamed 'Kirke's Lambs' on account of the Paschal Lamb embroidered on its colours. The following year the nickname gained an ironic twist, for the Regiment's savage behaviour in the aftermath of Monmouth's defeat at Sedgemoor was anything but lamb-like. Typically, Kirke was censured by the government not for his brutality but for selling pardons to suspected rebels before they could be tried.

In 1688, Kirke was one of those officers who, despite owing their careers to the patronage of King James II, joined the plot against him. Fearing that James planned to purge the English army of Protestant officers and replace them with Catholics, they decided to throw their lot in with William of Orange when he landed at Torbay. Kirke was duly arrested in Salisbury and accused of attempting to join William but was released when it was claimed that no evidence could be found against him. As it was, very few of James's troops did desert to William but the king lost his nerve. Believing

Percy Kirke

that he could no longer rely on his army, he fled to France.

Promoted to major-general by William, Kirke was sent to Ireland in 1689 and ordered to relieve Londonderry, which was besieged by forces loyal to James II. He eventually broke the siege but initially took a very cautious approach to the task and had to be prodded into action by his commander, Marshal Schomberg. Kirke took an active part in William's victory at the Boyne in July 1690 and in 1691 he was promoted to lieutenant-general. Kirke then joined King William's army in Flanders where he fell ill. He was taken to Brussels and died there on 31 October. It hardly seems surprising that his successor as colonel of the Queen's Regiment had to petition the Treasury for extra funds, claiming that Kirke had taken money intended to pay the regiment and 'applied it to his own use'.

Feversham had about 2,600 men at his disposal. In addition, 1,500 men of the Wiltshire Militia were quartered several miles away at Middlezoy. His six battalions of regular infantry, 1,900 men in all, were camped in front of Westonzoyland in regular lines of tents behind a wide shallow drainage ditch called the Bussex Rhyne. Space had been left between the tents and the Rhyne to allow the soldiers to form up. From left to right the regiments were: Kirke's; Trelawney's; the 2nd (Coldstream) Guards; two

battalions of the First Guards; and Dumbarton's. They were all equipped with the new flintlock muskets, with the exception of the men of Dumbarton's regiment, who still carried the older-style matchlocks.

The majority of Feversham's cavalry were quartered in Westonzoyland, while his guns were deployed facing west along the Bridgwater road – the most obvious route for Monmouth's troops to take, should they attack. Finally, detachments of cavalry and infantry were deployed in various locations across the moor to guard against a surprise attack, and patrols and scouts were sent out to look for the enemy. It seemed as though Feversham had covered every eventuality but one of his captains was taking no chances. According to Andrew Paschall, the rector of Chedzoy in 1685, who wrote two detailed accounts of the battle:

Only Captain Mackintosh, in the Scots regiment, believed over night, and would have ventured wagers upon it, that the Duke would come. He, in

View of the battlefield across Sedgemoor from Chedzoy church tower. On the night of 5 July, 100 royal horse and 50 dragoons under Sir Francis Compton were using Chedzoy as a base for their patrols, and Monmouth's army gave the village a wide berth.

The Grand Review of the British Army drawn up in battalion before the King at the Encampment on Hounslow Heath *by Willem van de Velde the Elder, c.1687. Seeing it as an essential instrument of royal power, James expanded his standing army, more than doubling its size following Monmouth's Rebellion in 1685. James's army was in a state of transition at the time of Sedgemoor. Many of his regiments had replaced their old-fashioned matchlock muskets with flintlocks. When the trigger was depressed a spring-loaded flint hit a piece of steel causing sparks which ignited the powder in the weapon's pan. However, although bayonets were becoming available, it can be seen that pikemen still made up a substantial proportion of his army.*

that persuasion, marked out the ground between the tents and the ditch, where his men should stand in case of an attack, and gave directions that all should be in readiness; and it was well he did so; for his regiment being in the right wing was to receive the first assault and main shock…

Informed of the royal deployments by Benjamin Godfrey, a local sympathiser, Monmouth came up with a daring plan. Instead of taking the direct route down the main road from Bridgwater he would lead his army out to the east, skirt round Chedzoy, and, guided by Godfrey across the moor, attack the royal camp on its least defended side. As Paschall put it, the plan was that 'the horse should advance first, and push into the King's camp, and mixing with the King's foot, endeavour to keep them from coming together', enabling Monmouth's infantry to take advantage of the confusion.

At about 10pm on Sunday 5 July, the rebel army set off along the Bristol road, under strict orders of silence. The hooves of their horses were muffled with rags and one gun that developed a squeaky wheel was left behind. At first the rebels' luck held out and they managed to avoid the royal cavalry patrols, which passed close by more than once. However, when they reached the Langmoor Rhyne, one of the drainage dykes that drained the moor, their guide could not find the way across. Eventually the crossing point was found but, as Monmouth's troops filed across, they were spotted by one of Feversham's scouts who fired a warning shot and galloped back to the royal camp repeatedly shouting 'Beat your drums, the enemy is come. For the Lord's sake, beat your drums.' Paschall graphically describes the frantic activity in the royal camp:

Now the drums beat, the drummers running to it, even barefoot for haste. All fly to arms. All are drawn out of their tents and in 5 battalions stand in the space between the tents and the ditch, (those) fronting the ditch not having their clothes on or arms all on and ready.

Looking north across Sedgemoor along the line of the rebel advance.

Monmouth had lost the element of surprise but the royal camp was now less than a mile away. The battle still hung in the balance. Lord Grey was sent ahead with the main body of rebel horse to attack, only to encounter the Bussex Rhyne, which was impassable to cavalry except by two cattle crossings, the Upper and Lower Plungeons. Whether Grey knew about the Rhyne is unclear. Paschall implies that he did and that he had been instructed to cross it by the Upper Plungeon. But in his confession, one rebel commander, Nathaniel Wade, stated that Godfrey had 'taken no notice of the ditch that lay in the way of our march', and King James concluded that Grey advanced 'not knowing anything of the ditch…'.

Desperately looking for a crossing point, Grey's men rode along the Rhyne in front of the royal positions. When Feversham's men realised they were the enemy, they opened fire causing Grey's untrained horses to bolt. According to Paschall, a second, smaller group of rebel cavalry under Captain Jones did locate the Plungeon but were driven off by a party of horse under Sir Francis Compton. By now, Monmouth's infantry were arriving on the scene, deploying out of their column of march and heading towards the royal army's right, for in the darkness they could see the glowing ends of the lighted match carried by Dumbarton's regiment. According to Wade:

The rout of the rebel horse, depicted on a 17th-century playing card. The failure of Monmouth's cavalry to find a way across the Bussex Rhyne was a key moment in the battle.

By that time I had put them in some order, and was preparing to pass the ditch (not intending to fire till I had advanced close to our enemies) Colonel Matthews was come up, and began to fire at a distance; upon which the battalion I commanded fired likewise, and after that I could not get them to advance.

The rebels initially had the advantage of numbers in the ensuing firefight, and their three guns inflicted heavy losses on Dumbarton's regiment. However, it was only a matter of time before the superior training and weaponry of the royal army began to tell. Furthermore, John Churchill, who commanded Feversham's infantry, had quickly reorganised the royal lines, sending regiments and guns from the left flank to the right in support of Dumbarton's regiment. Casualties mounted among Monmouth's infantry as the royal guns came into action.

To make matters worse, Feversham's cavalry had crossed the Rhyne by the two Plungeons, and were threatening the rebel flanks. When daylight arrived and Feversham could see what was happening, he ordered his

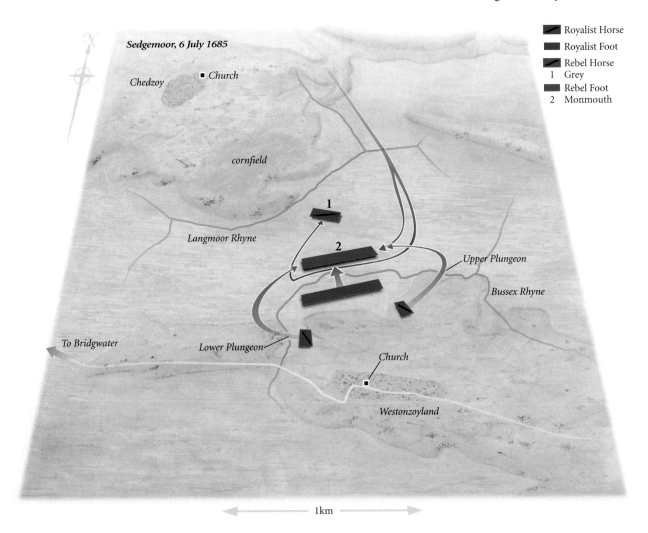

Royalist Horse
Royalist Foot
Rebel Horse
1 Grey
Rebel Foot
2 Monmouth

Sedgemoor, 6 July 1685

Chedzoy

Church

cornfield

Langmoor Rhyne

Upper Plungeon

Bussex Rhyne

To Bridgwater

Lower Plungeon

Church

Westonzoyland

1km

infantry also to cross the Rhyne. Monmouth's men broke completely.
James II later wrote:

> *…the day beginning to break, Lord Feversham, who was with the horse on the right, seeing no appearance of any more of the rebels horse, and that the pikes of one of their battalions began to shake, and at last open, ordered the foot to pass over the ditch to charge them; which they did. Which the rebels seeing, ran before they came to handy blows, and the five companies of grenadiers were ordered to follow the pursuit, and some of the horse and dragoons fell in with them and did great execution on them…*

At least 1,000 rebels fell in the battle and subsequent pursuit. The Royalists lost about 80, mainly from Dumbarton's regiment. Over 300 prisoners, some of them wounded, were locked up for the night in Westonzoyland Church, which later had to be thoroughly cleaned and fumigated. Some died there overnight, and the following day, 22 others were executed. The rest had to await the tender mercies of Judge Jeffreys' Bloody Assizes.

James Scott, Duke of Monmouth (1649–85)

Monmouth was born in the Netherlands in 1649, the natural son of the exiled Charles II and Lucy Walter, his mistress at the time. Although Charles acknowledged him as his son, Lucy Walter was not known for her chastity, and there were rumours that he was actually the child of Walter's previous lover, Robert Sidney. When he was only nine years old Monmouth was removed from his mother to be brought up by Lord Crofts. Lucy Walter died shortly after.

In 1662, 'James Crofts', as he was then known, was brought back to court. The following year, he was created Duke of Monmouth and married off to Anne Scott, the wealthy Countess of Buccleuch, whose surname he adopted. His recreational pursuits seem to have been typical of a Restoration courtier – hunting, racing, gambling, drinking, brawling and womanising. He had a succession of mistresses, including Elizabeth Waller, the daughter of the old Parliamentarian general, who bore him a daughter. Monmouth appears to have been affable and good looking but not particularly bright. It is said that when he was taken away from his mother he could neither read nor count, and that even as a 15-year-old, writing a letter would make him 'sigh and sweat.'

Monmouth does seem to have been a capable soldier, however. After service at sea against the Dutch he was made colonel of the King's Life Guards in 1669, and Captain General of the royal forces in the following year. In 1672, he commanded a brigade alongside the French in the Third Dutch War and distinguished himself at the siege of Maastricht. In 1678, he was again commander of a brigade, this time against the French, and the following year he defeated the Scottish Covenantor rebels at the battle of Bothwell Bridge.

As Charles II had no legitimate children (a claim that he had in fact married Monmouth's mother was denied) the heir to the throne was his Catholic brother James, Duke of York, a prospect viewed with alarm by much of the political nation. In many people's eyes Monmouth's royal blood, military reputation and solid Protestantism made him an attractive alternative, and attempts were made to exclude the Duke of York from the succession. Charles, determined that his brother should succeed to the throne, exiled Monmouth to Holland but he returned in 1680 and undertook a triumphant tour of the West Country. However, as parliamentary attempts to exclude York from the royal succession failed, Monmouth found himself

James Scott, Duke of Monmouth. Engraving after a 17th-century portrait by John Riley.

drawn into plots not only against James but also the king himself and, in 1684, he again went into exile in the Netherlands.

He returned the following year to lead a rising against James II, but within a month, his makeshift army had been crushed by James's professional soldiers at Sedgemoor and Monmouth was a prisoner. The king was unmoved by his nephew's pleas for mercy, and, on 15 July, Monmouth was beheaded on Tower Hill. It is said that the executioner took several blows of the axe to sever his head and had to finish the job off with a knife.

V ♦

Severall of ẙ Rebells hang'd upon a Tree

Rebels hanged from a tree, depicted on a 17th-century playing card. About 1,500 of Monmouth's men were killed in the battle and subsequent pursuit. Others were hanged without trial by Feversham's soldiers.

A close-run thing

Monmouth's night march has been described as a hare-brained scheme with little chance of success. However, Monmouth, who had considerable military experience, had probably come up with the best plan possible in the circumstances – a plan that came within a whisker of success.

Even though he had the advantage of numbers, Monmouth knew that his ill-equipped and poorly trained army would stand little chance against Feversham's regulars in a conventional pitched battle. However, he also suspected that, if he could catch them by surprise before they could form up, he might still prevail. He therefore concluded that his best option was to rely on the darkness to hide his troops from Feversham's patrols and to carry out a surprise attack on the Royalist camp from an unexpected direction. Indeed, this was essential since the obvious route from Bridgwater was covered by Feversham's guns.

It says much for Monmouth's leadership qualities that he was able to keep his army together as it crossed the moor and enforce total silence on the march. It was probably inevitable that his army would be spotted at some time but whether he was lucky to get as far as he did, or unlucky to be seen when he was so close to the enemy camp, is open to question. But it seems likely that he had got close enough for his cavalry to do real damage before Feversham's army could form up properly. Unfortunately for Monmouth, Grey was unable to find a way across the Bussex Rhyne and the opportunity was lost.

What of the royal army? The scout at Langmoor had done his job and raised the alarm but the other patrols had failed to find an army of over 3,000 men. It is clear that the Royalists were caught by surprise, and there certainly seem to have been flaws in Feversham's dispositions, especially in the way that his infantry and guns were unable to support each other. Edward Dummer who served with the Royal Train of Artillery at Sedgemoor later wrote:

At 2 o'clock this Morning (securely sleeping) Our Camp was Rouzd by the near approach of the Rebells; a darke Night and thick Fogg, covering the Moore, Supiness and a preposterous confidence of Our Selves, with an undervaluing of the Rebells, that many dayes before, had made us make such tedious Marches had put Us, into ye Worst circumstances of Surprize. Our Horse in Quarters, Some Near, Some Remote, Our Artillery distinct, & in a separate Post to that of the Camp, neither immediately accomodable to a Generall Resistance…

In the end, thanks to the foresight of Mackintosh, the tactical ability of Churchill and the determination of its soldiers, the Royalist army prevailed but it had, just for a few minutes, been a close-run thing.

'... *finding my own men not inclinable to stand*...'

About eleven o'clock that night, we marched out of the town. I had the vanguard of the foot, with the Duke's regiment; and we marched in great silence along the road that leads from Bridgwater to Bristol, until we came to the lane that passed into the moor where the King's army was. Then we made a halt for the horse to pass by, and received our orders; which were, that the horse should advance first, and push into the King's camp, and mixing with the King's foot, endeavour to keep them from coming together; that the cannon should follow the horse, and the foot the cannon, and draw all up in one line, and so finish what the horse had begun, before the King's horse or cannon could get in order. The horse advanced to the ditch, and never farther; but on the firing of some of the King's foot, ran out of the field. By that time our foot came up, we found our horse had gone, and the King's foot in order. I advanced within thirty or forty paces of the ditch, being opposite to the Scotch battalion of the King's, as I learnt since; and there was forced to make a full stop, to put the battalion in some order; the Duke having caused them to march exceeding swift after he saw his horse run, that they were all in confusion. By that time I had put them in some order, and was preparing to pass the ditch (not intending to fire till I had advanced close to our enemies) Colonel Matthews was come up, and began to fire at a distance; upon which the battalion I commanded fired likewise, and after that I could not get them to advance. We continued in that station firing for about an hour and a half, when it being pretty light, I perceived all the battalions on the left, running (who, as I since understood, were broken by the King's horse of the left wing), and finding my own men not inclinable to stand, I caused them to face about, and made a kind of disorderly retreat to a ditch a great way behind us, where we were charged by a party of horse and dragoons, and routed; above one hundred and fifty getting over the ditch.

This very clear account of the battle from a rebel point of view is part of the confession of Nathaniel Wade, who commanded the Red regiment in Monmouth's army at Sedgemoor. Wade was a Nonconformist lawyer from Bristol who, having been implicated in the Rye House Plot to kill Charles II, escaped to Holland and entered the service of the Duke of Monmouth. He acted as a go-between for the Duke and his fellow conspirator, the Earl of Argyl, before landing with Monmouth at Lyme in 1685.

After Sedgemoor – where he learned, like many other commanders have done before and since, that once advancing troops halt and open fire it is very hard to get them moving again – Wade escaped to Ilfracombe. He seized a vessel and put out to sea, only to be forced ashore by two of the king's frigates. He was later shot in the back and badly wounded while trying to avoid capture.

Despite his previous record, Wade saved his life by turning king's evidence and in Newgate Prison he made a detailed confession of his activities. James's government was clearly hoping that he would supply a long list of names of his fellow conspirators but, according to Wade, 'all the persons I can positively charge to have been concerned in it are either outlawed, dead or executed'.

Although his evidence did not yield the list of names hoped for, Wade was granted a full pardon. In January 1688, as part of James's efforts to court religious dissenters, Wade was made town clerk of Bristol. It was not a popular appointment and he was soon ousted. Nevertheless, he remained active in local affairs and was an enthusiastic member of the Bristol Society for the Reformation of Manners, which was formed to assist the authorities in 'discouraging prophaneness and debauchery' by 'discovering disorderly houses.' One wonders what Monmouth, his old commander, would have made of this. He also had shown an interest in such establishments, though for different reasons.

John Churchill, 1st Duke of Marlborough (1650–1722)

John Churchill was the son of an impoverished Royalist squire who rose to become by far the most successful general of his age and, for a short time at least, one of the leading statesmen in Europe. An undeniably brilliant soldier, Churchill remained in many ways a courtier at heart. The skills he honed in the late Stuart Court – charm, tact, diplomacy and the ability to dissemble – were to prove invaluable, both on the diplomatic stage and on campaign in his later years, when relatively few of the soldiers under his command were ever actually British.

Churchill began his career as a courtier and confidante to the future James II. Indeed, his sister, Arabella, was for a while the future king's mistress. In his early twenties he saw action with an English regiment in the service of France, fighting at the siege of Maastricht in 1673, and earning the praise of the great French Marshal Turenne. He then became an emissary for James and he and his wife, Sarah, developed a close relationship with James's daughter, the future Queen Anne. Although he served the king loyally during Monmouth's rebellion in 1685, three years later he was one of a number of leading officers whose defection to William of Orange led James to lose confidence in his army and flee the country. Created Earl of Marlborough as a reward, he fought successfully for William in Ireland in 1690 but his links with Anne were to lead to his dismissal from office. At this time, probably as an insurance policy, he seems to have opened up links with the exiled Jacobites but, in 1700, William appointed him commander of his forces in the Low Countries.

William's death and the accession of Anne in 1702 cemented Churchill's position. He was made a duke and, on the outbreak of the War of the Spanish Succession, was appointed commander of all allied forces. His diplomatic skills, particularly in gaining the support of the normally cautious Dutch for offensive operations were only matched by his brilliance on the battlefield. He displayed an unerring eye for ground, the knack of identifying weak spots in enemy lines and the ability, already demonstrated at Sedgemoor, to switch the positions of his troops. A typical Marlburian battle saw a series of feints designed to prepare the way for a devastating attack elsewhere. Notable victories won in this manner were Blenheim (1704), where he inflicted a crushing defeat on the Franco-Bavarians; Ramillies (1706), which led to the capture of much of the Spanish Netherlands; and Oudenarde (1708), which smashed a French counter-offensive. Throughout this period Marlborough had shown himself to be an accomplished planner and his march to the Danube in 1704 is still seen as a masterpiece of logistical organisation.

Marlborough's military career was to end on a sour note. His pyrrhic victory at Malp-laquet was greeted with much criticism at home, and when his Whig supporters lost influence at court in 1710 his days as commander were numbered. His wife was driven from court in January 1711 and he himself was dismissed at the end of that year. Threatened with corruption charges, he went into exile. Marlborough was reinstated by George I and oversaw the forces that defeated the 1715 Jacobite Rising, but in the following year he suffered a severe stroke. He died in 1722 and is buried in the chapel of Blenheim Palace.

Further Reading

Two websites provide invaluable information for anyone wanting to know more about the battles in this book. English Heritage's *Battlefield Reports* were produced in 1995 during the compilation of its register of 43 important English battlefields. Reports are available on the English Heritage website (www.english-heritage.org.uk) of all the battles covered here except Alton and Tresco, which do not feature in the register. The extremely useful *UK Battlefields Resource Centre* on the Battlefields Trust website (www.battlefieldstrust.com) draws quite heavily on the above but also includes maps, aerial photographs, alternative hypotheses and the results of more recent research, particularly in the fields of battlefield archaeology and the investigation of the historic landscape. New pages are added regularly.

With over 500 entries, M Rayner, *English Battlefields.* (Stroud: Tempus), 2004 is the most complete reference work on English battles and battlefields, although Tresco is not included. M Strickland and R Hardy, *The Great Warbow.* (Stroud: Sutton) 2005 covers all major British battles from Hastings to the mid-16th century. P Haigh, *The military campaigns of the Wars of the Roses.* (Stroud: Sutton) 1995 contains some lively accounts of the battles of the period while J Gillingham, *The Wars of the Roses: Peace and Conflict in 15th Century England.* (London: Phoenix) 2001 is particularly useful for information on the political and diplomatic background to the wars. J Wheeler, *The Irish and British Wars 1637-1654.* (London: Routledge) 2002 places the Civil War firmly in a British context while P Young and R Holmes, *The English Civil War.* (Ware: Wordsworth), 2000 (originally published 1974) remains the most readable account of its battles. The experiences of those who actually did the fighting are well covered in A Goodman, *The Wars of the Roses: the soldiers' experience.* (Stroud: Tempus), 2005 and C Carlton, *Going to the Wars; the experience of the british civil Wars 1638-1651.* (London: Routledge) 1992.

Biographical information about the majority of the leaders and generals referred to in this book can be found in H Matthew and B Harrison (eds) *The Oxford Dictionary of National Biography.* (Oxford: OUP) 2004.

The growing appreciation of the value of battlefield archaeology in locating and interpreting English battlefields is reflected in a number of recent publications. Produced to accompany the TV series of the same name, T Pollard and N Oliver, *Two Men in a Trench* Vol I. (London: Michael Joseph) 2002 offers a cheery introduction to the subject and includes chapters on Shrewsbury, Barnet and Flodden. Volume II 2003 includes Sedgemoor. J Cooksey (ed) *Battlefields Annual Review.* (Barnsley: Pen and Sword) 2005 looks at developments in the field and includes a report on ongoing work at Edgehill. G Foard *Naseby: the decisive campaign.* (Whitstable) 1995 is an excellent example of how archaeological evidence, notably the distribution of musket balls located by metal detector, a reconstruction of the landscape of the period, and an examination of the written sources with this information in mind can lead to a reassessment of a battle.

Detailed walks around the sites of most of the battles described in this book are included in D Clark *Battlefield Walks: The Midlands; The North; The South.* (Stroud: Sutton) 1993, 1995, 1996. J Humphrys, *Battlefield Hikes* Vols I and II. (London: English Heritage) 2003, 2004 are handy packs of waterproof laminated cards that combine interpreted walks with practical information on parking and refreshments. All the battles in this book are covered, with the exception of Myton, Alton and Tresco. A trail around civil war Tresco can be found in J Humphrys, J 'Journey of Discovery: Tresco 1651' in *BBC History Magazine* Vol 6, No 8, August 2005.

Select Bibliography

Primary source materials are listed under (1). Secondary works are listed under (2).

Maldon (1)
'The Battle of Maldon' in Rodrigues, L 1996 *Three Anglo-Saxon battle poems*. Lampeter: Llanerch Press
Swanton, M (ed) 2000 *The Anglo-Saxon Chronicles*. London: Phoenix
'The Life of St Oswald' extract in Whitelock, D (ed) 1979 *English Historical Documents c500–1042* (2nd ed). London: Methuen, 912-17

Maldon (2)
English Heritage 1995 *Battlefield Report: Maldon 991*
Cooper, J (ed) 1993 *The Battle of Maldon: fiction and fact*. London: Hambledon
Pollington, S 2002 *The English warrior from earliest times till 1066*. Hockwold-cum-Wilton: Anglo-Saxon Books
Scragg, D (ed) 1991 *The Battle of Maldon AD 991*. Oxford: Blackwell

Hastings (1)
Morton, C and Muntz, H (eds) 1972 *The Carmen de Hastingae Proelio of Bishop Guy of Amiens*. Oxford: Clarendon Press
Swanton, M (ed) 2000 *The Anglo-Saxon Chronicles*. London: Phoenix
William of Malmesbury 'Gesta Regorum Anglorum' extract in English Heritage 1995 *Battlefield Report: Hastings 1066*
William of Poitiers 'The deeds of William, Duke of the Normans and King of the English' in Douglas, D C and Greenaway, G W (eds) 1981 *English Historical Documents 1042–1189* (2nd ed). London: Methuen
Wilson D M 1985 *The Bayeux Tapestry: the complete tapestry in colour* London: Thames and Hudson

Hastings (2)
Barlow, F 2002 *The Godwins*. Harlow: Pearson
English Heritage 1995 *Battlefield Report: Hastings 1066*
Lawson, M K 2002 *The Battle of Hastings 1066*. Stroud: Tempus

Morillo, S (ed) 1996 *The Battle ofHastings: sources and interpretations*. Woodbridge: Boydell
Strickland M J (ed) 2000 *Anglo-Norman warfare*. Woodbridge: Boydell

Myton (1)
F W D Brie (ed) 1906 *The Brut or the Chronicles of England*. London: Early English Text Society. Translation in English Heritage 1995 *Battlefield Report: Myton 1319*
Denholm-Young, N (transl) 1957 *The life of Edward II by the so-called Monk of Malmesbury*. London: Nelson
Eyre-Todd, G (transl) 1907 *The Bruce: the history of Robert the Bruce King of Scots* (Prose translation). Edinburgh: Gowans and Gray (reprinted 1996 Edinburgh: Meercat Press)
'The Chronicle of Lanercost' in Rothwell, H (ed) 1975 *English Historical Documents 1189–1327* London: Eyre and Spotiswoode
'The Chronicles of Jean le Bel' quoted in Strickland, M and Hardy, R 2005 *The great warbow*. Stroud: Sutton 177–8

Myton (2)
English Heritage 1995 *Battlefield Report: Myton 1319*
Rothero C 1984 *The Scottish and Welsh wars 1250–1400*. London: Osprey

Shrewsbury (1)
Calvert, E (transl) 1898 'Annales Richard II et Henry IV' in *Transactions of the Shropshire Archaeological and Natural History Society*, 2nd series, Vol 10 295–305
Davies J S (ed) 1856 *An English Chronicle of the reigns of Richard II, Henry IV...* London: Camden Society, 64
Hardy, W (ed) 1887 *A collection of the chronicles and ancient histories of Great Britain, now called England, by John Waurin*. London

Shrewsbury (2)
English Heritage 1995 *Battlefield Report: Shrewsbury 1403*

Rose, A 2002 *Kings in the North: The house of Percy in British history*. London: Weidenfeld & Nicolson
Strickland, M and Hardy, R 2005 *The great warbow*. Stroud: Sutton

Towton (1)
'The Rose of Rouen' in *Archaeologia* **29**, 1842, 343–7
Letters from Richard Beauchamp and George Neville to Francesco Coppini in Hinds, A B (ed) 1912 *Calendar of State Papers and Manuscripts existing in the archives and collections of Milan*, Vol I 1385–1618. London: Public Record Office
Ellis, H (ed) 1809 *Edward Hall's Chronicle*. London
Ellis, H (ed) 1844 *Three Books of Polydore Vergil's English History*. London: Camden Society, 29
'Hearne's Fragment' in Giles, J A (ed) 1843 *Chronicles of the White Rose of York*. London: Bohn
Hardy, W and Hardy E (eds) 1891 *Jean de Waurin. Recueil des Chroniques D'Engleterre*. Volume V. London: Rolls Series
Riley, H T (ed) 1854 *The Croyland Abbey Chronicle*. London: Bone
Riley, H T (ed) 1872 *Registrum Abbatis Johannis Whethamsteade*. London

Towton (2)
Boardman, A W 2000 *The Battle of Towton* (2nd ed) Stroud: Sutton
English Heritage 1995 *Battlefield Report: Towton 1461*
Fiorato, V *et al* 2000 *Blood Red Roses: the archaeology of a mass grave from the Battle of Towton AD 1461*. Oxford: Oxbow Books

Barnet (1)
Adair, J 1968 'The Newsletter of Gerhard von Wesel, 17 April 1471' in *Journal of the Society for Army Historical Research*, **46**, 68
Bruce, J (ed) 1838 *Historie of the Arrivall of King Edward IV*. London: Camden Society
Halliwell, J O (ed) 1839 *John Warkworth. A chronicle of the first thirteen years of the reign of King Edward IV*. London: Camden Society

Thomas, A H and Thornley I D (eds) 1938 *The Great Chronicle of London*. London

Barnet (2)

English Heritage 1995 *Battlefield Report: Barnet 1471*

Hammond, P W 1993 *The Battles of Barnet and Tewkesbury* Stroud: Sutton

Ross, C 1974 *Edward IV* London: Eyre-Methuen

Stoke (1)

Andre, B 'Vita Henrici Septimi' in Gairdner, J (ed) 1858 *Memorials of King Henry the Seventh*. London: Roll Series (translation in Bennett, M 1987 *Lambert Simnel and the Battle of Stoke*. Stroud: Sutton)

Anoymous herald's report, quoted in English Heritage 1995 *Battlefield Report: Stoke 1487*

Doutrepont G and Jordogne O (eds) 1935 *Chroniques de Jean Molinet*. Brussels: Academie Royale (translation in Bennett, M 1987 *Lambert Simnel and the Battle of Stoke*. Stroud: Sutton)

Hay, D (transl) 1950 *The Anglica Historia of Polydore Vergil AD 1485–1537*. London: Camden Society

Lockyer, R (ed) 1971 *Francis Bacon. The history of the reign of King Henry the Seventh* (originally published 1622). London: Folio

Thomas, A H and Thornley I D (eds) 1938 *The Great Chronicle of London*. London: G W Jones

Stoke (2)

Bennett, M 1987 *Lambert Simnel and the battle of Stoke*. Stroud: Sutton

Chrimes, S B 1972 *Henry VII*. London: Eyre Methuen

English Heritage 1995 *Battlefield Report: Stoke 1487*

Flodden (1)

'Articules of the bataile bitwix the Kynge of Scottes and therle of Surrey...' in England, Record Commission 1836 *State Papers of King Henry VIII Part IV Correspondence Relative to Scotland and the Borders 1513–1534*. London

Ellis, H (ed) 1809 *Edward Hall's Chronicle*. London

Letter from Brian Tuke, Clerk of the Signet, to Richard Pace, Secretary to Cardinal Bainbridge, in Brown, R (ed) 1867 *Calendar of State Papers and Manuscripts relating to English Affairs existing in the archives and other collections of Venice...Vol II 1509–1519*. London: Stationery Office, 134

Laing, D (ed) 1867 '... the trewe encounter or batayle lately don between Englande and Scotlande' in *Proceedings of the Society of Antiquaries of Scotland* Vol VII. Edinburgh

'La Rocca de Scocesi' (The Rout of the Scots) translation in Mackenzie, WM 1931 *The Secret of Flodden*. Edinburgh: Grant and Murray

Letter from Thomas Ruthal, Bishop of Durham to Thomas Wolsey quoted in Smith, GG (ed) 1900 *The Days of James IV 1488–1513*. Edinburgh: Nutt

Flodden (2)

Barr, N 2001 *Flodden, 1513* Stroud, Tempus

English Heritage 1995 *Battlefield Report: Towton 1513*

Phillips, G 1999 *The Anglo-Scots Wars 1513–1550* Woodbridge: Boydell

Roundway Down (1)

Young, P and Tucker, N (eds) 1967 *Military Memoirs: Richard Atkyns and John Gwyn*. London: Longman

Chadwyck Healey C E H (ed) 1902 *Bellum Civile: Hopton's Narrative of his Campaign in the West (1642–1644) and other papers*. London: Somerset Record Society **18**. (Includes Colonel Walter Slingsby's account of the campaign)

Sir John Byron's relation to the secretary of the last western action between the Lord Wilmot and Sir William Waller BL 1103 d. 77/5

Letter from Captain Edward Harley to Sir Robert Harley in Historical Manuscripts Commission *Portland Manuscripts* Vol 3 112–13

A True Relation of the late fight between Sir William Waller's forces, and those sent from Oxford... BL E 61 (6)

Roundway Down (2)

Adair, J 1997 *Roundhead General: the campaigns of Sir William Waller*. Stroud: Sutton

Denton, B 1997 *Only in Heaven: the life and campaigns of Sir Arthur Hesilrige*. Sheffield: Sheffield Academic Press

Edgar, F T R 1968 *Sir Ralph Hopton*. Oxford: Clarendon Press

English Heritage 1995 *Battlefield Report: Roundway Down 1643*

Tincey, J 1990 *Soldiers of the English Civil War (2): Cavalry*. London: Osprey

Alton (1)

A narration of the great victory, (through Gods Providence) obtained by the Parliaments Forces under Sir William Waller...1643 BL E 78 (22)

Archer, E *A True Relation of the trained-bands of Westminster, the Green Auxiliaries of London, and the Yellow Auxiliaries of the Tower Hamlets... 1643* BL 101 b 64

'Colonel Joseph Bamfield's Apologie, written by himself and printed at his desire' quoted in Adair, J 1973 *Cheriton 1644* Kineton: Roundwood Press 56–57

Chadwyck Healey C E H (ed) 1902 *Bellum Civile: Hopton's Narrative of his Campaign in the West (1642–1644) and other papers*. London: Somerset Record Society **18**.

Webb, J and Webb, W (eds) 1873 *Military Memoir of Colonel John Birch...written by Roe, his Secretary...* London: Camden Society New Series Vol 7

Alton (2)

Adair, J 1973 *Cheriton 1644: the campaign and the battle*. Kineton: Roundwood Press

Hall, D and Gretton, F *Farnham during the Civil Wars and Interregnum 1642–1660*. Farnham: Farnham Castle Newspapers

Roberts, K 1989 *Soldiers of the English Civil War (1): Infantry*. London: Osprey

Select Bibliography continued

Tresco (1)

Severall Proceedings in Parliament: 10 April–17 April; 17 April–24 April; 24 April–1 May; 1 May–8 May 1651. BL Thomason Tracts 785.8, 12, 16, 20

A Perfect Diurnall: 14 April–21 April; 28 April–5 May; 5 May–12 May; 13 May–20 May 1651. BL Thomason Tracts 785.11, 19, 23, 27

Letter from Sir George Ayscue in *A Perfect Diurnall, 13 May–20 May 1651*

Lereck, J A 1651 *A true accompt of the reducement of the Isles of Scilly* BL E 638 (4)

Powell J R (ed) 1937 *The letters of Robert Blake.* Navy Records Society (includes two letters from Henry Leslie, Bishop of Down to Secretary Nicholas)

'St Mary's and St Agnes: articles of surrender' in Bowley, R L 2001 *Scilly at War.* St Mary's: Bowley p59–62

Tresco (2)

Adams, F and Adams, P 1984 *Star Castle.* St Mary's: Belvedere Press

Bowley, RL 2001 *Scilly at war.* St Mary's: Bowley

Capp, B 1992 *Cromwell's Navy* (new ed) Oxford: OUP

Powell, J R 1972 Robert Blake: *General-at-sea.* London: Collins

Sedgemoor (1)

Edward Dummer 'A brief journal of the Western Rebellion' in Davis J 1895 *History of the Second Queen's Royal Regiment.* London: Bentley p48–49

Lord Feversham's account, in Royal Commission on Historical Manuscripts 1904 *Report on the Manuscripts of Mrs Stoptford-Sackville,* Vol I. London: HMSO 16–19

King James II's account, in *Hardwicke State Papers* Vol II 1778 London: Strahan and Cadell 305–13

Andrew Paschall's account, in Heywood, S 1811 *A Vindication of Mr Fox's History of the Early Part of the Reign of James II,* Appendix 4, xxix–xlv

The confession of Nathaniel Wade in *Hardwicke State Papers* Vol II 1778 London: Strahan and Cadell p329–30

Sedgemoor (2)

Chandler, D 1685 *Sedgemoor 1685: from Monmouth's invasion to the Bloody Assizes.* London: Anthony Mott

Childs, J 1980 *The Army, James II and the Glorious Revolution.* Manchester: Manchester University Press

English Heritage 1995 *Battlefield Report: Sedgemoor 1685*

Guy, A J (ed) 1988 *1688: Glorious Revolution? The fall and rise of the British Army 1660–1704* London: National Army Museum

Places to visit

Battle of Maldon
Nearest town: Maldon
Battlefield location: 1 mile SE of the town centre
OS Explorer: 176
Grid Ref: TL 8605
Parking: Promenade car park, Maldon
Nearest train station: Witham
Riverside paths lead to the battlefield. Northey Island is a bird sanctuary maintained by the National Trust and should not be visited without permission.

Battle of Hastings
Nearest town: Battle
Battlefield location: in the grounds of Battle Abbey, *see* below
OS Explorer: 124
Grid Ref: TQ 7415
Parking: the car park is adjacent to Battle Abbey
Nearest train station: Battle

Battle Abbey & Battlefield, W Sussex
Tel: 01424 773792
Location: in Battle, at S end of High Street. Take the A2100 off the A21
www.english-heritage.org.uk/battleabbey
Admission to Battle Abbey is free to members of English Heritage. An audio guide to a brief circular tour of the battlefield is available.
www.english-heritage.org.uk/events provides details of the annual re-enactment of the Battle of Hastings or call 01424 775705.

Pevensey Castle, East Sussex
Tel: 01323 762604
Location: in Pevensey off the A259
www.english-heritage.org.uk/pevensey

Battle of Myton
Nearest town: Boroughbridge
Battlefield location: near the village of Myton-on-Swale, 3 miles W of Boroughbridge
OS Explorer: 299

Grid Ref: SE 4366
Parking: in the village
Nearest train station: York
There is good access to the presumed site of the battle, via rights of way and permissive paths.

Battle of Shrewsbury
Nearest town: Shrewsbury
Battlefield location: off the A5124, 3 miles N of Shrewsbury
OS Explorer: 241
Grid Ref: SJ 5117
Parking: in the battlefield car park
Nearest train station: Shrewsbury
A well-interpreted battlefield with a number of information panels. St Mary Magdalene Church, founded to commemorate the fallen, is in the care of the Churches Conservation Trust. For opening times visit their website at www.visitchurches.org.uk

Haughmond Abbey, Shropshire
Tel: 01743 709661
Directions: located 3 miles NE of Shrewsbury off the B5062
www.english-heritage.org.uk/haughmond

Warkworth Castle, Northumberland
Tel: 01665 711423
Directions: in Warkworth, 7^1/2 miles S of Alnwick, on the A1068
www.english-heritage.org.uk/warkworth

Battle of Towton
Nearest town: Tadcaster
Battlefield location: between villages of Saxton and Towton, off the A162, 3 miles S of Tadcaster
OS Explorer: 289/290
Grid Ref: SE 4738
Parking: in the villages
Nearest train station: Church Fenton
Much of this evocative battlefield can be explored by car.

Battle of Barnet
Nearest town: Barnet
Battlefield location: in the vicinity of Monken Hadley, on the A1000, 1 mile N of Barnet
OS Explorer: 173
Grid Ref: TQ 2497
Parking: in Barnet
Nearest train station: High Barnet underground
The exact location of the fighting is disputed. The nature of the terrain has changed since 1471 and there has been some suburban encroachment.

Middleham Castle, N Yorkshire
Tel: 01969 623899
Directions: located at Middleham, 2 miles S of Leyburn on the A6108
www.english-heritage.org.uk/middleham

Battle of Stoke
Nearest town: Newark
Battlefield location: SW of East Stoke on the A46, 3 miles S of Newark
OS Explorer: 271
Grid Ref: SK 7449
Parking: in East Stoke
Nearest train station: Newark Northgate
Although access to the presumed centre of the battlefield is restricted, an excellent circular walk is possible using tracks, rights of way and the pavement of the A46

Minster Lovell Hall, Oxfordshire
Directions: adjacent to Minster Lovell church; 2 miles W of Witney, off the A40
www.english-heritage.org.uk/minsterlovell

Hedingham Castle, Essex
(owned by the Lindsay family)
Tel: 01787 460261
www.hedinghamcastle.co.uk

Places to visit continued

Battle of Flodden

Nearest town: Coldstream
Battlefield location: nr Branxton village, 4 miles SE of Coldstream
OS Explorer: 339
Grid Ref: NT 8937
Parking: battlefield car park to the W of Branxton
Nearest train station: Berwick
Flodden is an extremely rewarding battlefield to visit, with excellent access by rights of way and permissive paths and a number of interpretation panels.

Battle of Roundway Down

Nearest town: Devizes
Battlefield location: 3 miles N of Devizes
OS Explorer: 173
Grid Ref: SU 0165
Parking: Roundway Hill Covert, at the end of track above Roundway Village
Nearest train station: Chippenham
A variety of walks are possible across this extensive battlefield.

Battle of Alton

Nearest town: Alton
Battlefield location: centred on St Lawrence's Church, Church Street
OS Explorer: 144
Grid Ref: SU 7139
Parking: in the town centre
Nearest train station: Alton
St Lawrence's Church still bears the scars of the battle.

Battle of Tresco

Nearest town: Hugh Town
Battlefield location: Tresco, Isles of Scilly
OS Explorer: 101
Grid Ref: SV 8915
Parking: Penzance
Nearest train station: Penzance
Getting to Tresco is an adventure in itself. A helicopter service runs directly to the island from Penzance airport. Alternatively the *Scillonian* passenger ferry runs from Penzance to Hugh Town, St Mary's where there is a regular local boat service to Tresco.

Battle of Sedgemoor

Nearest town: Bridgwater
Battlefield location: between Chedzoy and Westonzoyland, 3 miles E of Bridgwater
OS Explorer: 140
Grid Ref: ST 3535
Parking: on-street in Chedzoy or Westonzoyland
Nearest train station: Bridgwater
Although improvements in drainage have led to the disappearance of many of the watercourses that crossed Sedgemoor, including the pivotal Bussex Rhyne, the character of the battlefield remains essentially unchanged.

Etal Castle, Northumberland

Tel: 01890 820332
Directions: in Etal village, 10 miles SW of Berwick
www.english-heritage.org.uk/etalcastle

Farnham Castle, Surrey

Tel: 01252 713393
Directions: 1/2 mile N of Farnham town centre, on the A287
www.english-heritage.org.uk/farnham

Index

Figures in **bold** refer to illustrations

Index continued

Index continued

Picture acknowledgements

Maps

7, 15, 32, 41, 50, 61, 68, 69, 73, 88, 107, 117, 129, 136–7, 149, 151, 154, 171, 187 © English Heritage 2005/2006

Pictures

24–5, 29, 38, 46, 47, 62, 94, 100, 121, 124, 168 © English Heritage/NMR

82, 100, 166 © English Heritage

30, 59, 60, 64b, 70, 77, 78–9, 79, 96, 106, 109, 112, 114, 148, 157, 159, 160, 161, 163t&b, 168t, 170t&b, 173, 177 © Julian Humphrys

The author and publisher are grateful to the following sources for supplying pictures and illustrations.

95 © Fiona Powers 2006

10, 12t, 12b, 13t, 13b, 27, 44, 51, 56–7, 81, 85, 86–7, 88t&m, 98, 103, 118, 120, 145–1, 180, 182, 184, 186t © The Battlefields Trust

17, 28, 61b, 72, 87, 111, 113, 135, 164 © Ken and Denise Guest

11, 26, 32, 33, 36–7, 45, 50b (British Library Collection), 58, 97, 99, 134 (Tabley House Collection), 186b, 189 © The Bridgeman Art Library

54, 63, 65, 75, 92, 104, 116, 125, 138, 178 © The British Library

64t, 67, 71, 89, 102, 119, 142, 153, 162, 188 © National Portrait Gallery, London

30, 131, 132, 133, 136, 181 © Rowan Isaac

14 © The Museum of London

18 © Royal Coin Cabinet, Stockholm

20, 21 © The Trustees of the British Museum

23 © Humphrey Berridge

31, 115 © Mary Evans Picture Library/Douglas McCarthy

167, 172, 176 © Mary Evans Picture Library

48 © Dean and Chapter of York, York Minster

52 © The Douglas Museum

66, 93, 123, 126, 146, 158 © Board of Trustees of the Royal Armouries

73, 91 © Graham Turner Studio

76 © Biological Anthropology Research Centre, Department of Archaeological Sciences, University of Bradford

84 © Burgerbibliothek, Bern

105 © Hedingham Castle

108 © The Dean and Canons of Windsor

122 © Faculty of Advocates, Edinburgh

139t&b, 143, 144, 184–5 © National Army Museum

154 © The Trustees of the National Museums of Scotland

155 © Hampshire County Museum Service

169 © Star Castle Hotel

183 © Queen's Royal Surrey Regiment

It is a pleasure to thank the many people and organisations that have helped me during the writing of this book. I would particularly like to thank the staff of the British Library; Cambridge University Library; the English Heritage Library; Farnham Museum; Guildford Library; the National Army Museum Reading Room and Dr Williams Library for their courteous and efficient help. Warmest thanks are due to all my friends and former colleagues at the National Army Museum, especially Alastair Massie, Andy Robertshaw and David Smurthwaite who have generously shared their opinions, knowledge and expertise with me over the years.

I also owe a large debt of gratitude to many English Heritage members of staff. I would particularly like to thank Richard Beniston, Nerys Hayes, Emily Burns, Kellie Blake, Lisa Hampton, Rebecca McCaffrey, Alysha Sykes, Paul Stamper and especially Tracy Borman for their kindness and support. At English Heritage Publishing I would like to thank Adele Campbell, Val Horsler and Rob Richardson; gratefully acknowledge the work of Beck Ward Murphy in attempting to instil some Roundhead discipline into my Cavalier working habits; express my gratitude to my copy editor Naomi Waters for waiting for manuscripts with remarkable patience and carrying out picture research beyond the call of duty; and thanks to John Vallender and Christopher Evans for their splendid maps, and Simon Borrough for his excellent design work.

Thanks are also due to Ken and Denise Guest for their excellent re-enactment pictures; to Sarah Daniels, James Dunning, Dave Musgrove, Fiona Powers, Katherine Sawyer and Jo Woolley; to Emily Cooke and Brena Roche of Brookland Travel for organising my trips around the country; to Alison Weir for her advice and encouragement; to John and Charlotte Knight for their hospitality on Tresco and to Maria Merritt of the Etal Village Shop near Flodden for some of the best packed lunches in the country. A number of members of the excellent Battlefields Trust have been particularly helpful to me. I would especially like to acknowledge the assistance of Stephen Barker, Chris Scott, Alan Turton and Glenn Foard. Glenn's generous advice over battlefield photographs has been absolutely invaluable

Affectionate thanks are especially due to my family: to my parents for giving me a love of history; to my daughter Sarah, for allowing me onto the computer; to my son James, for demonstrating military tactics in the park behind our house; and to my wife, Catharine, for accepting that any form of DIY would be out of the question for a considerable period of time! Finally I would like to thank the hundreds of English Heritage members who have come on tours and battlefield hikes with me over the past four years. Their ideas and questions have been of infinite help in helping me to formulate my thoughts while their company has turned work into an absolute pleasure.

Julian Humphrys